Touring
the Springs of Florida

TOURING THE SPRINGS OF FLORIDA

A GUIDE TO THE STATE'S BEST SPRINGS

MELISSA WATSON

GUILFORD, CONNECTICUT
HELENA, MONTANA

FALCONGUIDES®

An imprint of Rowman & Littlefield
Falcon, FalconGuides, and Outfit Your Mind are registered trademarks of Rowman & Littlefield.

Distributed by NATIONAL BOOK NETWORK

Copyright © 2015 by Rowman & Littlefield
Maps: Design Maps Inc. © Rowman & Littlefield

British Library Cataloguing-in-Publication Information Available

Library of Congress Cataloging-in-Publication Data is available on file.

ISBN 978-1-4930-0147-7
ISBN 978-1-4930-1449-1 (e-book)

⊖™ The paper used in this publication meets the minimum requirements of American National Standard for Information Sciences—Permanence of Paper for Printed Library Materials, ANSI/NISO Z39.48-1992.

The author and Rowman & Littlefield assume no liability for accidents happening to, or injuries sustained by, readers who engage in the activities described in this book.

For my Besties . . .
Dawn McKinney, Irene Freer, Liz Martinez, Cheryl Giavagnorio,
Jenn Getter, and Shari Santos
You ladies bring pure joy into my life nearly every single day.
Thank you! All my love.

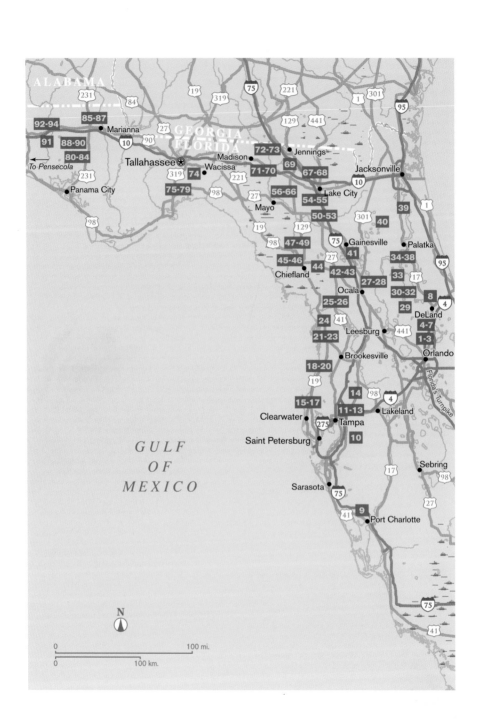

CONTENTS

North Region

ACKNOWLEDGMENTS

To the managers, rangers, and employees of the parks and springs: Joleen Dudley, Sally Vilberg, Dori Clark, Marcia Eining, Chris Hawthorne, Kelly Banta, Toby Brewer, Robyn Anderson, Kevin Pankau, Corky Williams, Amy Williams, Jerry Garrett, Jodi Schwarzenbach, Patricia Wisner, Mitchell Gentry, David Garcia, James Pellens, Jake Lasher, Tyler MacMillan, Prince Johnston, Susie Page, Kurt Huber, Sandro Huber, Lois Gossic, Connie Taylor, Steve Bowen, Terri Propst, George Kanaris, Joe Bishop, Jeff Toby, Carol Androvich, Scott Jacob, Randall Talbott, Mark Giblin, Melisa Thompson, Karen Kerby, Larry Steed, Sandra Leeper, Jonah Snelling, Mike Gainey, Kevin Champion, Hal Kirk, Jody Pack, Ryan Maier, Craig Savanna, Cliff Barnett, Becky Newell, Keri Walker, Carmen Maldomado, Barbara Suggs, Mike Herrin, Melissa Gulvin, Chris Anastasiou, Brit Catrell, Michelle Waterman, Robin Will, Kathy Richardson, Ludovica Weaver, Cheyenne Stemple, Robert Brooks, Erin Bryce, Edwin McCook, Jennifer Roberts, Amy Conyers, Scott Crosby, Jeffrey Gordon, Peter Salco, Tricia Wisner, Julie Clevinger, Ricky Lyons, Lisa Baltus, Victoria Modin, Judy Staley, Thomas Kamermayer, Amanda Kimmer, Durr Richard, Brian Polk, John Weston, Trent Hatcher, Edd Sorenson, Paul Heinerth, and Brandon. You are all a wealth of knowledge and took the time to go above and beyond with me. Your help on this book was a valuable tool to ensure its accuracy! Thank you!

A special thanks to Judy and her friend for letting me pitch a tent in their yard during the government shutdown.

I must give a shout out to my production team at Falcon Guides! They are the unsung heroes. So much goes on behind the scenes, and rarely do they get credit for their hard work and dedication. Without these people, this text would surely suffer. Thank you! Katie Benoit who has been extremely helpful, and worked on several of my books. Paulette Baker, who has tediously copyedited several of my books to perfection. Ellen Urban, the project manager on this book, for her patience and expertise. Roberta Monaco, for her extraordinary proofreading. And last, but certainly not least, John Burbidge. I know you're no longer with FalconGuides, but you guided me through my very first books and are the reason I am a successful author today. Thank you!

To my niece Christina Payton, for being my pack mule right after I had shoulder surgery. She spent some time on the road with me and helped Mikey and I cover about twenty springs while I was incapacitated.

To my nephew Cory Payton, for adding adventure and lots of fun while we explored the Wacissa River.

To Dawn McKinney. Not only for being my "person," my BB, and BFF, but also for lending me your underwater camera. It was an invaluable tool in capturing some amazing underwater photos.

Thank you all!

INTRODUCTION

Have you ever seen an eagle fly? Soaring high overhead, so smooth and regal. With silent wings but a distinctive call, maneuvering freely with the wind beneath it.

Watched the sun set over a pristine, peaceful lake? A single giant blaze of orange, slowly sinking into the horizon. As the orb slowly sets you realize what a gift it is to witness the miracle of nature right before your eyes. Flocks of pelicans perfectly align in the air, floating in flawless unison like a choreographed dance.

These are just a few of the sights you'll see when you venture out to explore the marvelous Sunshine State of Florida. Although Florida is best known for its beautiful beaches as the waves flawlessly lap upon the sand, what most people don't realize, is that beyond the beaches, beneath the ground below our feet, is an underground circuit of tunnels and windows filled with water that's just waiting to well up. From here, what's known as the aquifer, each spring is born. Most springs in this book gush out of the earth by the millions of gallons per day. Springs are "ranked" based on the amount of water they put out each day. These rankings are known as "magnitude," so when I refer to a first-magnitude spring, this is the biggest and best spring there is. A first-magnitude spring puts out over 64 million gallons of water every single day! It's hard to imagine that it's possible to put out that much freshwater daily, but these beautiful, blue springs do. Florida has twenty-seven first-magnitude springs just waiting for you to explore—to swim, snorkel, tube, and dive in. A second-magnitude spring puts out an impressive 6.5 to 64 million gallons each day and often are just as gorgeous as the first magnitudes. The final category you'll see in these pages contains the smaller, third-magnitude springs. These springs may have less volume, but typically what they lack in volume, they make up for with character. Even a third-magnitude spring puts out between 64 thousand and 6.5 million gallons of water daily, which is still impressive.

Florida has over 700 confirmed springs, scattered throughout the state. Most are smaller than third magnitude, and some are surrounded by private property and just not worth the effort to reach by boat. In researching this book, I personally visited over 400 of these springs. I then narrowed the field down to the best 140 springs in the state. Within these pages you'll find the cream of the crop, just waiting for you to get outside and enjoy. Along with the best springs, you'll also find a few sinks. In most cases, I included the sinks due to their close proximity to their sister spring.

So what is the difference between a sink and a spring? A spring flows from below, and the water actually goes somewhere—forming a spring run, much like a creek, that eventually ends up in a river. A sink is basically a hole in the ground that's filled with water. But the water doesn't come from above, like from a lake or a pond. Instead these "holes" tie into the aquifer, so the sinks are filled with crystal-clear springwater from below.

As you begin your journey to the Florida springs, you'll notice that several of the premier spring sites are found in clusters or groups, such as Ginnie Springs, Kings Bay, or Merritt's Mill Pond. You'll find rivers flowing pure brilliant blue water like the Rainbow and Silver, each fed by over a hundred springs. Inviting emerald oases such as Rock Springs and Wekiwa and pale baby blue pools like Lithia, Pitt, and Williford are just waiting for your discovery. Grab a towel, bring a camera, don your mask and snorkel, and prepare to get wet as you begin an adventure unlike any other—*Touring the Springs of Florida*.

How to Use This Guide

As you thumb through this book, you'll notice that it's been broken down into geographic regions. Because Florida is such a large state, there are five major regions commonly designated: South, East Central, West Central, North, and Panhandle. Each region is further broken down into smaller geographic areas based on the nearest town. Overview maps are provided for each region, and detailed maps for each specific area help you find your way around. You'll then see essential information for each spring. Here's a brief explanation of each category:

General description: A quick description of the springs, important information to pique your interest, and certain facts may be found here. While this comes in handy, I recommend reading "The Spring" to get a full description of the springs, activities allowed, and specific information.

Location: This is the spring's physical address; you'll also get a general idea of where the spring is in reference to nearby towns.

Development: Springs are designated "Primitive" or "Developed." Basically, a spring with concrete walls around it or built-up platforms is considered "developed." If there's nothing but natural banks surrounding the spring, it's "primitive." However, a "primitive" spring can still be found within a developed park. It just means the park didn't alter the spring from its natural state.

Best time to visit: Most of the springs are open year-round, but a handful are closed for a few months during winter. This information will be listed here.

Restrictions: Here you'll find the hours of operation and other pertinent information, such as whether pets, SCUBA diving, or alcohol are allowed.

Access: The springs are either "drive to," "hike to," or "boat to." "Drive to" springs still require a short walk from the parking lot. The "hike to" springs are all easy hikes; the longest one is only 5.5 miles round-trip. When I refer to a "boat to" spring, I mean one reached by paddling a canoe or kayak. Some of the waterways can accommodate small motorboats, but make sure you read the specifics before heading out.

Fees: Some springs have no fee; others do. Each fee is listed with a symbol that represents a range: $ = $0–$10, $$ = $11–$20, and $$$ = more than $20. Most of the parks that require a fee have a staffed gate. But some of the springs have self-pay stations near the entrance, so you may need to have exact change (singles) to put in an envelope. Some additional activities, such as camping and canoe rentals, require an additional fee.

Water temperature: All temperatures in this book are represented in degrees Fahrenheit. You may notice a pattern in the water temperature of the springs. That's because temperature is a direct result of latitude. For example, the only warm spring in the state is also the farthest south. In the central regions the temperature sits around 72°F. But as you work your way north, the temperature of the water drops to a brisk 68°F. While that might sound quite chilly, the Florida sun warms you up quick enough.

Nearby attractions: This is where you'll find other nearby parks and activities.

Services: If a spring has restrooms, food, or lodging on-site, it will be listed here. Some of the "restrooms" may be a vault toilet. Beyond that, I've listed the nearest town that has restrooms, food, gas, and lodging.

Camping: "On-site" means there is a full-service campground on the property. If there is only primitive camping on-site, that is listed along with the name of the nearest park or two that have a full-service campground.

Management: This section lists the agency that maintains the spring.

Contact: Any pertinent contact information is listed here, along with websites where you can get more information on the spring.

Maps: Here you'll find the page number and quadrant where you'll find the springs using the *DeLorme: Florida Atlas & Gazetteer*. While I've used DeLorme's maps on all my travels, there are some errors in the Florida version, especially in the Mayo area and Lafayette and Suwannee Counties. Several county roads are marked wrong on their maps. With this in mind, I urge you to pay attention to my specific driving directions and to the maps provided in this guidebook.

GPS coordinates: I've included GPS coordinates for every spring.

Finding the spring: I've done my best to provide explicit driving directions from the junction of two main roads all the way to the spring. While I found some errors in *DeLorme: Florida Atlas & Gazetteer*, I still recommend it. These maps are a valuable tool and include highways, state roads, county roads, and many forest service roads as well.

The Spring: Here you'll find the meat and potatoes of the spring. Detailed descriptions; pros and cons; activities you can participate in, such as swimming or SCUBA diving; and any other important information about the spring and the surrounding area. If the park has mountain bike trails or excellent birding, you'll find that information here.

For Your Safety

As you venture out to see Florida's natural wonders, keep in mind that these springs are pure and primeval. There is no switch where you can turn the flow on or off, and most springs are deep near the center. There are usually no lifeguards on duty, so you must know your own limitations. If you're not a strong swimmer, don a life vest or bring a floatation device. But make sure you read that spring's restrictions, since some springs don't allow floats or inner tubes. *Always* watch your children closely! Drowning can be quick and silent, and it only takes a few moments to happen. Even if your children know how to swim, you *cannot* underestimate the strength of the water as it pours out of the aquifer at a rate of millions of gallons per day.

Weather: Although we do have the occasional cold front in Florida, most of the time the temperature ranges from the 70s to over 100°F. Humidity runs high as well, so the springs are a perfect way to cool off.

Water: By simply looking at a spring's water, you can see how crisp and clear and pure it is. Some of the springs are even used by bottling companies and sold in stores as drinking water. But before the water hits the stores, it goes through an entire purification process. Although it appears perfect, and looks as though you could just gulp it down, there are still minerals and bacteria in the water that are not fit for consumption. Make sure you bring plenty of drinking water along. The Florida sun gets very hot, especially at midday, and it's important to stay hydrated in the heat.

Poison ivy, oak, and sumac: All three of these plant irritants are found in the forests of Florida. If you know how to identify them, you may save yourself some unpleasant itching. A nice little rule of thumb is "leaves of 3, let it be," since poison ivy and oak both typically have three leaflets to a leaf.

Bugs, bees, and ticks: Depending on when and where you visit, you may run into biting mosquitoes or pesky gnats, especially in the early-evening hours of the summer months. Bug spray containing DEET seems to deter both mosquitoes and ticks, but be sure to rinse it off before you swim. As for ticks, these heat-seeking parasites are sneaky little buggers. You may not even feel a tiny tick embedding itself under your skin. It's a good idea to do a thorough "tick check" each time you leave a forested area, and again later when you take a shower or before you go to bed. If you do find a tick, tweezers work well for removal.

Wildlife: Florida has some unique species that you should be aware of. While the chilly water of the springs doesn't sound like a place you'd find an alligator or snake, these reptiles occasionally do wander into a spring run. Alligators usually just want to be left alone, but they are a wild animal and can be potentially dangerous. If you see an alligator, enjoy the sight from a distance; take pictures, but do *not* interact with it. While most are harmless, alligators can swim and run faster than any human. Most snakes are nonvenomous. But Florida does have four venomous species: rattlesnakes, copperheads, coral snakes, and water moccasins. The first three are found on land only, but the water moccasin is found both on land and in water. They're quite territorial and will swim after a canoe if you enter an area where they're nesting. I've never seen a moccasin at the head of a spring, but I have seen them in wooded coves that I've wandered into with a canoe. If you see a snake, simply back away slowly, giving it space. Remember, when you visit a park, forest, or spring, you're a guest in the home of *all* wildlife, whether it's a cute and cuddly river otter or a scaly snake.

Pets: I'm a big fan of dogs and animals in general. As a matter of fact, my big dog, Mikey, goes on all my trips. But I've noticed that many of the parks with springs are not pet friendly, which is not indicative of Florida parks in general. Perhaps it's the possibility of alligators, or maybe it's the swimming nature of the parks, because they don't want unattended animals left tied up by the waterside. Make sure you read the restrictions to see if pets are allowed before bringing them along. Also, make sure you bring a water bowl and *lots* of water for them. Dogs don't have the luxury of cooling off in the spring. Always keep them on a leash, and *always* pick up after them.

For Mother Nature's Safety

Unlike other natural water bodies, the springs of Florida survive under unique circumstances. The water that ends up on the ground from rain, lawn sprinklers, car washings, etc., all gets soaked up into the porous ground of Florida and then filters itself through the earth before it finally ends up in the intricate system of underground windows and tunnels known as the aquifer. The water that emerges from every spring in this book comes from the aquifer. It seems unreal that all these springs, even those putting out 70 million gallons of water a day, can be sustained by the aquifer, but they are.

Because of this cycle, and where the water comes from, there are a few simple things you can do at home to help protect the spring's environment. When looking at a massive spring we tend to think of it as untouchable, untaintable, but unfortunately that's just not so. The Hightower Spring entry (#90) is a perfect example. Sometimes it's invasive aquatic vegetation that chokes off a spring. Sometimes it's silt. When visitors repeatedly wade in the sandy bottom of a spring, silt gets kicked up and, over time, clogs the flow. In a case like this, we are simply loving the spring to death. In other cases, it's a grander scheme of things that harm the good underwater vegetation such as eelgrass. Eelgrass is a sign of a healthy spring, but when you use pesticides or too much fertilizer on your lawn, it ends up being absorbed into the aquifer and eventually kills off the eelgrass. This in turn deteriorates the health of a spring. By using eco-friendly fertilizer, or simply less fertilizer, you can help protect our springs. If you live on the water, plant a buffer zone between the lawn and shoreline, which helps prevent fertilizer and grass clippings from entering the water system. Have your septic tanks inspected regularly. Leaks allow bacteria to enter the aquifer. Never dump anything down a storm drain. Again, all water dumped on the ground ends up in the aquifer, and eventually in the precious springs we swim in. It comes down to this: A spring is only as healthy as its springshed. So please do your part to protect it, and the glorious springs of Florida.

Wildlife: I spoke a bit about wildlife above, but there's one important fact I left for here: Never feed *any* wildlife! Not even the squirrels, otters, fish, or turtles. Often these cute critters cannot digest people food, so you may be doing them more harm than good. More important, especially in the case of bears or alligators, these animals will then associate people with food. This inadvertently makes them a "nuisance," and a potential danger. The park service will euthanize a "nuisance" animal to protect the public. Please do not be the reason for an animal's unnecessary death. Instead, help keep wildlife wild.

Catholes: If no restrooms or portable toilets are available and you *must* go in the forest, dig a "cathole" to bury your solid waste *at least* 200 feet from any water source. Same goes if you have to urinate. Please go *at least* 200 feet from the water rather than in it.

Litter: I implore you to put trash where it belongs—in a trash can! If there is no trash can, or it's full, please don't leave trash beside the can. The wind blows, or a heavy rain hits, and the trash ends up in the water or woods. Please pack it in—pack it out, especially if you hike or boat to a spring.

Leave No Trace: Simply put, when you leave a spring, it should be just as you arrived (if not cleaner). "Take nothing but pictures, leave nothing but footprints." This leaves less impact on the environment, and allows other visitors to appreciate the natural beauty of their surroundings.

Spring Finder

Most picturesque:

3   Rock Springs
18 Weeki Wachee Springs
23 Homosassa Springs
24 Kings Bay/Crystal River: Three Sisters and Parker Island Springs
26 Rainbow Springs
28 Silver Springs
30 Juniper and Fern Hammock Springs
32 Silver Glen Springs
42 Blue Grotto
43 Devil's Den
53 Ginnie Springs
54 Ichetucknee Head Spring
85 Jackson Blue Spring
86 Merritt's Mill Pond: Shangri-La Spring
88 Cypress Spring

Most populated:

3   Rock Springs
7   Volusia Blue Spring
8   De Leon Springs
9   Warm Mineral Springs
12 Sulphur Springs
18 Weeki Wachee Springs
23 Homosassa Springs
24 Kings Bay/Crystal River: Tarpon Hole
25 KP Hole Park: Rainbow River Springs
26 Rainbow Springs
29 Alexander Springs
52 Big Blue Spring
53 Ginnie Springs
54 Ichetucknee Head Spring
85 Jackson Blue Spring
93 Vortex Spring

Least populated:

20 Eagle's Nest Sink
21 Chassahowitzka Springs
22 Bluebird Springs
34 Beecher Spring
35 Sulfur Spring
36 Mud Spring
57 Ruth Spring
59 Owens Spring
65 Allen Mill Pond Spring
68 Blue Sink
69 Suwannee Springs
70 Falmouth Spring
71 Anderson Spring
74 Wacissa Springs Group
77 Cherokee Sink
84 Devil's Hole Spring
88 Cypress Spring
90 Hightower Spring
94 Holmes Blue Spring

Best swimming holes:

3 Rock Springs
18 Weeki Wachee Springs
26 Rainbow Springs
30 Juniper Springs
32 Silver Glen Springs
44 Levy Blue Spring
46 Fanning Springs
52 Big Blue Spring
53 Ginnie Springs
54 Ichetucknee Head Spring
70 Falmouth Spring
76 Wakulla Spring
81 Pitt Spring
85 Jackson Blue Spring
92 Ponce de Leon Springs

Best for snorkeling:

2 Wekiwa Springs
3 Rock Springs
7 Volusia Blue Spring
24 Kings Bay/Crystal River: Tarpon Hole and Three Sisters
25 KP Hole Park: Rainbow River Springs
26 Rainbow Springs
29 Alexander Springs
32 Silver Glen Springs
45 Manatee Springs
46 Fanning Springs
53 Ginnie Springs
54 Ichetucknee Head Spring
73 Madison Blue Spring
85 Jackson Blue Spring
86 Merritt's Mill Pond: Shangri-La Springs
92 Ponce de Leon Springs

Best for SCUBA (open-water):

17 Hudson Grotto
19 Hospital Hole
24 Kings Bay/Crystal River: Tarpon Hole
25 KP Hole Park: Rainbow River Springs
27 Paradise Springs
42 Blue Grotto
43 Devil's Den
58 Troy Spring
63 Wes Skiles Peacock Springs State Park: Orange Grove Sink
93 Vortex Spring

Best for cave diving:

19 Hospital Hole
27 Paradise Springs
53 Ginnie Springs: Devil's Eye and Devil's Ear Springs
56 Little River Spring
63 Peacock Springs
64 Lafayette Blue Springs
73 Madison Blue Spring
85 Jackson Blue Spring
86 Merritt's Mill Pond
91 Morrison Springs
93 Vortex Spring

Best for family fun:

3   Rock Springs
18 Weeki Wachee Springs
44 Levy Blue Spring
52 Big Blue Spring
53 Ginnie Springs
54 Ichetucknee Head Spring
60 Royal Spring
61 Convict Spring
76 Wakulla Spring
78 Camp Indian Springs
85 Jackson Blue Spring
93 Vortex Spring

Best paddle routes:

2   Wekiwa Springs
3   Rock Springs
8   De Leon Springs
18 Weeki Wachee Springs
21 Chassahowitzka Springs
24 Crystal River/ Kings Bay
25 KP Hole Park: Rainbow River Springs

26 Rainbow Springs
28 Silver Springs
29 Alexander Springs
30 Juniper Springs
32 Silver Glen Springs
54 Ichetucknee Head Spring
74 Wacissa Springs Group
82 Gainer Springs Group
86 Merritt's Mill Pond Springs Group
88 Cypress Spring
94 Holmes Blue Spring

Author's Favorites:

3   Rock Springs
7   Volusia Blue Spring
24 Crystal River/Kings Bay: Three Sisters Springs
26 Rainbow Springs Group
28 Silver Springs
29 Alexander Springs
30 Juniper Spring
32 Silver Glen Springs
42 Blue Grotto
43 Devil's Den
46 Fanning Springs
52 Big Blue Spring
53 Ginnie Springs
54 Ichetucknee Head Spring
60 Royal Spring
81 Pitt Spring
82 Gainer Spring #2
85 Jackson Blue Spring
86 Merritt's Mill Pond: Shangri-La Springs
88 Cypress Spring
91 Morrison Springs
93 Vortex Spring

Map Legend

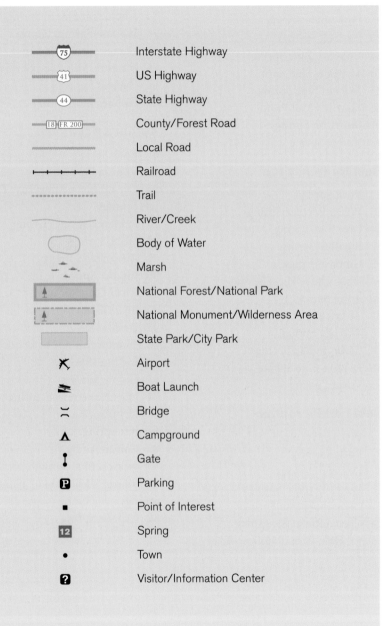

75	Interstate Highway
41	US Highway
44	State Highway
18 / FR 200	County/Forest Road
	Local Road
	Railroad
	Trail
	River/Creek
	Body of Water
	Marsh
	National Forest/National Park
	National Monument/Wilderness Area
	State Park/City Park
✗	Airport
	Boat Launch
	Bridge
Λ	Campground
	Gate
P	Parking
▪	Point of Interest
12	Spring
•	Town
?	Visitor/Information Center

EAST CENTRAL REGION

West Indian manatees are friendly and curious.

The eastern central part of the state may have fewer springs than other regions, but most of them pack a punch. Wekiwa and Rock Springs are fabulous for snorkeling, and offer some of the best paddle opportunities in the state. Green Springs has milky emerald-green water unlike any other you've seen. Volusia Blue is a manatee refuge in winter, when you'll see hundreds of playful manatees enjoying the warmer waters of this precious spring. De Leon is not only rich in history but the spring has an enormous swim area. Take an eco-tour, paddle through untouched wilderness, snorkel a spring run, or witness entire families of endangered manatees. Where else can you visit Disney World one day and wake up the next to float on the crystal-clear water of a pristine spring? Right here, in the East Central region of the fabulous Sunshine State.

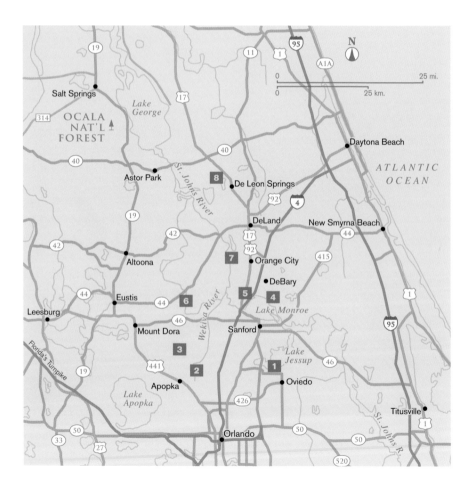

General description: Located within a tiny Seminole County park, the brown, murky water of Mineral Spring follows a short spring run out to the southern banks of Lake Jessup.

Location: 1988 Spring Ave., Oviedo; on the south side of Lake Jessup

Development: Primitive

Best time to visit: Year-round

Restrictions: Open 8 a.m. to sunset

Access: Drive to

Fee: No fee

Water temperature: 72°F

Nearby attractions: Little Big Econ State Forest, Black Hammock Wilderness Area, Cross Seminole Trail

Services: All services in Oviedo and Winter Springs

Camping: Wekiwa Springs State Park

Management: Seminole County Leisure Services

Contact: (407) 788-0405; http://seminolecountyfl.gov/parksrec/PassiveParksandBoatRamps/overlook.aspx

Map: *DeLorme: Florida Atlas & Gazetteer:* Page 80 C3

GPS coordinates: N28 42.010' / W81 14.283'

Finding the spring: From the junction of CR 419 and FL 417 (Central Florida Greenway) near Oviedo, drive west on CR 419 for 0.5 mile to a right onto Spring Avenue. Follow Spring Avenue for 0.6 mile to Overlook Park, on the left.

From the junction of CR 419 and FL 434 in Winter Springs, drive east on CR 419 for 3.7 miles to a left on Spring Avenue and follow directions above.

The Spring

As you pull into the tiny county park, the spring is tucked away to the left (west) of the parking lot. Murky brown water creates a short spring run that passively flows out to Lake Jessup. With no visible boil, and dark tones to the water, you might not even know this was a spring if you hadn't been told. A single picnic shelter acts as a focal point in the small grassy field that forms Overlook Park. Sitting amid massive oak trees, the shelter houses several picnic tables, a charcoal grill, and a trash can and offers outstanding views of Lake Jessup. A short, buggy boardwalk skirts the edge of the park along the lakeshore. You can fish from the small dock or launch a canoe or kayak and explore even farther.

Clearly Lake Jessup is the highlight. A public boat ramp is located about 12 miles away off FL 46, where it crosses the northeast portion of the lake. If you don't have your own boat, you can book a guided airboat tour with Black Hammock Adventures. They not only offer airboat tours but also have a restaurant, bar, and wildlife exhibits. For more details: www.theblackhammock.com.

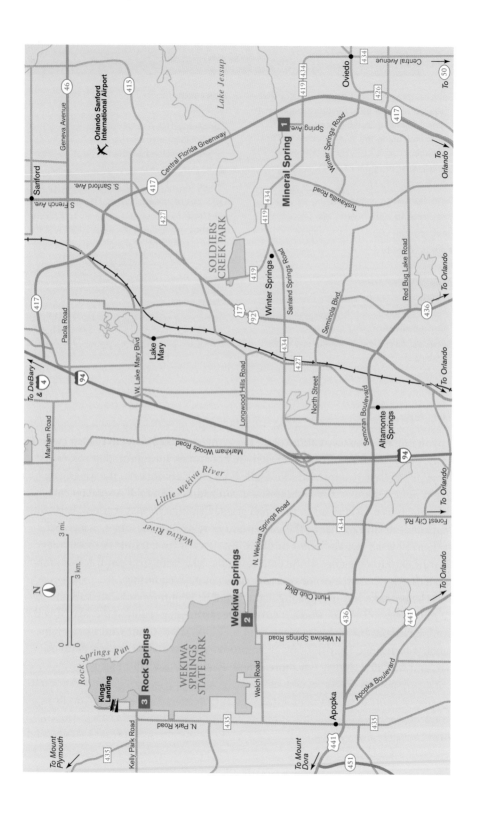

General description: Packed with activities, Wekiwa Springs State Park has something for everyone. Swim, snorkel, hike, bike, paddle, or horseback ride. Whether you're in the water or out, you're sure to have fun at this wonderful park.

Location: 1800 Wekiwa Circle, Apopka

Development: Developed

Best time to visit: Year-round

Restrictions: Open 8 a.m. to sunset

Access: Drive to

Fees: $

Water temperature: 72°F

Nearby attractions: Kelly Park (Rock Springs), King's Landing Canoe Rental, Seminole State Forest, Wekiva Island

Services: Restrooms, limited food on-site; all services in Apopka

Camping: On-site

Management: Florida Parks Service

Contact: (407) 884-2009; www.florida stateparks.org/WekiwaSprings/

Map: *DeLorme: Florida Atlas & Gazetteer:* Page 80 C1

GPS coordinates: N28 42.717' / W81 27.633'

Finding the springs: From I-4 near Altamonte Springs, take exit 94 (FL 434) and drive west on FL 434 for 0.8 mile to a right onto Wekiwa Springs Road. Travel for 4.2 miles to the park, on the right.

From the junction of FL 436 and US 441 in Apopka, drive east on FL 436 for 1.8 miles to a left on North Wekiwa Springs Road. Travel for approximately 2.9 miles to the park, on the left.

The Springs

One of the many wonderful things about this spring is that although it sits in the middle of a busy town, it's almost as though you're magically transported away from the noise and traffic the minute you enter the park. The hustle and bustle instantly fade away, replaced with the sounds of a gentle breeze blowing through the trees and the birds softly singing. A grassy hillside leads down to the dark green water of the springs, and impressively big oak trees add character to the scenery. The springs form a large swim area circled by a cement walkway. Snorkelers enjoy the scenery below, while the occasional local swims laps above. A wooden footbridge crosses over the spring run as it begins its journey out to the Wekiwa River. Beyond the footbridge you'll find the kiosk for canoe and kayak rentals. But first you must pay for your rental at the park's concession at the top of the hill. While you're there, pop into the Nature Center, where they have wildlife exhibits and historical artifacts. The paddling route is one of the best in the area, with wildlife viewing at its core. You're likely to see fish leaping from the water as hawks cry out from above. Along the banks and up on logs, turtles and alligators lazily soak up the sun. If you're lucky, you may see deer near the banks as well. Birdlife is plentiful, and the park has a birding checklist that you can mark off as you see the wide variety of species. Along the boardwalk/nature trail near the spring, you're likely to see pileated woodpeckers, colorful cardinals, and butterflies flit about.

If you're up for more hiking, an extensive hiking trail system covers more than 13 miles. The park also has an 8-mile equestrian trail and equestrian camping. Nine miles of trail are dedicated to mountain bikers, and they are also allowed on the horse trails. There is no drinking water anywhere along the trails, so bring lots of water. This spectacular state park also has a full-service campground, group campsites, and primitive trailside sites; they even have campsites that can only be reached by canoe or kayak. Reservations are required for most of the camping and can be made at www.reserveamerica.com. If you're still not entertained, the park has a volleyball net and horseshoe pit. Bring the family and enjoy it all.

General description: Rock Springs is full of life—and character! It's among my favorites. Caves, rocky limestone ledges, footbridges, and a swift current of crystal-clear water all add to the allure. Wildlife is abundant, and birdlife abounds. If you want to appreciate this place in all its glory, visit on a weekday to avoid the crowds. When you have this place to yourself, you realize that it truly is paradise.

Location: 400 E Kelly Park Rd., Apopka

Development: Partially developed

Best time to visit: Year-round

Restrictions: Open summer: 8 a.m. to 8 p.m., winter: 8 a.m. to 6 p.m.; no alcohol, pets, fishing, SCUBA diving, boats

Access: Drive to

Fees: $

Water temperature: 72°F

Nearby attractions: Wekiwa Springs State Park, Seminole State Forest

Services: Food, restrooms, showers on-site; all services in Apopka

Camping: On-site

Management: Orange County Culture and Parks

Contact: (407) 254-1902; www.ocfl.net/ CultureParks/Parks.aspx?m=dtlvw&d=22
Kings Landing; (407) 886-0859; http:// kingslandingfl.com

Map: *DeLorme: Florida Atlas & Gazetteer:* Page 79 B3

GPS coordinates: N28 45.383' / W81 30.1'

Finding the spring: From the junction of US 441 and CR 435 (N. Park Road) in Apopka, drive north on CR 435 for approximately 5.9 miles to a right onto W. Kelly Park Road. Travel for 0.25 mile and the road bends left. The park is on your right.

From the junction of CR 435 and FL 46 in Mount Plymouth, drive south on CR 435 for 3.9 miles to a left onto W. Kelly Park Road and follow directions above.

The Springs

Squirrels, raccoons, turkeys, and deer are abundant in Kelly Park. I've even seen a black bear, bald eagle, and bobcat here. Although it's within the city limits of Apopka, you'd never know it. If it weren't for crowds of kids dropped off by school buses on the weekends, you'd think you were deep within the forest. Rolling grassy hills and massive oak trees with Spanish moss dangling from their limbs add to the appeal. Amid the trees you'll find a shaded picnic area with tables and charcoal grills. A few volleyball nets and a playground greet you before you reach the concession stand. Here you can get snacks, buy a mask and snorkel, or rent a tube to float down the spring run. Beyond the concession, the main swimming area comes into view. A small sandy beach sits to the left, and to the right a few footbridges make the scenery picturesque. The spring run flows downstream, drifting past the swim area to what's known as second and third landings. Completely natural and untouched, these landings are as pretty as the head springs themselves. You can reach them via the hiking trails that pass through the park. A boardwalk follows the spring run upstream about 0.1 mile and leads to the head springs. Here another footbridge crosses the spring run, painting a perfect picture. Beyond the bridge, you see two perfect caves in the tall bank that acts as a backdrop to the springs. Rocky limestone ledges make

Rocky ledges add to the scenery at Rock Springs.

an ideal launch site for tubers and give snorkelers a great place to jump out into the water. Large boulders below the surface add to the scenery as the current sweeps you away under the footbridge and down the spring run. Fish and turtles scramble to get out of the way as you float downstream. The blue green water is crisp and pure and breathes new life into your soul. The minute you get out in the swim area, you're ready to head back up to the head spring and do it again.

The campground is excellent, although at times the sound of the leaf blower drowns out the sounds of nature. Beyond swimming, snorkeling, and tubing, I recommend heading down the street to Kings Landing. From here you can rent a canoe or launch your own and paddle down the Rock Springs Run. The run is surrounded by state-owned land, so all you'll see is wilderness and wildlife as you paddle downstream. A shuttle service is available, or you can paddle out and back. Either way, the water is immaculate!

Early-morning steam rises from the spring run near third landing.

General description: A short walk leads to the enticing milky green water of Green Springs. A deck overlooks the spring on one side and a bench rests on the other, giving you a perfect place to sit and stare, hypnotized by the emerald-green color of the water. Although this is one of Florida's few sulfur springs, there's no sulfur smell in the air.

Location: 994 Enterprise/Osteen Rd., Enterprise; about 1 mile south of Deltona

Development: Primitive

Best time to visit: Year-round

Restrictions: Open sunrise to sunset; no swimming or fishing

Access: Drive to

Fee: No fee

Water temperature: 76°F

Nearby attractions: Spring to Spring Trail, East Central Region Rail Trail, Central Florida Zoo and Botanical Gardens, Lake Monroe Park, Gemini Springs Park, Blue Springs State Park

Services: Restrooms on-site; all services in Deltona and DeBary

Camping: Primitive at Gemini Springs Park; full-service camping at Blue Springs State Park, Lake Monroe Park

Management: Volusia County Parks, Recreation and Culture Division

Contact: (386) 736-5953; www.volusia .org/services/community-services/parks -recreation-and-culture/parks-and-trails/ park-facilities-and-locations/ecological -nature-parks/green-spring-park.stml

Map: *DeLorme: Florida Atlas & Gazetteer:* Page 80 B3

GPS coordinates: N28 51.767' / W81 14.85'

Finding the spring: From I-4 near DeBary, take exit 108 to DeBary Avenue (CR 4162) and drive east for 1 mile to a right onto Main Street. Travel for 0.5 mile to a left onto Lake Shore Drive and drive east for 1 mile to a left into the park.

Note: CR 4162 is named Dirksen Drive west of I-4 and Doyle Road east of Providence Boulevard.

The Spring

Green Springs Park is tucked away in a neighborhood just north of Lake Monroe. Within the park, benches line paved paths along the walkway that leads to Green Springs. Early Native Americans thought the spring had healing properties, and it's easy to see why. Emerald-green water greets you, and a small wooden deck overlooks the inviting spring pool. Although the pool is clearly marked with "No Swimming" signs, a rope swing hangs over the spring, and local kids leap into the deep, milky water on a daily basis. There's a playground and a picnic shelter, and "trails" crisscross the park. A paved bike path leads to both the East Central Region Rail Trail and Volusia County's Spring to Spring Trail. The Spring to Spring Trail is a multiuse trail that's open to bicyclists, skaters, and those on foot. The trail was still under construction in 2014, but when it's finished, visitors will be able to spring hop between Gemini, Green, Blue, and De Leon Springs along the 26-mile paved path. The opaque green spring run leads out to Lake Monroe, which can be accessed at Lake Monroe Park. If you have a canoe or kayak, you can launch at Mariner's Cove Park, which is east on Enterprise Osteen Road.

Milky emerald-green water forms a perfect pool at Green Springs.

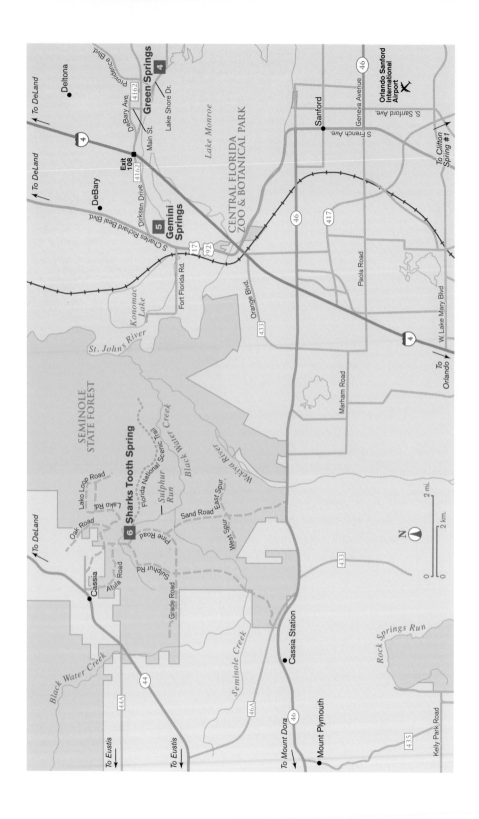

General description: Two springs welcome you at this lovely county park, and a 0.25-mile stroll leads you to both before looping back over a bridge that gives you fantastic views of the spring run. Due to bacteria in the water, the swim area is closed, but you can still rent a canoe and explore the spring run firsthand. If you prefer to stay on dry land, you can fish, hike, bike, and even bring your pooch along to play in the dog park.

Location: 37 Dirksen Dr., DeBary

Development: Primitive

Best time to visit: Year-round

Restrictions: Open sunrise to sunset; no swimming or glass containers

Access: Drive to

Fee: No fee

Water temperature: 73°F

Nearby attractions: Blue Springs State Park, Spring to Spring Trail, East Central Regional Rail Trail, Central Florida Zoo and Botanical Gardens, Lake Monroe Park, Green Springs Park

Services: Restrooms on-site; all services in DeBary

Camping: Primitive camping on-site; full-service camping at Blue Springs State Park, Lake Monroe Park

Management: Volusia County Parks, Recreation and Culture Division

Contact: (386) 736-5953; www.volusia .org/services/community-services/parks -recreation-and-culture/parks-and-trails/ park-facilities-and-locations/ecological -nature-parks/gemini-springs-park.stml

Map: *DeLorme: Florida Atlas & Gazetteer:* Page 80 B2

GPS coordinates: N28 51.767' / W81 18.683'

Finding the spring: From I-4 in DeBary, take exit 108 onto Dirksen Drive (CR 4162) and drive west for 1.5 miles to a left into the park. Once inside the park, turn right and follow the road back to the western parking lot.

From the junction of CR 4162 (Dirksen Drive) and US 17/US 92 in DeBary, drive east on CR 4162 for 0.3 mile to a right into the park and follow directions above.

The Spring

What a charming community park, where families come to enjoy the playground or take a stroll to see the springs. You can canoe, fish, hike, or bike; they even have a dog park. Overlooks offer views of both springs as crystal-clear water flows from the small boils all the way out to Lake Monroe. Although the water appears crisp and clean, there's no swimming due to bacteria in the water—not to mention alligators camouflaged among the lily pads. Fishing is allowed from the fishing pier on the east side of the park, but you must have a permit.

Although the park is not well marked, to see the springs, head to the western portion of the park. From here follow the paved path that leads southeast beyond the playground. You'll walk by open grassy fields that are perfect for a family picnic. Or, if you'd prefer, you can rent a pavilion for the day. A big red barn, used as a maintenance shed, adds to the ambience. A bridge over a small spillway forms a loop in the path and leads you back from the far side of the springs; amazing views of the glassy water can be seen from here. A primitive camping area, canoe launch, and canoe rentals are all available on-site. Volusia County's Spring to Spring Trail

Gemini Springs has several viewing platforms.

skirts the northern edge of the park. Upon completion, the trail will be a whopping 26-mile multiuse trail on which bikers, skaters, and those on foot will be able to spring hop between Gemini, Green, Blue, and De Leon Springs.

This wonderful park serves as a peaceful getaway from the hustle and bustle of everyday life.

General description: Perhaps the smallest spring in this book, yet full of life and character. Due to its size, this tiny spring and spring run are *extremely* environmentally sensitive. I urge you to stay on the trail and footbridge. A permit and gate code must be obtained from Seminole State Forest before gaining access.

Location: Within Seminole State Forest; about 7 miles west of Sanford

Development: Primitive

Best time to visit: Year-round except during hunt dates (check website prior to visiting as hunt dates vary)

Restrictions: Open sunrise to sunset; permit and gate code required prior to arrival

Access: Hike to; 0.1 mile one way

Fees: $

Water temperature: 72°F

Nearby attractions: Blue Springs State Park, Wekiwa Springs State Park, Rock Springs, Rock Springs Run State Preserve, Lower Wekiva River Preserve State Park

Services: Restrooms on-site; all services in Sanford

Camping: Primitive camping on-site by permit/reservation only (backcountry camping does not require a permit unless vehicles will be left at trailhead overnight); full-service at Blue Springs State Park, Wekiwa Springs State Park

Management: Florida Department of Agriculture and Consumer Services

Contact: (352)360-6675; www.freshfrom florida.com/Divisions-Offices/Florida-Forest-Service/Our-Forests/State-Forests/Seminole-State-Forest

Map: *DeLorme: Florida Atlas & Gazetteer:* Page 80 B1

GPS coordinates: N28 52.4' / W81 26.4'

Finding the spring: From the junction of FL46 and CR431 (Orange Boulevard) near Sanford, drive west on FL 46 for approximately 3.8 miles to the entrance to the state forest on the right. Follow the road north for 0.3 mile to a gate. From the gate, follow the main road (Sand Road) in a generally northern direction. You'll pass a check station, and several roads and trails head off in both directions. Ignore them all and continue driving north on Sand Road. At 2.7 miles you'll cross a bridge over Blackwater Creek. Continue from the bridge for another 0.2 mile until you come to a T where Pine Road heads to the right and Grade Road heads left. Go right, following Pine Road for 0.8 mile to the parking area for Sulphur Camp, on your right.

From the junction of FL 46 and CR 46A North near Cassia Station, drive east on FL46 for approximately 2.2 miles to the entrance to the state forest on the left and follow directions above.

The Spring

This tiny spring is extremely environmentally sensitive. I *implore* you to stay on the trail and footbridge to view this trickling spring. From the parking area, hike generally north through the campsite, following the orange-blazed Florida National Scenic Trail. You'll come to a fork and see two orange blazes on a tree. Whenever you see two blazes on the same tree, it indicates that the trail is making a distinct turn in the direction of the top blaze mark. At this particular fork, you'll see a side trail that goes straight ahead (north) as the Florida Trail heads left (west) and begins to climb. Go right onto the small side trail; it quickly brings you to a footbridge over the shallow, narrow spring run. Look upstream from the footbridge and you'll see that the land rises a bit. At the base of this rise, crystal-clear water comes out of the ground from seemingly nowhere. While all springs come up out of the ground, Sharks Tooth seems more dramatic. Perhaps because it's on such a small scale that you can actually visualize it, you gain a different perspective. The spring run forms its own tiny creek, with rapids, minnows, and crawfish. At its widest visible point, the creek is about 6 feet wide, yet the run flows for about 800 feet before merging into Sulphur Run.

As you approach the spring, you'll see signs urging you to stay on the trail. Please heed the signs! This is a *very* environmentally sensitive area. Do your part to protect it. If you go traipsing around the area you will damage the spring, and you may end up clogging it to where it never flows again. Also, the best view of the spring is from the footbridge. If that's not enough to encourage you to stay on the path, you should also know that this forest has ticks galore. I picked up about half a dozen while staying on the trail. I can't imagine how many I'd have picked up if I'd gone off-trail.

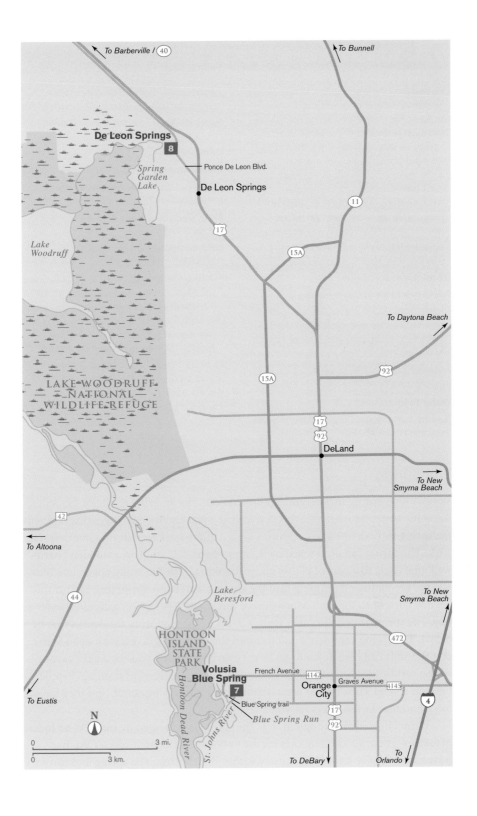

General description: A 0.25-mile walk along a wooden boardwalk gives you a bird's-eye view of the spring. To reach the spring boil by water, you must swim or float upstream 0.25 mile as well. All water activities are prohibited from mid-November through mid-March due to the presence of manatees. Although you can't swim or paddle with the manatees, it's a superb and rare opportunity to view this endangered species in their own natural environment, so don't forget your camera.

Location: 2100 W. French Ave., Orange City; about 6 miles southwest of DeLand

Development: Primitive

Best time to visit: Open year-round

Restrictions: Open 8 a.m. to sunset; pets allowed in designated areas only; closed to swimming, diving, and paddling from Nov 15 to Mar 15

Access: 0.25-mile hike or swim

Fees: $

Water temperature: 72°F

Nearby attractions: DeLand Museum of Art, DeLand House Museum, Lake Beresford Park, Gemini Springs Park, Green Spring, Seminole State Forest

Services: Food, restrooms on-site; all services in Orange City

Camping: On-site

Management: Florida Parks Service

Contact: (386) 775-3663; www.florida stateparks.org/bluespring/default.cfm

Map: *DeLorme: Florida Atlas & Gazetteer:* Page 80 A2

GPS coordinates: N28 56.85' / W81 20.383'

Finding the spring: From US 17/US 92 and CR 4145 (Graves Avenue), drive north on US 17/US 92 for 0.25 mile to a left onto French Avenue. Travel for 0.4 mile to a four-way stop sign. Continue straight across and travel for another 1.6 miles to the park on your left.

From US 17/US 92 and FL 44 in DeLand, drive south on US 17/US 92 for 5.1 miles to a right onto French Avenue and follow directions above.

The Spring

Volusia Blue Spring makes quite an impression. The amazing clarity of the water, the chilly temperature that leaves you feeling alive, and the manatees that frequent the spring run are just a few reasons I keep coming back to visit this amazing state park. The spring can be reached by walking about 0.25 mile on a wooden board-walk that leads to a pair of platforms overlooking it. But to really appreciate Blue Spring, I recommend jumping into the chilling water and swimming against the healthy current to the boil, which gushes out about 104 million gallons of water a day. The spring is quite popular with SCUBA divers exploring the depths that lie below. The spring vent drops 120 feet into the earth, and divers with open-water certifications can dive down to 60 feet. To go any deeper, you *must* have cave-diving certification. *Always* dive within your limits and level of training. People have died here! Tube rentals are available at the concession stand, and they have food, and nice hot showers for when you get out.

From November through March, the spring is inhabited by many West Indian manatees. These gentle giants are on the national endangered species list, but fortunately they've found a sanctuary within Blue Spring. The spring and spring

A 0.25-mile swim or hike leads to Volusia Blue Spring.

run are designated as a federally protected manatee refuge. As a result, the park is closed to *all* water activities when manatees are present. But you can still view the spring and these friendly "sea cows" from the swim platform and overlooks.

The boardwalk not only leads to the spring but also follows the run all the way out to the St. Johns River. At 310 miles, the St. Johns is Florida's longest river, and Blue Spring is the largest spring on the river. The park offers 2-hour guided eco-tours on the St. Johns River Cruise, or you can rent a canoe or kayak and explore on your own. Fishing is allowed in designated areas, as long as you have a freshwater fishing license.

If you prefer dry land, the park has trails for hiking and mountain bikes. Their campground is superb, and there are rental cabins available. You can also step back in time on a self-guided tour of the historic Thursby House, which was built in 1872. Enjoy this marvelous park as I have time and time again.

During winter, manatees flock to the warmer waters of Volusia Blue Spring.

General description: Surrounded by concrete, the large swim area mimics an oversize swimming pool with a good-size picnic area overlooking it. Huge oak trees offer shade and add to the scenery as the spring pours out about 19 million gallons of clear greenish water each day.

Location: 601 Ponce de Leon Blvd., De Leon Springs

Development: Developed

Best time to visit: Year-round

Restrictions: Open 8 a.m. to sunset

Access: Drive to

Fees: $

Water temperature: 72°F

Nearby attractions: Lake Woodruff National Wildlife Refuge, Blue Spring State Park, Hontoon Island State Park, Seminole State Forest, Lake George State Forest

Services: Restrooms, food on-site; all services in De Leon Springs

Camping: Blue Spring State Park, Alexander Springs Recreation Area

Management: Florida Parks Service

Contact: (386) 985-4212; www.florida stateparks.org/deleonsprings/

Map: *DeLorme: Florida Atlas & Gazetteer:* Page 74 C2

GPS coordinates: N29 08.05' / W81 21.767'

Finding the spring: From US 17 and FL 11 in DeLand, drive north on US 17 for 4.7 miles to a left onto Ponce de Leon Boulevard at the easy-to-miss sign for De Leon Springs State Park. Travel for 0.8 mile to the park directly in front of you as the road bends right.

From US 17 and FL 40 in Barberville, drive south on US 17 for 6.4 miles to a right onto Ponce de Leon Boulevard and follow directions above.

The Spring

Steeped in history dating back at least 6,000 years, and touted as one of Florida's original "fountains of youth," De Leon Springs remains a popular destination for both locals and out-of-towners. The park often fills to capacity, especially on weekends and holidays during the summer, forcing them to turn people away at the gate. I recommend arriving early or visiting on a weekday if you want to guarantee entry. The spring itself is surrounded by concrete, forming a sizable swim area with the feel of a large, spring-fed swimming pool. Multiple access points make it easy to take a dip in the greenish-hued water from all sides; they even have a lift and ramp for wheelchair access. You may occasionally see SCUBA divers in the spring, but this is by special permit for instructional purposes only. No recreational diving is allowed. At its deepest point the spring is about 30 feet, and snorkelers plunge down to get a closer look, but access into the spring cave is not permitted. At the far end of the spring, the water passes over a rocky spillway, forming a gorgeous little waterfall that begins the wide spring run.

You can rent a canoe, kayak, or pedal boat and venture down the spring run and out to Lake Woodruff National Wildlife Refuge, where birding and fishing opportunities are prime. Depending on water levels, you can also launch your own boat, up to 22 feet, at the park's boat ramp. A few trails give you the opportunity

A great blue heron shows off its impressive wingspan.

to explore by land, including a 4-mile hiking trail, and a 0.5-mile paved path that's wheelchair accessible. A large shaded picnic area overlooks the spring, with pavilions, tables and charcoal grills scattered throughout. Also overlooking the spring run is a unique restaurant, the Old Spanish Sugar Mill. You can order snacks and sandwiches at the take-out window or be seated inside and enjoy their famous pancake breakfast. The restaurant stands in the same location where a sugar mill once stood back in the 1800s. Stop in the park's visitor center and take a journey through time to see how this location has evolved throughout the years.

SOUTHWEST
REGION

This barred owl was spotted in the early-morning hours.

A single spring is found within this region of the state, which is why you don't see an overview map for the area. The region is best known for its white sandy beaches and islands such as Captiva, Sanibel, and Marco. Museums and culture welcome you in Sarasota, while cozy little beach towns such as Bradenton Beach and Anna Maria Island offer spectacular sunsets. Amid these treasures you'll find Florida's only inland spring in the southern part of the state. It's also the state's only warm spring, with daily temperatures ranging from 84°F to 87°F. Bring a towel, a mask and snorkel, and enjoy the warmer water of Warm Mineral Springs.

General description: This heavily populated spring is the only warm spring in the state. Averaging about 84°F to 87°F, it's especially enjoyable on the cooler days of Florida's "winter." Buoy lines act as partitions, dividing the large swim area into different sections. Grassy hillsides surround the springs and slope down to its banks. Bring a chair, a towel, and even a beach umbrella, since there aren't many trees around to offer shade.

Location: 12200 San Servando Ave., North Port; about 11 miles east of Venice

Development: Developed

Best time to visit: Year-round

Restrictions: Open 9 a.m. to 5 p.m.; no balls or throwing objects; no rafts or floats (noodles are the only floatation device allowed except for children's safety floatation devices); no alcohol, glass, or pets

Access: Drive to

Fees: $$–$$$

Water temperature: 84°F to 87°F

Nearby attractions: Myakka River State Park, Myaka State Forest

Services: Restrooms, showers, food on-site; all services in North Port

Camping: Myakka River State Park, Myakka River RV Resort, Rambler's Rest RV Resort

Management: City of North Port Parks and Recreation; run by a private concessioner

Contact: (941) 426-1692; www.cityof northport.com/index.aspx?page=1334

Map: *DeLorme: Florida Atlas & Gazetteer:* Page 97 D3

GPS coordinates: N27 03.6' / W82 15.6'

Finding the spring: From the junction of US 41 and CR 777 near North Port, drive east on US 41 for 2.5 miles to a left onto Ortiz Boulevard. Travel for 0.8 mile to the park, on the right.

From the junction of US 41 and CR 776 (Veterans Boulevard) in Port Charlotte, drive west on US 41 for approximately 8.2 miles to a right onto Ortiz Boulevard and follow directions above.

From I-75 near Venice, take exit 191 and drive south on N. River Road for approximately 5.5 miles to a left onto US 41. Travel east for 2.5 miles to a left onto Ortiz Boulevard and follow directions above.

From I-75 in North Port, take exit 182 and drive south on Sumter Boulevard for approximately 4.6 miles to a right onto US 41. Travel east for approximately 2.7 miles to a right onto Ortiz Boulevard and follow directions above.

The Spring

Built in the 1950s, the spring was privately owned until recently, when it was obtained by the city of North Port. Visions of the past remain in the murals, mosaics, and original tile work that decorate the property. Massage rooms, a sauna, and a cafe still stand, some of which will be reopened in the near future. Colorful blossoms line the pathways throughout the grounds, and butterflies flit from flower to flower. As you emerge from the first tunnel that leads to the spring, you almost immediately feel a wave of peace and serenity settle in around you. Legend has it that Warm Mineral Springs was the original "Fountain of Youth" sought after by Juan Ponce de Leon in the early 1500s. Who knows, there may be some truth to the healing properties of this large spring pool. Fed by two cold spring vents and one warm vent, it has the highest mineral content of any spring in the United States and the third highest in the world. The spring has also found

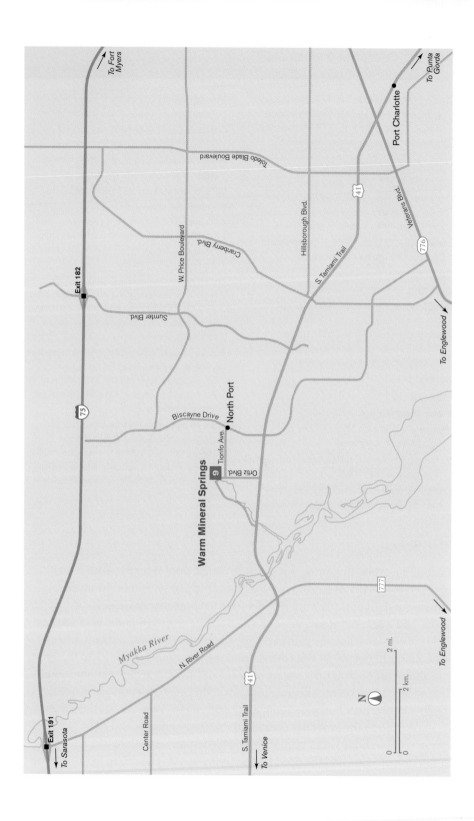

its place on the US National Register of Historic Places, partly because of its underwater archaeological significance. The remains of several prehistoric humans and creatures have been extracted from the spring, including saber tooth tigers and giant sloths.

Today, strings of buoys seem to separate the spring into sections, and there's a children's area as well. Lifeguards are on duty from 9 a.m. to 5 p.m. except for Christmas and Thanksgiving, which is a good thing, since the spring is surprisingly deep, reaching depths of up to 240 feet in the center. Despite its depth, SCUBA diving is not allowed in the spring, but you're welcome to bring a mask and snorkel and explore from the surface.

WEST CENTRAL
REGION

This amazing river otter seemed to pose for the camera.

ow! Some of the prettiest springs you'll ever lay eyes upon are found right here in the western central part of the state. They've got the crown jewels of the Ocala National Forest, with Juniper, Alexander, and Silver Glen Springs. In the town of Crystal River, you can swim with manatees as you explore a cluster of clear, crisp springs in Kings Bay. The magical Silver and Rainbow Rivers flow brilliant blue water over miles at a time. Each of these rivers is fed by more than a hundred springs, and the Silver River has earned the status of National Natural Landmark. At Weeki Wachee you can enjoy a mermaid show in the bright blue water or feel the rush as you zip down one of three waterslides. Take a glass-bottom boat tour, or paddle a pristine river. See alligators and turtles in their natural environment while bald eagles soar overhead. Venture out onto miles of trails where you can hike, mountain bike, horseback ride, or hop on an ATV. From waterwheels to wildlife, mermaid shows to museums—they've got it all, right here in the spectacular west central region of the state.

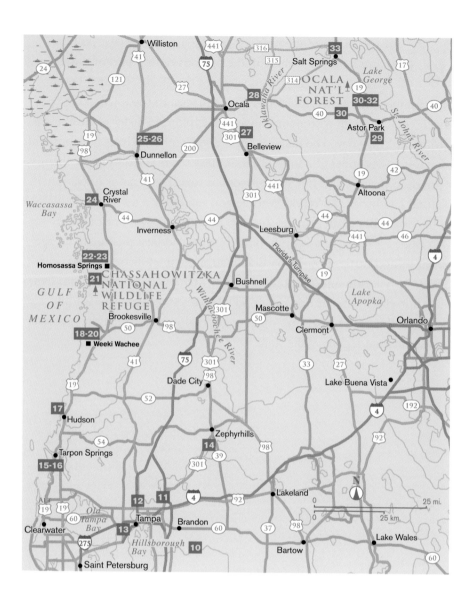

General description: The pale blue inviting water of Lithia Springs is unmistakable, and this is one of the few springs with a life guard on duty at all times. While you can see the spring from outside the swim area, a small additional fee is required to take a dip. But I assure you, it's worth it.

Location: 3932 Lithia Springs Rd., Lithia; about 5 miles southeast of Brandon

Development: Developed

Best time to visit: Year-round

Restrictions: Open spring: 8 a.m. to 6 p.m. Mon–Fri, 8 a.m. to 7 p.m. Sat–Sun; summer: 8 a.m. to 7 p.m.; fall/winter: 8 a.m. to 6 p.m.; no alcohol; no pets allowed in the swim area

Access: Drive to

Fees: $

Water temperature: 72°F

Nearby attractions: Fish Hawk Nature Preserve, Fish Hawk Sports Complex, Alafia River Canoe Rentals, Alafia River State Park, Alderman's Ford Regional Park

Services: Restrooms on-site; all services in Brandon

Camping: On-site

Management: Hillsborough County Parks, Recreation & Conservation Department

Contact: (813) 744-5572; www.hillsboroughcounty.org/Facilities/Facility/Details/Lithia-Springs-Regional-Park-7938

Map: DeLorme: Florida Atlas & Gazetteer: Page 92 B1

GPS coordinates: Lithia Major: N27 51.987' / W82 13.827'; Lithia Minor: N27 51.920' / W82 13.862'

Finding the spring: From the junction of CR 640 (Lithia Pinecrest Road) and FL 60 in Brandon, drive south on CR 640 for 6.9 miles to a right onto Lithia Springs Road. Travel for 1.4 miles to the park, on the right.

From the junction of CR 640 (Lithia Pinecrest Road) and FL 39 in Pinecrest, drive north on CR 640 for 4 miles to a left onto Lithia Springs Road and follow directions above.

The Spring

Each time I visit Lithia Springs it seems to get prettier and prettier, and I'm astounded that more people aren't out enjoying the pale baby blue water of the spring. It seems that word hasn't yet gotten out that right in the heart of Brandon is this wonderful hidden gem. The main spring, Lithia Major, has a huge swimming area encircled by a narrow sandy beach. Behind part of the beach stands a tall cement wall, with staircases that lead down to the beach in a few different spots. In the center of the spring, a large grate covers the vent where the water pushes out. If you're a decent swimmer, the water is shallow enough that you can dive down and touch the grate. Above the cement wall is a shaded grassy area, and the park charges a small additional fee to access the swim area. This spring is easily the highlight of the park and is visible without having to enter the swim area.

The remainder of the park is shaded by massive oak trees that add to the allure. There are plenty of places to have a picnic, and there's a playground, volleyball net, and campground on-site. They rent canoes, or you can bring your own to explore the winding Alafia River. A second and smaller spring, Lithia Minor,

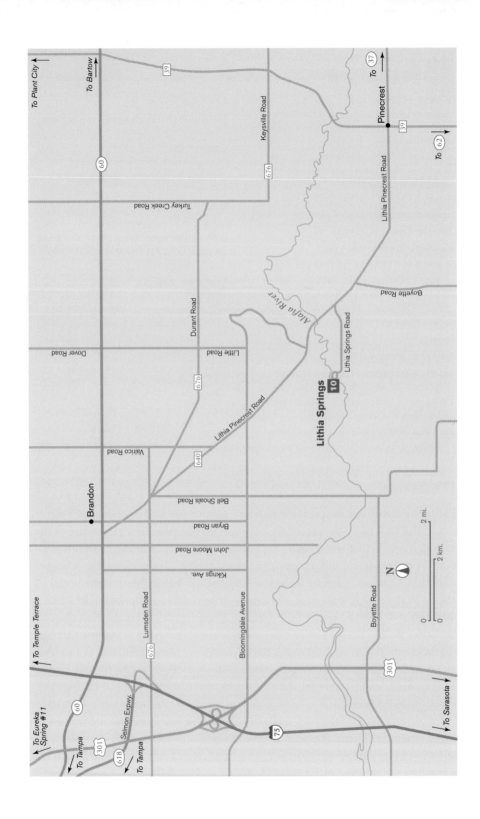

Inviting pale blue water awaits at Lithia Major Springs.

is also found within the park. This little beauty is blocked off for environmental protection, but you can view it through a chain-link fence. The spring is crystal clear, pristine, and full of fish. To see it, walk south on the sidewalk to the left of the main spring. As you follow the spring run downstream, the sidewalk ends at a chain-link fence overlooking Lithia Minor.

General description: Covered in duckweed, these inactive springs are certainly not the highlight of Eureka Springs Regional Park. The boardwalk "trail" and gardens, however, are quite lovely. If you're in the area, it's worth a visit, but I wouldn't go out of my way to see this one.

Location: 6400 Eureka Springs Rd., Tampa; about 4 miles southeast of Temple Terrace

Development: Primitive

Best time to visit: Year-round

Restrictions: Open 9 a.m. to 5 p.m. Mon–Fri, 8 a.m. to 6 p.m. Sat–Sun

Access: Drive to

Fee: $

Water temperature: 72°F

Nearby attractions: Sulphur Springs Pool, Busch Gardens theme park, Adventure Island water park, Hillsboro River State Park, Fort Foster State Historic Park, Lower Hillsborough Wilderness Preserve

Services: All services in Tampa

Camping: Hillsborough River State Park

Management: Hillsborough County Parks, Recreation & Conservation Department

Contact: (813) 744-5536; www.hillsborough county.org/facilities/Facility/Details/7934

Map: *DeLorme: Florida Atlas & Gazetteer:* Page 83 D3

GPS coordinates: N28 00.35' / W82 20.75'

Finding the spring: From US 301 near the I-4 overpass in Tampa, drive north on US 301 for 0.3 mile to a right onto E. Sligh Avenue. Travel for 0.2 mile to a right onto Maple Lane. Follow Maple Lane and the road bends left; after 0.5 mile the road becomes Eureka Springs Road. Continue another 0.8 mile to the park, on the left.

From the junction of US 301 and FL 580 (Harney Road) near Temple Terrace, drive south on US 301 for approximately 1.6 miles to a left onto E. Sligh Avenue and follow directions above.

The Springs

As you drive through the peaceful neighborhood on your way to this county park, it seems like an odd location. Sounds from I-4 drone in the background and planes fly overhead from the nearby Tampa Executive Airport. Although the park is named for Eureka Springs, the springs are not the highlight. In fact, the springs were so covered with duckweed when I visited, that from afar they looked like a grassy field rather than a body of water.

Follow the gravel path south from the park entrance for less than 0.1 mile directly to the springs. Near the park entrance there's a self-pay fee station and a covered picnic pavilion that's available for rent. Be sure to bring along a few singles, since the fee station is rarely staffed. A well-built boardwalk leads you through the park's swampy floodplain for about 0.5 mile and shows off an amazing amount of plant life diversity. That and the gardens are certainly the highlights of the park. In the late 1930s this parcel of land was developed as a botanical garden, and in 1967 it was donated to the county. Today lily pads line the canal that passes through the park, and the gardens are full of showy blossoms and native plant species. A small greenhouse, a gazebo, and benches here and there offer several ways for you to appreciate nature's beauty.

The great egret stands more than 3 feet tall.

General description: Sulphur Springs pool and park is a great treat for the people of Tampa and fun for the whole family, but you should know that the pool is not spring fed. Actually, the spring sits behind a chain-link fence, completely isolated. Some of the spring's water is used for municipal uses; the rest pours over a spillway, forming a small man-made waterfall. The water then follows a short spring run surrounded by the park as it heads out to the Hillsborough River.

Location: 701 E. Bird St., Tampa

Development: Developed

Best time to visit: Year-round

Restrictions: Open 10 a.m. to 6 p.m. Mon–Fri; 10 a.m. to 5 p.m. Sat–Sun (hours vary for adult or children swims; call ahead to confirm); no alcohol, glass containers, or pets

Access: Drive to

Water temperature: 72°F

Nearby attractions: Eureka Springs, Palma Ceia Spring, Hillsborough River State Park, Busch Gardens theme park, MOSI Museum of Science & Industry

Services: All services in Tampa

Camping: Hillsborough River State Park

Management: City of Tampa Parks & Recreation

Contact: (813) 931-2156; www.tampagov .net/parks_search_webapp/ParkDetail .aspx?nbr=137

Map: *DeLorme: Florida Atlas & Gazetteer:* Page 83 D2

GPS coordinates: N28 01.267' / W82 27.1'

Finding the spring: From I-275 in Tampa, take exit 49 and drive east on Bird Street for 0.2 mile to the large parking area on the right (just west of the El Camino Building).

From the junction of US 41 (Nebraska Avenue) and FL 580 (Busch Boulevard) in Tampa, drive south on US 41 for approximately 0.7 mile to a right onto E. Bird Street. Travel for 0.1 mile to the large parking area on the left (just west of the El Camino Building).

From the junction of US 41 (Nebraska Avenue) and US 92 (Hillsborough Avenue) in Tampa, drive north on US 41 for approximately 1.8 miles to a left onto E. Bird Street and follow directions above.

The Spring

Smack dab in the middle of Tampa, less than a minute from the highway and surrounded by city streets, you'll find Sulphur Springs Pool and Park. The spring itself, although it's on the same property, is completely isolated from the swimming pool. Both walled and fenced off, the spring is due east of the swimming pool, and the pool is not spring fed. Instead, it's a typical chlorinated swimming pool that you'd find in any backyard throughout the state. The pool has a wonderful children's area where fountains flow freely; there's also a section for adults to swim laps. Obviously convenient to the city, this is a refreshing place to cool off from the heat of the Florida sun at any time of the year. A mural showcasing some of Florida's native wildlife can be seen behind the spring—an attempt to give it a natural feel. While you can view the spring through the fence, you cannot swim, snorkel, or dive in it. The water pours over a spillway, creating a small but pleasant man-made waterfall. From the spillway, a wide spring run flows out to the Hillsborough River.

The park has a separate entrance just west of the pool, and between the pool and park, the spring run is surrounded on both sides. As you approach the park, a large white gazebo stands out before anything else. The gazebo and picnic shelters can be reserved and rented for special occasions. Most of the park is composed of picnic areas, and a small footbridge crosses the spring run near its confluence with the river. A playground keeps the kids entertained, but there were a few homeless people loitering in the park during my visit, so don't let the kids wander too far.

General description: Within Fred Ball Park, the walls surrounding this hundred-plus-year-old spring/fountain are shrouded in vegetation. There's no way to swim, snorkel, or play in the spring; it simply acts as a showpiece for this small peaceful park.

Location: 2621 Bayshore Blvd., Tampa

Development: Developed

Best time to visit: Year-round

Restrictions: Open sunrise to sunset; no alcohol

Access: Drive to

Water temperature: 72°F

Nearby attractions: Ballast Point Park, Eureka Springs, Sulphur Springs Pool & Park, Busch Gardens theme park, MOSI Museum of Science & Industry

Services: All services in Tampa

Camping: Hillsborough River State Park

Management: City of Tampa Parks & Recreation

Contact: (813) 274-8615; www.tampagov .net/parks_search_webapp/ParkDetail .aspx?nbr=46

Map: *DeLorme: Florida Atlas & Gazetteer:* Page 91 A2

GPS coordinates: N27 55.317' / W82 29.3'

Finding the spring: From the Selmon Expressway (FL 618) in Tampa, take exit 3 and drive east on W. Bay to Bay Boulevard. Travel for 0.1 mile to where the road ends at Bayshore Boulevard. Turn left and drive northeast for 0.2 mile to a left onto Rubideaux Street. Travel for 0.1 mile to the park, on the right.

From the junction of Bayshore Boulevard and the Selmon Expressway (FL 618) bridge in downtown Tampa, drive southwest on Bayshore Boulevard for 2.4 miles to a right onto Rubideaux Street and follow directions above.

The Spring

A single narrow path leads east from the parking area to Palma Ceia Spring. Built in 1906, the cloudy green springwater is now fed by a pump, keeping the fountain flowing day and night. This small city park has minimal amenities, but it sits within view of the Hillsborough Bay. While the view of the bay is lovely, during low tide the odor wafting on the steady breeze is unpleasant at best. Benches line the lawn, and a couple of loveseat swings offer a resting place. There's a charming gazebo, which you can rent out for the day, but it's on the small size. A handful of picnic tables rest alongside the path leading to the spring, but don't be surprised if they're occupied by the homeless.

General description: Designed as an educational experience, Crystal Springs Preserve is only open to groups of 15 people or more. Reservations are required, so you must plan your trip in advance.

Location: 1609 Crystal Springs Rd., Zephyrhills

Development: Developed

Best time to visit: Year-round; reservations required.

Restrictions: Open 9 a.m. to 6 p.m.; open to groups only (group sizes 15 to 100 people) by reservation only. Visitors must wear closed-toed shoes that can get wet and muddy.

Access: Drive to

Fees: $$$

Water temperature: 72°F

Nearby attractions: Hillsborough River State Park, Withlacoochee State Forest, Green Swamp Wildlife Management Area

Services: All services in Zephyrhills and Plant City

Camping: Hillsborough River State Park

Management: Crystal Springs Preserve

Contact: (813) 715-9707; www.crystal springspreserve.com

Map: *DeLorme: Florida Atlas & Gazetteer:* Page 84 C1

GPS coordinates: N28 10.933' / W82 11.117'

Finding the spring: From the junction of CR 535 and FL 39 (Chancey Road) in Zephyrhills, drive west on CR 535 for 0.4 mile to a left onto Crystal Springs Road. Travel for 1.8 miles to the preserve, on your right.

From the junction of CR 535 and US 301 in Zephyrhills, drive east on CR 535 for 0.1 mile to a right onto Crystal Springs Road and follow directions above.

The Spring

Although it's Pasco County's nicest spring, Crystal Springs is kept under a tight lock and key. It took numerous attempts via phone, e-mail, and normal post to gain access to the property for the purposes of this guide. You'll find it's nearly impossible to step foot on the property as an individual, so plan ahead, since you must have a group of fifteen to one hundred persons to visit. Once you do gain access, you'll find this is one of the best educational facilities in the state when it comes to the spring's environment. Along with the spring, which is second magnitude and pumps out about 30 million gallons a day, the property also has a living laboratory, a nature center, and ample opportunities for wildlife viewing. The 525-acre preserve has boardwalks and trails and even a butterfly garden. Most often school and church groups visit the spring, but any group of fifteen or more people is welcome. Reservations are required, and they have a user-friendly interactive calendar on their website to book your trip. A nominal fee is charged, and it's worth every penny. This is an amazing educational tool, and I applaud them for the environmental awareness they promote.

Nonvenomous black racer snakes often lie in leaves to soak up the sun while waiting for their prey.

General description: You might think that the cement walls surrounding the spring gave Wall Spring its name, but actually the spring was named for the Wall family, who owned it for many years. Today this second-magnitude spring is just one of the many things to see within the county park that houses it. I recommend taking a stroll on the boardwalk out to the bayou. The opportunities for birding and viewing wildlife are wonderful.

Location: 3725 DeSoto Blvd., Palm Harbor; about 2 miles south of Tarpon Springs

Development: Developed

Best time to visit: Year-round

Restrictions: Open 7 a.m. to dusk; no swimming, or alcohol; no fishing in the spring

Access: Drive to

Water temperature: 74°F

Nearby attractions: Fred Marquis Pinellas Trail, Tarpon Springs, Werner-Boyce Salt Springs State Park, Honeymoon Island State Park, Caladesi Island State Park, Jay B. Starkey Wilderness Park, Fred Howard Park, A.L. Anderson Park, Brooker Creek Preserve, John Chestnut Park

Services: Restrooms on-site; all services in Palm Harbor

Camping: Dunedin Beach Campground, Hillsborough River State Park

Management: Pinellas County Parks & Conservation Resources

Contact: (727) 582-2100; www.pinellascounty .org/park/21_Wall_Springs.htm

Map: *DeLorme: Florida Atlas & Gazetteer:* Page 82 D3

GPS coordinates: N28 06.383' / W82 46.333'

Finding the spring: From the junction of Alternate US 19 (Palm Harbor Boulevard) and FL 816 (Alderman Road) in Crystal Beach, drive north on Alternate US 19 for 0.8 mile to a left onto Brevard Street. Travel for less than 0.1 mile to the park, at the end of the road.

From the junction of Alternate US 19 and FL 880 (Klosterman Road) near Tarpon Springs, drive south on Alternate US 19 for 1.3 miles to a right onto Brevard Street and follow directions above.

The Spring

Locals frequent this lovely community park, but it's more often to access the Fred Marquis Pinellas Trail than to visit the spring. This paved path runs right by the park and covers nearly 40 miles from St. Petersburg to Tarpon Springs. People bike, skate, walk, and jog along the old railroad grade. I often wonder if these travelers even realize that there's a beautiful spring and bayou within the park. Two large playgrounds stand out, and paths crisscross between picnic areas. There's a butterfly garden, a climbing wall for the kids, and the park seems very dog friendly. A boardwalk leads you around the spring and then follows the spring run out to several fishing piers alongside the bayou.

A perfectly circular cement wall surrounds the spring. It then flows over a small spillway, creating a man-made waterfall that forms the beginning of the spring run. Fish are plentiful, birdlife is abundant, and wildlife viewing is optimal along the multiuse trails that extend out by the bayou. At the time of my visit, the park was in the process of rebuilding the observation tower that burned down in 2013. Hopefully it will be finished soon. The tower offers visitors scenic views of the Gulf of Mexico, and although there's no swimming allowed anywhere in the park, all in all it's a nice place to visit.

This brazen raccoon was caught red-handed.

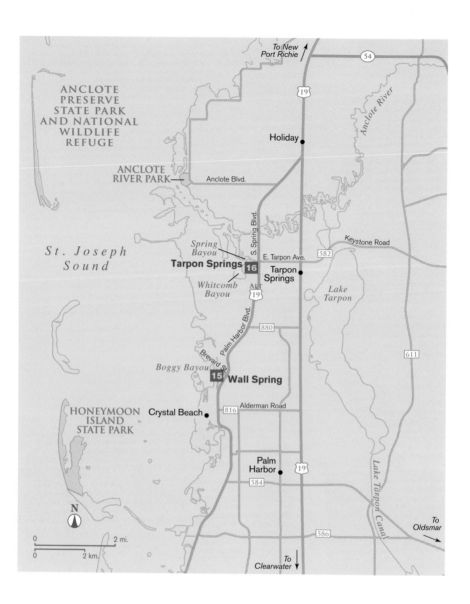

General description: At the turn of the twentieth century, this area was known as the "Golden Crescent," renowned for the famous actors, artists, and government officials who were drawn to it. Today it's easy to see the appeal of this quaint little coastal town. Adjacent to the spring bayou is a small park. On any given day there's a bustle of activity as locals walk their dogs, stroll along the water's edge, or lay a blanket out for a picnic.

Location: W. Tarpon Ave. at Spring Blvd., Tarpon Springs

Development: Developed

Best time to visit: Year-round

Restrictions: Open 7:30 a.m. to dusk

Access: Drive to

Water temperature: 72°F

Nearby attractions: Tarpon Springs Sponge Docks, Suncoast Primate Sanctuary, Tarpon Springs Aquarium, Wall Spring, Howard Park, Anclote River Park, Anclote Preserve State Park and National Wildlife Refuge, Honeymoon Island State Park, Jay B. Starkey Wilderness Park

Services: All services in Tarpon Springs

Camping: Dunedin Beach Campground, Hillsborough River State Park

Management: City of Tarpon Springs Recreation Department

Contact: (727) 942-5610; www.tarpon springschamber.com/community-info/parks#.U6wedUnD_wp

Map: *DeLorme: Florida Atlas & Gazetteer:* Page 82 C3

GPS coordinates: N28 08.783' / W82 45.583'

Finding the spring: From the junction of CR 582 (Tarpon Avenue) and Alternate US 19 in Tarpon Springs, drive west on W. Tarpon Avenue for less than 0.1 mile to a T at Spring Boulevard. Turn left here and follow S. Spring Boulevard for 0.1 mile to a right onto Beekman Lane. The park is on the right, immediately after the turn.

The Spring

In the quaint little town of Tarpon Springs you'll find Craig Park, a simple neighborhood park that circles the Spring Bayou. On any given day, locals walk their dogs, jog, or stroll around the circumference of Tarpon Springs. But each year on January 6 this tiny town park fills with people by the thousands. People travel here from all over the world to celebrate the religious tradition known as the Epiphany. On this day the Spring Bayou transforms, mimicking traditions typically found in the Greek Isles. The bayou is first blessed by the clergy of the Greek Orthodox faith, after which a cross is thrown into the water. Teenage boys then leap into the chilly water to retrieve the cross. It's said that the boy who brings it back will be blessed for the year to come. This tradition has been celebrated here at Tarpon Springs for more than a century. A monument on the south side of the park honors the Epiphany, and on the north side of the park another monument honors our troops that have been lost at war.

Although the spring boil is no longer active, manatees still frequent the bayou in wintertime, seeking warmer waters. While you're in town, you may also want to visit the wharf, the Sponge Docks, and the downtown historic district.

General description: This local SCUBA diving location is directly across the street from the dive shop that owns it. While the popular sink doesn't look like much from above, it's an entertaining and unique dive site. Those with open-water certifications are welcome to dive here, but you must first register at Scuba West before making your descent.

Location: 6815 Tower Dr., Hudson

Development: Primitive

Best time to visit: Year-round

Restrictions: Open 10 a.m. to 6 p.m. Mon—Fri; 8 a.m. to 5 p.m. Sat—Sun. All visitors must register at the dive shop.

Access: Drive to

Water temperature: Gradient temperature depending on depth

Nearby attractions: Werner-Boyce Salt Springs State Park, Wall Spring, Weeki Wachee State Park, Hospital Hole

Services: All services in Hudson

Camping: Chassahowitzka River Campground, Dunedin Beach Campground

Management: SCUBA West Dive Shop

Contact: (727) 863-6911; www.scubawest .net/HudsonGrotto/tabid/187/Default .aspxscuba

Map: *DeLorme: Florida Atlas & Gazetteer:* Page 82 B3

GPS coordinates: N28 20.75' / W82 42.067'

Finding the sink: From the junction of US 19 and FL 52 in Jasmine, drive north on US 19 for 1 mile to a left onto Tower Drive. Travel for 0.1 mile to the dive shop, on the right.

From the junction of US 19 and FL 595 near Hudson, drive south on US 19 for approximately 5.8 miles to a right onto Tower Drive and follow directions above.

The Sink

Hudson Grotto is a privately owned sink that's located directly across the street from Scuba West, the dive shop that owns it. The dive shop also has a swimming pool and barbecue grill on the property, creating a perfect setting for patrons to get their dive certifications right on the premises. Prior to visiting the grotto, you must register at the dive shop. Once you've registered, you can stay all night if you want. Although people don't typically come just to swim in the murky look-ing water of the grotto, they are more than welcome to, and the fee is the same whether you swim, snorkel, or dive. The water is brackish, and the temperature is gradient with the Gulf of Mexico.

Quite honestly, Hudson Grotto doesn't look that impressive from the surface, but divers tell me it's a unique diving destination. With a car, a sunken boat, a statue of Buddha, fossils, fish, turtles, and a magical chalice, this hourglass-shaped sink offers plenty to see within its depths. The grotto is about 140 feet deep, and all divers are welcome, but you must show proof of certification when you register.

Red-shouldered hawks are identified by a reddish hue on the upper third of their body and long yellow legs.

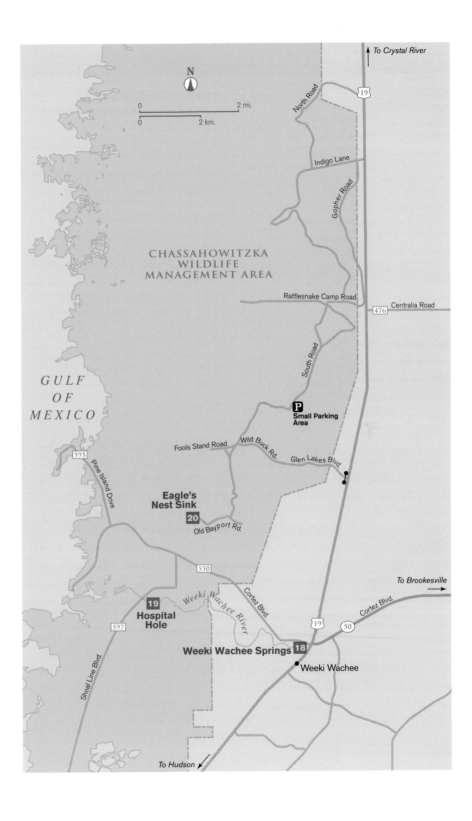

General description: What fun this fabulous state park is. The park is famous for its mermaid shows, but that's just one of many attractions you'll find here. They offer river cruises that take you along the Weeki Wachee River, which is fed by a brilliantly blue first-magnitude spring. You can swim and snorkel in the spring run, which is accessed from a small swim beach. But perhaps the most fun you'll have here is zooming down the water slides that are open seasonally.

Location: 6131 Commercial Way, Spring Hill, in the town of Weeki Wachee

Development: Developed

Best time to visit: Year-round

Restrictions: Open 9 a.m. to 5:30 p.m.; no pets allowed

Access: Drive to

Fees: $–$$

Water temperature: 74.2°F

Nearby attractions: Hospital Hole, Chassahowitzka Springs and Wildlife Management Area, Eagle's Nest Sink, Ellie Schiller Homosassa Springs Wildlife State Park

Services: Food, restrooms on-site; all services in Weeki Wachee

Camping: Chassahowitzka River Campground

Management: Florida Park Service

Contact: (352) 592-5656; www.florida stateparks.org/weekiwachee/

Map: *DeLorme: Florida Atlas & Gazetteer:* Page 77 D1

GPS coordinates: N28 30.033' / W82 34.383'

Finding the spring: From the junction of US 19 and FL 50 (Cortez Boulevard) in Weeki Wachee, drive south on US 19 for 0.1 mile to the park, on your right.

From the junction of US 19 and FL 595W (Osawaw Boulevard) in Spring Hill, drive north on US 19 for 5 miles to the park, on your left.

The Spring

Grand and fabulous Weeki Wachee Springs. If I were to label any of Florida's state parks a "theme park," it would be Weeki Wachee. But I assure you that I use the theme park moniker as a compliment. You won't see a life-size Mickey Mouse or Donald Duck strolling around the grounds; however, they do have an area cordoned off where you can take your picture with a real-life mermaid. That's right—one of the ongoing attractions at Weeki Wachee is a live mermaid show. The park has an underwater theater room where you'll see mermaids swimming along to modern-day music. The occasional turtle and fish are apt to swim by as well, since the mermaids swim in the heart of Weeki Wachee Springs. The theater can seat 400 people, and it still fills up. The mermaids use the original breathing system that was installed back in the 1940s. It's amazing how easy they make it look, but when you swim in the run of this first-magnitude spring, you'll realize how strong the current is—170 million gallons of water gush out daily. As you gaze at the spring, the cobalt blue color of the water is mind-boggling.

Beyond the spring you'll see Weeki Wachee's "Buccaneer Bay." This is where you'll find a sandy beach alongside the swimming area. You'll also see the park's water-slides just waiting for you to zoom down before plunging into the crisp, cool water of

These waterslides at Weeki Wachee are a blast.

the spring. The slides are open seasonally. Opposite the swim beach is the main body of the park. Here you'll find pathways that lead throughout to fountains, gift shops, restaurants, and wildlife shows that go on throughout the day. Peacocks roam freely among the people, strutting their stuff and even begging for a scrap of food or a french fry from an unsuspecting diner. The park also offers a river cruise, which is included in the price of admission. The cruise takes you on an enjoyable voyage downstream where you're likely to see lots of birdlife. If you're lucky, you may see a mating pair of bald eagles or an anhinga drying his wings in the sun. The occasional otter playing in the water or an alligator soaking up the sun are also possible sightings.

You can rent a canoe or kayak from the concessioner in the parking lot, but this is a one-way trip. It takes a few hours to cover the 5.5-mile river before they pick you up at the end and shuttle you back. I'm an avid paddler, and I love this trip. I just suggest that you take in all there is to see within the state park before heading out on the river, or you might miss something. The magnitude of the spring creates a swift current, moving at about 5 mph. It's quite an experience to paddle this many miles on a crystal-clear river, and there are only a few in the state to rival the beauty of this one.

General description: Although Hospital Hole is reached by boat, it's a very short paddle and well worth the effort. Not only is the spring pretty, but the entire Weeki Wachee River is gorgeous to paddle on.

Location: 7244 Shoal Line Blvd., Spring Hill; about 6 miles west of Weeki Wachee

Development: Primitive

Best time to visit: Year-round

Restrictions: Rogers Park open 24 hours; no alcohol, no pets allowed in the park except for loading and unloading from a boat

Access: Boat to; 0.2 mile upstream

Fees: $

Water temperature: 72°F

Nearby attractions: Weeki Wachee State Park, Eagle's Nest Sink, Hudson Grotto, Chassahowitzka National Wildlife Refuge, Chassahowitzka Wildlife Management Area

Services: All services in Weeki Wachee

Camping: Chassahowitzka River Campground

Management: Hernando County Parks and Recreation

Contact: (352) 754-4031; www.co.hernando.fl.us/parks_rec/Parks/Park_detail.asp?Key=22

Map: *DeLorme: Florida Atlas & Gazetteer:* Page 77 D1

GPS coordinates: Canoe Launch: N28 31.856' / W82 37.657'; Hospital Hole: N28 31.833' / W82 37.417'

Finding the spring: From the junction of CR 597 (Shoal Line Boulevard) and CR 550 (Cortez Boulevard) near Weeki Wachee, drive south on CR 597 for 1.4 miles to a left onto Patterson Drive. Travel for less than 0.1 mile to the park, on the left.

The Spring

A quick and easy upstream paddle leads to one of the lesser known springs in this book. Paddle south from Rogers Park, and in the second bend to the left, you can't help but notice the pool of clear water welling up on the right (south) side of the river. This is Hospital Hole. Legend has it that ill fish would come to the spring to heal before heading back out to the Gulf of Mexico. To this day, schools of fish and manatees can often be seen basking in the clear springwater.

Although the spring is only reached by water, it's very popular with the local SCUBA diving community. Open-water divers can dive in the spring, but at the 70-foot depth, a thick layer of hydrogen sulfide blocks off all the ambient light beyond it. For this reason, as well as the spring's heavy silt content, you must have cave-diving certification to dive beyond the 70-foot mark. Too many people have died in SCUBA accidents because they dove beyond the level of their training. I urge you to heed all warnings. I've met with several body recovery specialists, and most often these accidents were avoidable.

If you don't dive, you can still appreciate the beauty of this spring from above. And if you're feeling ambitious, you can continue paddling upstream for another 5 miles to Weeki Wachee State Park, where the head springs for the river are located. Rogers Park has a launch site for canoes and kayaks and a separate ramp for small motorboats. There's a sandy beach near the swim area, a playground, and a sand volleyball court. All in all, this small local park packs a punch. If you don't have your own canoe or kayak, you're in luck. The Upper Deck Restaurant is right across the river from the park. Along with a full menu and bar, they also offer canoe and kayak rentals.

A manatee calf may stay with its mother for up to two years.

General description: I hate to start out on such a serious note, but for the sake of public safety, I must. *Numerous* people have died diving at Eagle's Nest Sink because they were not properly trained or ignored the large signs posted regarding the difficulty of this extremely advanced dive site. There are several *minimum* requirements listed below that you must meet before diving here. For your own safety, and to spare those who do the body recoveries, please dive within your limits.

Location: Within Chassahowitzka Wildlife Management Area; off US 19 between the towns of Weeki Wachee and Homosassa Springs

Development: Primitive

Best time to visit: Year-round

Restrictions: Open 24 hours; day-use permit required

Access: High-clearance, four-wheel-drive vehicles recommended

Fees: $; You must display your pass in the windshield

Water temperature: 72°F

Nearby attractions: Weeki Wachee State Park, Hospital Hole, Ellie Schiller Homosassa Springs State Park

Services: All services in Weeki Wachee and Homosassa Springs

Camping: Chassahowitzka River Campground

Management: Florida Fish and Wildlife Conservation Commission

Contact: (352) 592-5715; http://myfwc.com/hunting/wma-brochures/sw/chassahowitzka

Map: *DeLorme: Florida Atlas & Gazetteer:* Page 77 D1

GPS coordinates: N28 33.317' / W82 36.567'

Finding the sink: From the junction of US 19 and CR 480 in Chassahowitzka, drive south on US 19 for 4.4 miles to a right onto Indigo Lane. Travel for 0.1 mile to a left onto Gopher Road. (**Note:** Stop at the self-pay station here before proceeding into the WMA.) Follow Gopher Road south for 2 miles to a T intersection. Go right here, continuing to follow Gopher Road, and after 0.1 mile come to another intersection. Go left again, continuing south on Gopher Road. After 0.7 mile come to a fork. The left leads east to a gate; go right, now following Rattlesnake Camp Road west. After 0.8 mile turn left onto South Road. Travel for 2.4 miles and you'll see a small parking area on the left (east) side of the road. Turn right here and travel for 0.5 mile to a left turn (you're now heading south again). Follow this dirt road south for 0.8 mile, passing Wild Buck Road. Continue on the dirt road south; after 0.4 mile you'll also pass Fools Stand Road. From this intersection, continue south on the unmarked dirt road that you've been on for another 1.3 miles to a T intersection. Turn right here onto Old Bayport Road and follow it west for 0.7 mile to where it dead-ends at the parking area for Eagle's Nest Sink. **Note:** This area is very complicated, and there are dirt roads running every which way. Please follow these directions very closely so that you don't get lost!

From the junction of US 19 and CR 476 East (Centralia Road), drive north on US 19 for 3 miles to a left onto Indigo Lane and follow directions above.

The Sink

Eagle's Nest is by far the most difficult location to find within this book. With such a demanding drive, after 11-plus miles on bumpy dirt roads, you might expect something spectacular. But in reality, a single boardwalk leads out to what seems to be an isolated pond at the far south end of this massive wildlife management area. Perhaps it's the perfect stillness of the dark green water, or maybe it's the fact that I'm well aware of the history of this sink. Whichever it may be, I almost instantly felt a chill and an eerie feeling in the air as I stared out over the calm water of Eagle's Nest Sink. Completely isolated and surrounded by brush, this is not my idea of a perfect swim hole. Also, there's really nothing eventful to see if you snorkel. So unless you're an advanced cave diver, skip this one and instead head over to Weeki Wachee or Hospital Hole. They're far more entertaining.

So why would I include this one? Aside from the urgings of several experienced cave divers, I also opted to help bring awareness to the extreme dangers of cave diving. Eagle's Nest Sink has unfortunately been the site of *numerous* fatalities. Despite the very large signs warning of the danger and difficulty of this particular dive site, people still attempt to dive here without proper training. There is *no* cavern, *no* entrance room, *no* place to get acclimated, and *no* room for error. If you don't meet the minimum requirements, do *not* SCUBA dive here. The National Speleological Society's Cave Diving Section (NSS-CDS) and the National Association for Cave Diving (NACD) have made the following recommendations for SCUBA diving at Eagle's Nest. And remember, these are the bare *minimum* requirements:

Full Cave Diving Certification

Trimix Certification

Appropriate experience with deep cave dives

If it's your first time diving here, they also advise that you go with someone familiar and experienced with this particular dive site.

I wish you the best experience in all your underwater endeavors, but please use caution and common sense at all times when you visit any of the springs in this book—especially when it comes to cave diving.

General description: Seemingly in the middle of nowhere, you'll find the Chassahowitzka River Campground and Chassahowitzka Springs. You can get a glimpse of the clear springwater from the dock near the boathouse, but to really see the head spring and the several other springs within the Chassahowitzka National Wildlife Refuge, you'll need to rent a boat, grab a map, and get out on the water.

Location: 8600 W. Miss Maggie Dr., Chassahowitzka; about 6 miles south of Homosassa Springs

Development: Primitive

Best time to visit: Year-round (closed Christmas Day)

Restrictions: Open 8 a.m. to 6 p.m.; no alcohol, swimming, or SCUBA diving

Access: Drive to, but ideally by boat

Fees: $

Water temperature: 72°F

Nearby attractions: Chassahowitzka National Wildlife Refuge, Chassahowitzka Wildlife Management Area, Ellie Schiller Homosassa Springs Wildlife State Park, Eagle's Nest Spring, Weeki Wachee Springs State Park, Hospital Hole

Services: Restrooms on-site; all services in Chassahowitzka and Homosassa Springs

Camping: On-site

Management: Citrus County Parks and Recreation

Contact: (352) 382-2200; after hours: (352) 601-8612; www.citruscountyparks .com/Default.aspx?id=28 or www .chassahowitzkaflorida.com

Map: *DeLorme: Florida Atlas & Gazetteer:* Page 77 C1

GPS coordinates: N28 42.933' / W82 34.567'

Finding the spring: From the junction of CR 480 (W. Miss Maggie Drive) and US 19 in Chassahowitzka, drive west on CR 480 for 1.5 miles to a right into Chassahowitzka River Campground. Follow the signs for another 0.1 mile to the boat ramp, at the end of the road.

The Spring

In the tiny town of Chassahowitzka, (pronounced CHAZZ-a-wiz-ga) you'll find the Chassahowitzka River Campground. The campground is just like any other full-service campground, but what makes this one special is its location at the head of the Chassahowitzka River. Several springs are found along the river, but you can get a glimpse of the head spring from the boat ramp. The spring has been in great peril in years past, but thanks to the efforts of the Southwest Florida Water Management District and local volunteers, today this spring is on its way to good health.

The campground office doubles as a camp store and boathouse. You can rent a canoe, kayak, or johnboat and venture out onto the clear running river, but make sure you get a map before you embark. The river has many twists and turns and offshoots, and it's easy to get turned around if you don't have a good map and compass. The head spring is just upstream from the boathouse and reached by a quick easy paddle. Wildlife viewing, birding, and fishing opportunities are endless along the river.

American alligators regulate their body temperature by basking in the sun.

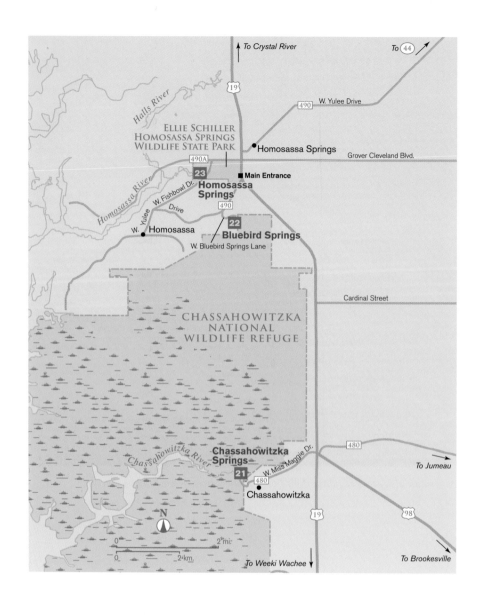

General description: Although there's no obvious boil, or big beautiful spring with a swim area, this peaceful park still has its appeal. The narrow, clear spring run is surrounded by grassy fields. If you want to get away from the crowds, this is your place; but if you're looking for more, or wanted to swim, head down the road to Weeki Wachee Springs instead.

Location: 8750 W. Bluebird Springs Ln., Homosassa Springs

Development: Primitive

Best time to visit: Year-round

Restrictions: Open sunrise to sunset; no swimming, or alcohol

Access: Drive to

Water temperature: 72°F

Nearby attractions: Ellie Schiller Homosassa Springs State Wildlife Park, Chassahowitzka Springs, Chassahowitzka Wildlife Refuge, Chassahowitzka Wildlife Management Area, Crystal River/Kings Bay Spring group, Weeki Wachee Springs

Services: Restrooms on-site; all services in Homosassa Springs

Camping: Chassahowitzka River Campground

Management: Citrus County Parks and Recreation

Contact: (352) 527-7540; www.bocc.citrus .fl.us/commserv/parksrec/parks/bluebird/ bb_park.jsp?PARKID=7

Map: *DeLorme: Florida Atlas & Gazetteer:* Page 77 B1

GPS coordinates: N28 47.333' / W82 34.767'

Finding the spring: From the junction of CR 490 (W. Yulee Drive) and US 19 in Homosassa Springs, drive southwest on CR 490 for 0.6 mile to a left onto W. Bluebird Springs Lane. Travel for 0.1 mile to the park, at the end of the road.

The Spring

Dedicated as a park in 1927, this small plot of land harbors the spring vents that form Bluebird Springs. The springs are primitive, and the 5.5-acre park is simple but pleasant. A playground and volleyball court offer entertainment, and a picnic area and pavilion with a charcoal grill provide a place to enjoy a day outdoors with the family. The whole family! Citrus County has recently added a dog park on the premises. The fenced in area is suitable for dogs of all sizes, and they've provided water fountains and plenty of shade for your four legged friends to enjoy a day in the park as well.

Grassy fields surround the spring and run. The spring vents and run issue out perfectly clear water, and they don't appear to be that deep. There is no swimming allowed anywhere within the park. It's a peaceful and quaint location, but if you're looking for a first-magnitude spring, head over to Homosassa Springs (#23). Unfortunately, there is no swimming there either, so if you want to take a dip, head down the road to Weeki Wachee Springs (#18); you won't be disappointed!

Sandhill cranes flourish in the wetlands of Florida.

General description: Although you can't swim in the blue-green water of Homosassa Springs, I highly recommend a visit. You can view the spring from above or go down into the underwater room called the "fishbowl." The view from here is fabulous and gives you insight into the abundant variety of fresh- and saltwater fish congregating below. Even manatees occasionally pass by the windowed walls. The park features many of Florida's native species of mammals, reptiles, and birds. Make sure you bring a camera. You're going to want to keep these memories for years to come.

Location: 4150 South Suncoast Blvd., Homosassa

Development: Developed

Best time to visit: Year-round

Restrictions: Open 9 a.m. to 5:30 p.m. (last tickets sold at 4:45 p.m.); no pets (the park provides complimentary kennels at the main entrance on US 19); no alcohol, swimming, or fishing

Access: Drive to

Fees: $–$$

Water temperature: 72°F

Nearby attractions: Historic Yulee Sugar Mill Ruins, Crystal River/Kings Bay Spring group, Chassahowitzka Springs, Chassahowitzka Wildlife Refuge, Chassahowitzka Wildlife Management Area, Withlacoochee State Forest

Services: Restrooms and food on-site; all services available in Homosassa Springs

Camping: Chassahowitzka River Campground

Management: Florida Park Service

Contact: (352) 628-5343; www.florida stateparks.org/homosassasprings/default.cfm

Map: *DeLorme: Florida Atlas & Gazetteer:* Page 77 B1

GPS coordinates: N28 47.95' / W82 35.317'

Finding the spring: West Entrance: From the junctions of CR 490A (Halls River Road) and US 19 in Homosassa Springs, drive west on CR490A for 0.5 mile to a left onto W. Fishbowl Drive. Travel for 0.3 mile to the parking area, on the left.

Main entrance: From the junctions of US 19 and CR 490A in Homosassa Springs, drive south on US 19 for approximately 0.25 mile to the visitor center, on the right.

The Spring

Unlike any other state park in Florida, Ellie Schiller Homosassa Springs Wildlife State Park not only has springs but also abundant native wildlife exhibits. Black bears to bald eagles, otters to owls, bobcats, deer, alligators, and crocodiles can all be seen here. To really appreciate all the wildlife and extensive birdlife takes a few hours. Manatees meander into the spring, and there's a room known as the "fishbowl," where you can view the scenery from underwater. The clear blue-green water of the spring is tidally influenced; as a result, this spring is home to a large collection of both freshwater and saltwater fish.

Throughout the day the park puts on educational programs; you can watch park personnel feed the animals while learning about their habitat, range, and lifestyle. There is no swimming allowed in the spring, but with all the wildlife exhibits, you won't be at a loss of things to see or do. There's a picnic area in what's known as the "Garden of the Springs," or you can grab a bite at the concessioner, which has indoor and outdoor seating. Pets are not allowed in the main body of the park, but outdoor kennels are provided near the visitor center free of charge. So if you're on the road with your pet, you can still stop in and enjoy the exhibits. Just make sure you leave plenty of water for your pet so that you can take your time and enjoy all there is to see at this phenomenal state park.

You can reach the park by driving directly to the west entrance off Fishbowl Drive, but there's limited parking. Another option is to enter via the visitor center off US 19. From there, the park has a tram and a guided boat tour that takes you to the west entrance by land or by water.

24

The Springs of Crystal River/Kings Bay: Tarpon Hole (aka Kings Spring), Parker Island, Hunter, Jurassic, House, Magnolia, Idiot's Delight, and Three Sisters Springs

General description: Over 70 springs have been located within the Crystal River/Kings Bay area, and likely hundreds of smaller springs and seeps exist throughout this 600-acre tidal bay. Here I have highlighted the top eight. The only way to reach almost every spring in the bay is by boat. Having a map of the springs is extremely helpful in finding your way around. I recommend printing one out before you embark, or grabbing one at Pete's Pier, which is the boat ramp I reference all the springs from. Hunter Springs is the only one that can be reached by either land or water. I urge you to use caution as you head out to explore. Kings Bay is the largest natural thermal refuge for manatees in the country, and boating accidents are the second biggest cause of manatee mortality. "No Wake" signs are there for a reason, so please slow down and keep your eyes peeled for these gentle endangered animals.

Location: Pete's Pier: 1 SW First Place, Crystal River; springs found throughout Kings Bay

Development: Primitive

Best time to visit: Open year-round; Nov–April is optimal for manatee viewing

Restrictions: No littering

Access: Boat to; distances vary

Fees: $–$$

Water temperature: 72°F

Nearby attractions: Crystal River Preserve State Park, Crystal River Archaeological State Park, Ellie Schiller Homosassa Springs Wildlife State Park, Chassahowitzka Wildlife Management Area, Rainbow Springs State Park

Services: All services in Crystal River

Camping: Chassahowitzka River Campground, Rainbow River State Park

Management: Southwest Florida Water Management District (SWFWMD); US Fish & Wildlife Service (USFWS)—Crystal River National Wildlife Refuge

Contact: SWFWMD: (352) 796-7211; www.watermatters.org; US Fish & Wildlife Service: (352) 563-2088; www.fws.gov/crystalriver/; Pete's Pier: (352) 795-3302

Map: DeLorme: Florida Atlas & Gazetteer: Page 76 A1

GPS coordinates: Pete's Pier: N28 04.646' / W82 35.836'

Finding the spring: Pete's Pier: From the junction of US 19 and FL 44 East in Crystal River, drive south on US 19 for 0.4 mile to a right onto Kings Bay Drive. Travel for 0.6 mile to a right onto SW 1st Place. Drive 0.2 mile to the boat ramp, at the end of the road.

From the junction of US 19 and CR 44 in Crystal River, drive north on US 19 for 0.6 mile to a left onto SE Kings Bay Drive and follow directions above.

TARPON HOLE SPRING (aka Kings Spring)

Location: At the south end of Kings Bay; in the middle of the bay, southeast of Banana Island

GPS coordinates: N28 52.9' / W82 35.65'

The Spring

Probably the most surprising spring in this group, and the most populated, is Tarpon Hole. I say surprising because it literally is out in the middle of the bay, with no land nearby except for Banana Island. These types of springs that discharge out into open water are aptly known as submarine springs. Buoy lines

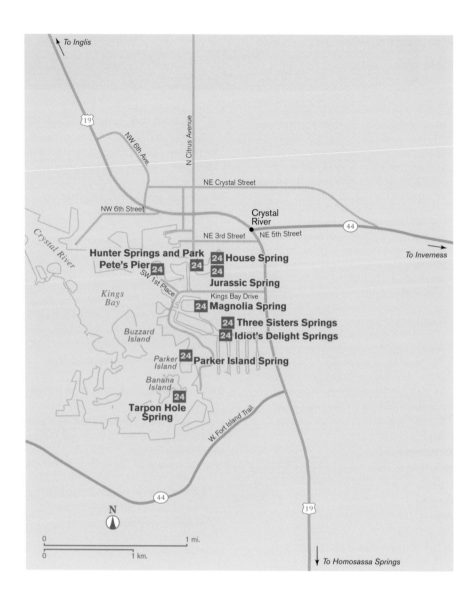

To Inglis

19

NW 6th Ave.

N Citrus Avenue

NE Crystal Street

NW 6th Street

Crystal River

NE 3rd Street   NE 5th Street

44

To Inverness

Crystal River

Hunter Springs and Park
Pete's Pier 24

SW 1st Place

24 **House Spring**

24
24
Jurassic Spring

Kings Bay

Kings Bay Drive

24 **Magnolia Spring**

24 **Three Sisters Springs**

24 **Idiot's Delight Springs**

Buzzard Island

Parker Island 24 **Parker Island Spring**

Banana Island

24
Tarpon Hole Spring

W. Fort Island Trail

44

N

19

0 ————————— 1 mi.

0 ————————— 1 km.

To Homosassa Springs

surround the spring itself, and in the winter months, a floating dock sits near the spring and acts as a visitor center and information kiosk for the Crystal River National Wildlife Refuge. SCUBA divers and snorkelers flock to Tarpon Hole in hopes of swimming with the manatees that frequent the spring. If you miss the opportunity to swim with a real manatee, a plaque and brass manatee statue rest on the floor near the spring vent. Legend says that if you rub this manatee's belly, it is sure to bring you good luck. This is a popular stopping point for the many boat tours that venture out into Kings Bay and the Crystal River.

PARKER ISLAND SPRING

Location: Northeast side of Parker Island (mouth of spring)

GPS coordinates: N28 53.133' / W82 35.633'

The Spring

This is the smallest spring on the bay, but it's still quite pretty and has lots of character. Clear water flows from two distinct spring vents, with a hint of blue shining through. When in season, a patch of beautiful blue irises stands at the mouth of the spring run, enhancing the scenery of this peaceful little spring. Parker Island is part of the National Wildlife Refuge and also a protected bird sanctuary. For this reason, you must stay in your boat and view the springs from the mouth of the run. Bring binoculars along to enjoy some bird watching while you're here.

HUNTER SPRINGS

General description: Hunter Springs is the only spring on the Kings Bay/Crystal River that can be reached by both boat and land. It's found in a small cove, known as Hunters Cove, on the northeast side of the bay, and a large swim area is buoyed off to protect swimmers from incoming boat traffic.

Location: 104 NE 1st Ave., Crystal River

Development: Developed

Best time to visit: Year-round

Restrictions: Open 8 a.m. to sunset; no dogs, alcohol, buses, RVs, or trailers of any kind (***Note:*** The health department discourages swimming until 24 hours after heavy rainfall.)

Access: Drive to or boat to

Fees: By boat:$–$$; no fee by land

Services: Restrooms on-site; all services in Crystal River

Management: City of Crystal River

Contact: www.crystalriverfl.org/index.asp ?Type=B_LIST&SEC=%7B607CC37E -4964-4967-8E36-1FC827923F13%7D

GPS coordinates: N28 53.667' / W82 35.55'

Finding the spring: Hunter Springs Park: From the junction of US 19 and FL 44 East in Crystal River, drive south on US 19 for less than 0.1 mile to a right onto NE 3rd Street. Travel for 0.4 mile to a left onto NW 1st Avenue. Travel for 0.3 mile to the park, at the end of the road.

From the junction of US 19 and FL 44 West near Crystal River, drive north on US 19 for 0.9 mile to a left onto NE 3rd Street and follow directions above.

The Spring

Hunter Springs is the only spring in this group that can be reached by either boat or land. The small, but active, Hunters Spring Park overlooks a small cove in the northeastern part of Kings Bay. The park has a sand volleyball court, picnic tables, charcoal grills, and a few picnic shelters, but primarily it comprises an open grassy field alongside the water. At one end of the parking lot is a narrow canoe/kayak launch site; at the other end is a sidewalk that leads to a single set of cement steps providing convenient access to the swim area. A sea wall frames the spring and swim area on one side, and it's buoyed off on the other side to protect swimmers from boat traffic. Plans are in motion for this park to get a complete make-over.

Kings Bay is a popular destination for viewing the endangered Florida manatee

The transformation should be complete by the end of 2016, when the sea walls will be replaced with a living shoreline, among other changes and upgrades.

To reach Hunter Springs by boat, follow the driving directions to Pete's Pier. From Pete's Pier, head north in Kings Bay, hugging the right (eastern) shoreline. You quickly come to a point on the right and a pair of tiny islands in front of you. Go right here, around the point, and follow the channel due east. You'll pass a wide opening on the right and then a narrow one. After you pass the narrow opening, the land you see in front of you, coming out to a point on the left, is Hunter Springs Park. The spring sits behind the buoy line.

JURASSIC SPRING

Location: East of Hunter Springs; in Hunters Cove on the northeast side of the bay

GPS coordinates: N28 53.683' / W82 35.417'

The Spring

About 0.1 mile east of Hunter Springs on the southeast side of the cove, you'll see a PVC pipe on top of the water that runs between two docks and blocks off the entrance to a tiny cove with buildings on each side. This is Jurassic Spring. The spring is surrounded by private property, so it can only be viewed from the main channel of the cove. From this viewpoint, the spring appears blue-green, but it also looks as though it needs a little protection from encroaching aquatic plants and lyngbya, a blue-green algae (cyanobacteria) that can grow like a weed. Hunters Cove is a freshwater part of the bay, which is part of why it struggles with the heavy intrusion of lyngbya. Most other parts of the bay are too salty for its survival.

HOUSE SPRING

Location: East of Jurassic Spring; in Hunters Cove on the northeast side of the bay

GPS coordinates: N28 53.75' / W82 35.4'

The Spring

House Spring is even more obscured than Jurassic. The spring is less than 0.1 mile north of Jurassic Spring and sits to the left of a house, hence its name. You'll see a much narrower PVC pipe on top of the water, blocking off the narrow spring run. A swimming pool–type slide sits out in the yard and drops swimmers straight out into the spring. Unfortunately, a natural land bridge keeps you from getting a good view of the spring.

MAGNOLIA SPRING

Location: South of Pete's Pier; in the middle of a side canal on the way to Idiot's Delight and Three Sisters Springs

GPS coordinates: N28 53.433' / W82 35.55'

The Spring

As you leave Pete's Pier, head south, keeping your eye out to the left (east) side of the bay. You'll see a small bridge that goes over a narrow finger canal. Head southeast down that canal, passing a canal opening on your left and right, and then another on just the left. About halfway up this second canal on the left, in the middle of the canal you'll see a small patch of clear water with a passive boil. This is Magnolia Spring. While most people simply pass it by on their way to Three Sisters Spring, this too is a popular spot for manatees during the winter months.

IDIOT'S DELIGHT SPRINGS

Location: On the east side of the bay; about halfway up, on the northern bank of a canal. The two springs that make up Idiot's Delight straddle the mouth of the Three Sisters Spring Run.

GPS coordinates: N28 53.274' / W82 35.343'

The Spring

While Idiot's Delight is beautiful with its crystal-clear water, it's often missed or overshadowed by the remarkable beauty of Three Sisters Springs. Idiot's Delight is composed of two separate springs located at the mouth of Three Sisters Spring Run. They sit on opposite sides of the entrance like guardians keeping watch. Both springs are buoyed off to keep boats out, and manatees are found here as well.

THREE SISTERS SPRINGS

Location: The spring is located on the east side of the bay, about halfway up. If you look at a map, you'll see a canal system on the east side of the bay. Three Sisters sits on the northern bank of a canal that is on the north side of this system. It's off the only canal that runs due east and west, about 0.4 mile east of the bridge you must pass under to reach the spring.

Restrictions: No SCUBA diving or motorized underwater propulsion devices; open Nov 15–Mar 31: no anchoring or disembarking/embarking of vessels in the spring

GPS coordinates: N28 53.317' / W82 35.35'

Three Sisters Springs are the crown jewel of Kings Bay.

The Spring

The crown jewel of Kings Bay, and by far my favorite spring in the bay, is Three Sisters Springs. The prettiest baby blue water you've ever seen flows from three different spring vents, giving Three Sisters an atypical free-form shape. Manatees frequent the springs seeking warmer waters in winter, and the United States Fish and Wildlife Service (USFWS) keeps a close eye on the springs and these endangered gentle giants, protecting them from errant snorkelers and kayakers trying to get a closer look.

It's difficult to describe the beauty that unfolds before you as you explore Three Sisters. I believe part of the reason this spring is in such perfect health is the contributions of the USFWS and Southwest Florida Water Management District (SWFWMD) and the help of volunteers who also keep a watchful eye on the springs. Another contributing factor is that up until now the only way to reach the spring is by boat. For this reason, it doesn't see the same flow of traffic that many other springs in the state do. Not only do you have to reach the spring by boat, but once you arrive at the mouth of the spring run, you must then swim or kayak up the short run to reach the boils. In the near future, you may be able to access this spring by land via a shuttle sevice offered by the USFWS.

To find the spring, follow the directions above for Magnolia Spring. From Magnolia continue southeast on the canal; you'll come to a T, where you intersect another canal. This is the only waterway in the area that runs due east and west. Go left here (east) and in less than 0.1 mile you'll see the buoys that block off Idiot's Delight Spring on the left (north). Pilings at the mouth of the spring run ensure that only kayaks and swimmers enter the spring. This spring is *not* to be missed!

General description: KP Hole Park gives you easy access to the stunning Rainbow River. On a good day, the visibility in the river is nearly 250 feet, and at its worst it's more than 100 feet. I recommend taking the water taxi upriver and diving, snorkeling, or floating your way back down to the park. The river is fed by over one hundred springs and is one of the most beautiful waterways in the state.

Location: 9435 SW 190 Avenue Rd., Dunnellon

Development: Developed

Best time to visit: Year-round

Restrictions: Open 8 a.m. to 8 p.m. in summer; 8 a.m. to 5 p.m. in winter; no food or drink in disposable containers anywhere on the Rainbow River

Access: Drive to

Fees: $

Water temperature: 73°F

Nearby attractions: Rainbow River State Park, Silver Springs State Park, Paradise Springs, Blue Run Park

Services: Restrooms, food on-site; all services in Dunnellon

Camping: Rainbow Springs State Park, Silver Springs State Park

Management: Marion County Parks

Contact: (352) 489-3055; www.kphole.org

Map: *DeLorme: Florida Atlas & Gazetteer:* Page 71 D2

GPS coordinates: N29 05.233' / W82 25.75'

Finding the spring: From the junction of US 41 and CR 484 in Dunnellon, drive north on US 41 for 2.1 miles to a right onto SW 99th Place. Travel for 1.1 miles to a left onto SW 190th Avenue immediately after crossing the railroad tracks. Travel for 0.5 mile to the park, on your right.

From the junction of US 41 and FL 40 West near Dunnellon, drive south on US 41 for approximately 2.4 miles to a left onto SW 99th Place and follow directions above.

The Spring

Before you get your hopes up, I must tell you that although the park is named KP Hole, there is no KP Hole spring. However, this small county park sits along the banks of the magical Rainbow River, and I do *not* use the term "magical" lightly. The Rainbow River runs clear blue over its entire length of 5.7 miles. Rainbow Springs (#26) forms the headwaters of the river, but it's also fed by more than one hundred other springs. The park has roped off a small swim area in the river, or you can rent a canoe or kayak and experience one of the nicest paddle routes in the state. They have a boat ramp in the park, so you can launch your own boat for a small fee ($). Tube rentals ($$) and an air station are available on-site, and you can take a 4-hour float trip downstream and catch a shuttle back to the park.

Another way to see the river is to hop on the Rainbow River Water Taxi. The pontoon boat taxis will take you upstream about a mile and literally drop you off in the water. Many SCUBA divers take advantage of this, but it's also cool to snorkel or tube downstream. And I mean that both figuratively and literally—the river's temperature is 72°F to 73°F. Some people are sensitive to the extended cold exposure, so you may want to wear a full or shorty wet suit. Snorkelers and divers alike must carry a "diver down" flag while on the river, so plan ahead. It's also a good idea to stay off to the side and out of the main navigable channel.

The park also has a small concession stand and a few picnic tables if you need a snack after all this fun in the water. This river is near and dear to my heart, and I'm pleased to say that it's littered with springs rather than trash, in part because no food or drink is allowed on the water taxi and no disposable containers of any kind are allowed on the river. Please do your part to help keep this river immaculate. For more information on the water taxi, visit www.rainbowriverwatertaxi.com or call (352) 427-0457.

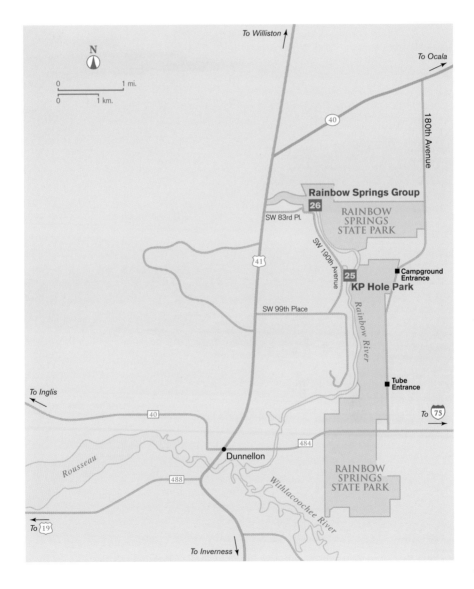

Visitors tube, paddle, snorkel, and dive in the unspoiled Rainbow River.

General description: Astounding! This really is paradise. A virtual garden of Eden, with a number of beautiful bonnie blue springs as an added bonus. Brick and stone walkways weave through tropical gardens overlooking the river. Flowering plants, waterfalls, and a butterfly garden are just part of the attraction. The glorious Rainbow River is fed by over one hundred springs, and the headwaters of the river are right here in this magnificent state park.

Location: 19158 SW 81st Place Rd., Dunnellon

Development: Partially developed

Best time to visit: Year-round

Restrictions: No alcohol, tubes, floats, or rafts (noodles are the only floatation devices allowed); no fishing within 1,700 feet of the head spring; no pets allowed in the springs; no food or drink in disposable containers anywhere on the Rainbow River

Access: Drive to

Fees: $

Water temperature: 72°F

Nearby attractions: KP Hole Park, Blue Grotto, Devil's Den, Blue Run Park

Services: Restrooms on-site; all services in Dunnellon

Camping: On-site

Management: Florida Park Service

Contact: (352) 465-8555; www.florida stateparks.org/rainbowsprings/default.cfm

Map: *DeLorme: Florida Atlas & Gazetteer:* Page 71 D2

GPS coordinates: N29 06.15' / W82 26.25'

Finding the spring: From the junction of US 41 and CR 484 in Dunnellon, drive north on US 41 for approximately 3.9 miles to the park, on your right.

From the junction of US 41 and FL 40 near Dunnellon, drive south on US 41 for 0.6 mile to the park, on your left.

The Spring

Stunning! Words cannot describe the brilliant blue beauty you're about to experience when you visit Rainbow Springs State Park. Forming the headwaters of the magical Rainbow River, you'll find the first-magnitude Rainbow Springs pushing out more than 400 million gallons of water a day. It's truly hard to fathom that much water pouring out of the ground—and this is only the fourth-biggest spring in the state! The park has three distinct entrances. One is for the campground, which is on the east side of the river off SW 180th Avenue. A second entrance is for tubing. This too is on the east side of the river, downstream from the campground and also accessed via SW 180th Avenue. (***Note:*** Tubing is not allowed at the main entrance or headwaters.) And then there is the main entrance to the park, where a Chattahoochee stone path leads you to the fee booth.

Almost immediately after entering the park, the scenery unfolds and you are transported into the most beautiful setting you could ever imagine. You're instantly afforded stunning views of the spring pool below. To the right, a large grassy hillside slopes down toward the water. To your left, pathways made of brick and stone lead you through gardens and past waterfalls as you explore the park. That's right; I said waterfalls, in Florida. There are actually a few scattered throughout the gardens of the park—remnants of years gone by, when the land

The immaculate Rainbow River is fed by more than one hundred springs.

surrounding the spring was a popular amusement park. The park closed down in the 1970s, and the state acquired the land in the 1990s, creating the fabulous state park you see before you. A walkway leads past the grassy hillside and takes you to a large swim area where you can swim and snorkel in the head spring. The pathway then continues to a canoe launch, where you can rent a canoe or kayak. You can launch your own vessel from here, but it's a long haul and a steep hill to drag your boat. If you ask me, it's worth the price to rent a boat instead. If you're set on taking your own canoe or kayak out, a better option is to launch at KP Hole Park (#25) and head upstream. It's about 1.4 miles via the river to reach the head spring.

The gardens, waterfalls, and head spring are not all there is to see at this fabulous state park. As you look out over the spectacular river, you'll notice patches and pools of brilliant blue. That's because this river is fed by over one hundred additional springs. It's literally littered with springs. I highly recommend taking a kayak out. You not only will see spring after spring as you paddle on one of Florida's finest waterways but will also be privy to a wide variety of birdlife, including bald eagles! Without a doubt, Rainbow Springs and the entire Rainbow River are among my favorites.

General description: The entrance to this privately owned spring is small but beautiful. But like many things in life, you can't judge a book by its cover, because below the surface, the spring opens up into a giant cavern. People come from all over the world to dive here, and the spring has options for both open-water and cave divers. The downside is that if you don't dive, you cannot visit—no swimming or snorkeling is allowed in the spring.

Location: 4040 SE 84th Lane Rd., Ocala; about 3 miles north of Belleview and 7 miles south of Ocala

Development: Primitive

Best time to visit: Year-round except on holidays (Call ahead to check the schedule.)

Restrictions: Open 9 a.m. to 5 p.m. Thurs—Fri, 8 a.m. to 5 p.m. Sat—Sun; closed Mon—Wed; SCUBA diving only, no swimming, or snorkeling

Access: Drive to

Fees: $$$; cash only

Water temperature: 74°F to 77°F

Nearby attractions: Santos Mountain Bike Trail System, Silver Springs State Park, Ocala National Forest, Florida Horse Park

Services: Restrooms, full dive gear rentals, air fills on-site; all services in Ocala

Camping: Silver Springs State Park, Santos Campground

Management: Privately owned

Contact: (352) 368-5746; www.florida diveconnection.com/paradise-springs/

Map: DeLorme: Florida Atlas & Gazetteer: Page 72 D2

GPS coordinates: N29 5.917' / W82 4.867'

Finding the spring: From the junction of US 441 and FL 25 in Belleview, drive north on US 27 for approximately 3.7 miles to a right onto SE 84th Lane Road. Travel for approximately 0.2 mile to the railroad tracks. Cross over the tracks and immediately turn right onto SE 36th Court. Travel for less than 0.1 mile to a left that puts you back on SE 84th Lane Road. Travel 0.1 mile to Paradise Springs, straight ahead just before the road bends right.

From the junction of US 441 and CR 328 (SE 80th Street) near Ocala, drive east on CR 328 for 0.2 mile to a right onto SE 36th Court just after crossing the railroad tracks. Travel south for 0.5 mile to a left onto SE 84th Lane Road and follow directions above.

The Spring

Unlike most other springs in the state, Paradise Springs is fed by two different aquifers, at two different temperatures. One is 72°F degrees and the other 78°F, so the water blends together and warms this spring up to about 74°F to 77°F daily. The spring pool is small but deep blue in color, and it's absolutely gorgeous. Unfortunately, there is no swimming or snorkeling allowed here. This is strictly a SCUBA diving destination, and a popular one at that. People come from all over the world to dive here. The first room is a giant cavern, and depending on your experience and comfort level, you can dive down to 100 feet with an open-water certification. There are fossils embedded in the walls, and a small Buddha statue smiles back at you. To go beyond the 100 foot mark, you must be a certified cave diver.

The spring is family owned and operated, and they are very nice people. They do bottle fills and rent out equipment on-site, making it quite convenient to dive here. When you enter the property, you must first stop at the office to take care of business. After the waivers are signed and fees are paid, they have a couple of picnic tables where you can prep your gear. From there a path leads down to the spring, where a submerged platform makes for an easy entrance and exit. They also offer night dives, but you must call ahead to make a reservation. Quite honestly, it's always a good idea to call ahead at this location, since they are a small family-run business. They also offer classes from open-water through cavern-diving certifications. There are no visitors allowed on the property, unless you're diving. The owners ask that if you need additional information, visit the website or call ahead; they'll be happy to help you.

General description: If it was up to me, some of our natural springs would be on the Natural Wonders of the World list, including this one. Silver Springs is a group of many springs that form the magnificent Silver River, and it has the amazing claim to fame of being the biggest spring in the world. That's right, I said world! While you can't swim in the river, you can canoe, kayak, or take a glass-bottom boat tour to get a better view of this spectacular waterway.

Location: 1425 NE 58th Avenue, Ocala

Development: Developed

Best time to visit: Year-round

Restrictions: Open 8 a.m. to sunset; no swimming or fishing

Access: Drive to

Fees: $

Water temperature: 72°F

Nearby attractions: Ocala National Forest, Paradise Springs

Services: Food, restrooms on-site; all services in Ocala

Camping: On-site

Management: Florida Park Service

Contact: (352) 236-7148; www.florida stateparks.org/silversprings/default.cfm

Map: *DeLorme: Florida Atlas & Gazetteer:* Page 72 C2

GPS coordinates: N29 12.96' / W82 03.177'

Finding the spring: From the junction of FL 40 and FL 35 near Ocala, drive east on FL 40 for 0.1 mile to the park, on the right.

From the junction of FL 40 and FL 326 near Ocala, drive west on FL 40 for 1.3 miles to the park, on the left.

The Spring

Spanning more than 5,000 acres, Silver Springs State Park has three distinct entrances and four distinct areas to explore. The first entrance, the River Side entrance is located off FL 35, south of FL 40 on the southwest side of the river. This is where you'll find a system of trails that are open to hiking and mountain biking, the park's campground, and the park's main museum. I highly recommend a visit to the museum, which has the skeletal remains of a woolly mammoth standing tall. This is the most complete mammoth skeleton in the state, and it was recovered from within the head spring itself. The second entrance is on FL 40, about 1.25 miles east of FL 35 on the northeast side of the river. This is where you'll find the trails dedicated to those on horseback. You must call ahead before you access this section of the park. If you don't have your own horse, you can call Cactus Jacks at (352) 266-9326. They offer horse rentals by the hour.

The third entrance is the Spring Side entrance, which is located on FL 40, just west of FL 35. This is where you'll find the springs and headwaters of the Silver River. But before I get to that, at the far southeast end of this parking lot, you'll also find a canoe/kayak launch, where you'll pay a small fee ($) to launch your own vessel. No motorized boats are allowed, and there's no fishing in the river. From the northwest end of this large parking lot, you can access their water park, Wild Waters, which is open seasonally. A separate fee is required to enter the

A perfect resting place overlooks the Silver River.

water park, but it's well worth the money! They have several water slides, a wave pool, and an area for the little ones. It's just good clean fun!

And now, on to the grand finale . . . Silver Springs and the Silver River. This is the biggest spring in the world! If I say nothing more, you should know that you *must* go here! But I do have so much more to say about this magical place, I don't even know where to start. As you enter the newly formed state park, tall trees tower overhead and you're greeted with freely flowing fountains, pacifying you with the pleasant sound of moving water. After you pass through the grand gates near the entrance, the river comes into view, and you instantly see why I call it magical. As you gaze upon the river, you see so many shades of blue. From deep cobalt to teal, from deep sky to royal blue, it's hard to believe that the water truly comes out of the ground looking like this, but it's true. And this is why the Silver River is protected and designated as a National Natural Landmark.

You'll be hypnotized by this amazing spring-fed river, but once you snap out of your trance, you'll see there's almost like a mini shopping plaza near the head-waters. They have a pizza place, an ice-cream shop, and a second museum with an on-site archaeologist to answer questions. In fact, this is the only state park in Florida with its own dedicated archaeologist. The "plaza" is also where you'll find the kiosk to pay the fee for the glass-bottom boat tour, which I *highly* recommend. Unless you're going to paddle on the river, this is the very best way to see several springs along the river, as well as learn quite a bit of history and fun facts about the springs, the river, and the park. The boat captains have been guiding these

For more than one hundred years, glass-bottom boat tours have been running on the glorious Silver River.

tours for decades, from when this was a privately owned theme park–type tourist attraction. They possess a wealth of knowledge and make the trip fun; if you pay attention to what they say along the tour, you'll enjoy some dry humor. You're certain to see birdlife and turtles and may even spy an alligator sunning itself on the banks or lying over a tree root.

When you finish the glass-bottom boat tour, a sidewalk path leads past the boats and around to the far side of the spring. Here you'll see a statue or two and pretty flowering plants. On one occasion I spied a 9-foot alligator lying on the bank just 20 feet from the sidewalk, so keep your eyes peeled, and your children close by. The American alligator can sprint up to 40 mph, so I wouldn't take any chances. Well-behaved pets are allowed in the park, as long as they remain on-leash at all times. They are not allowed on the boat tour, but the park offers kennels near the entrance, where you can board your pet while you take the tour. But you must quickly retrieve them when you're done. This is Florida. It's far too hot to leave your pet unattended for any length of time. Make sure you bring a bowl and lots of water to leave with your pet while you enjoy the tour.

As you look out over the Silver River, just think—it's fed by over a hundred springs, which collectively put out more than 850 million gallons of water every single day. And the water that flows into this river is 99.8 percent pure when it comes out of the aquifer below. It's hard to imagine that that much water lies under the ground beneath our feet. But here it is, in all its glory, flowing freely in this miraculous natural state. Obviously, Silver Springs is among the front runners of the Author's Favorites.

General description: Alexander Springs easily makes the Author's Favorites list, and it's the only first-magnitude spring in the state that's found on national forest property. True blue water pours out, forming the wide spring run that adds to the scenery at this serene spring. The large picnic area overlooking the spring fills up quickly on weekends and holidays. If you don't like crowds, and want to see this spring at its best, I suggest visiting on a weekday.

Location: 49525 CR 445, Altoona; about 10 miles northeast of Altoona and 10 miles southwest of Astor

Development: Primitive

Best time to visit: Year-round

Restrictions: Open 8 a.m. to sunset; no fishing, boating, pets, or bicycles in the swim area; designated areas for fishing; boats are allowed in the spring run

Access: Drive to

Fees: $

Water temperature: 72°F

Nearby attractions: Billies Bay Wilderness, Alexander Springs Wilderness, Great Florida Birding Trail, Florida National Scenic Trail, Juniper Springs Recreation Area, Lake Woodruff National Wildlife Refuge, Lake George State Forest.

Services: Food, restrooms on-site; all services in Astor

Camping: On-site

Management: Ocala National Forest—Seminole Ranger District; run by private concessioner

Contact: (352) 669-3522; www.fs.usda.gov/recarea/ocala/recarea/?recid=32209

Map: *DeLorme: Florida Atlas & Gazetteer:* Page 73 D3

GPS coordinates: N29 04.883' / W81 34.55'

Finding the spring: From the junction of CR 445 and FL 19 near Alexander Springs, drive east on CR 445 for 5 miles to the recreation area, on the left.

From the junction of CR 445A and FL 40 in Astor Park, drive south on CR 445A for approximately 0.6 mile to a left onto CR 445. Travel for approximately 5.8 miles to the recreation area, on the right.

The Spring

River otters frolic in the spring run at dawn and dusk, deer roam freely through the property, and the spring is top notch. Bright blue water flows down the wide spring run at a rate of 70 million gallons a day. A large picnic area sits alongside the spring. It takes a little bit of a swim to actually get out over the spring boil, but when you do, you'll see two distinct openings, one at each end of a large hole in the ground. A small amount of aquatic vegetation constantly moves with the flow of the water, as if holding on for dear life. The park has a fantastic wooded campground and a trail that shortcuts from the campground to the day-use area, so you can walk from your campsite directly to the spring. The day-use area consists of the large picnic area near the spring, a smaller picnic area near the "camp store," and a canoe launch site. They rent canoes, or you can launch your own.

You're likely to see turtles, alligators, lots of birdlife, and possibly an otter or manatee in the spring run. The run is extremely long, covering about 8 nautical miles before its confluence with the St. Johns River. A hiking trail/boardwalk meanders through the park and leads to a platform overlooking the spring run.

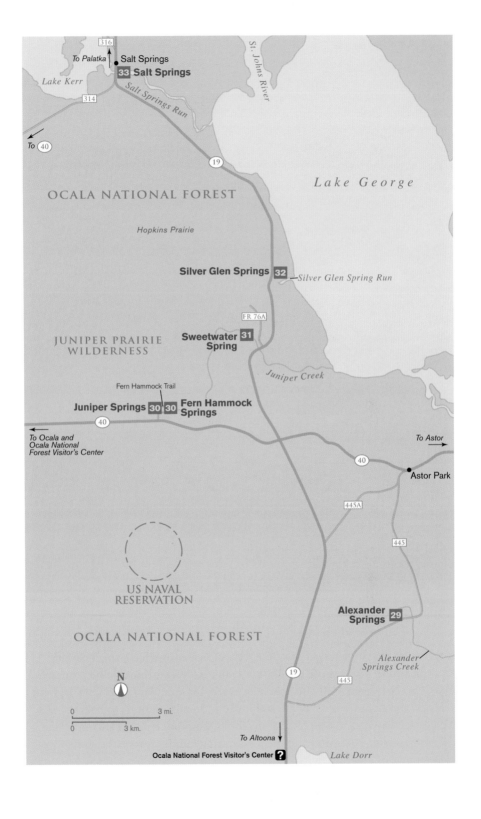

A skin diver explores Alexander Springs.

If you're looking for a longer hike, the recreation area also has a small parking lot dedicated to hikers, since the Florida Trail passes right through the property. The Ocala National Forest also has trail systems for mountain bikers, off-highway vehicles, and equestrians. Wildlife is abundant, from black bears to bobcats, and bald eagles, hawks, and ospreys soar overhead. *Caution:* Hunters are out by the dozens in season, so if you're on the trails during hunting season, be sure to wear blaze orange or other bright colors.

General description: With a working waterwheel at the far end of the spring and brilliant blue hues gleaming in the sun, Juniper easily stands out as an Author's Favorite. There's a campground, a canoe launch, hiking trails, a swim area, and access to Fern Hammock Springs within the wonderful recreation area that surrounds Juniper Springs.

Location: 26701 FL 40, Silver Springs; about 11 miles west of Astor and 22 miles east of Ocala

Development: Developed

Best time to visit: Year-round

Restrictions: Open 8 a.m. to sunset; no bikes, alcohol, or pets in the swimming area (pets allowed in the campground); no wading in the spring run

Access: Juniper: Drive to; Fern Hammock: Hike to; an easy 0.4-mile one way

Fees: $

Water temperature: 72°F

Nearby attractions: Ocala Shooting Range, Sweetwater Cabin, Silver Glen Recreation

Area, Alexander Springs Recreation Area, Lake George

Services: Restrooms, food on-site; all services in Astor

Camping: On-site

Management: Ocala National Forest—Lake George Ranger District; run by private concessioner

Contact: (352) 625-3147; www.fs.usda.gov/recarea/ocala/recarea/?recid=34064

Map: DeLorme: Florida Atlas & Gazetteer: Page 73 C2

GPS coordinates: N29 11.017' / W81 42.75'

Finding the spring: From the junction of FL 40 and FL 19 in Healing Waters, drive west on FL 40 for 4.4 miles to the Juniper Springs Recreation Area, on the right.

From the junction of FL 40 and FL 314A near Waldena, drive east on FL 40 for approximately 11 miles to the Juniper Springs Recreation Area, on the left.

JUNIPER SPRINGS

The Spring

Juniper Springs Recreation Area lies almost dead center in the Ocala National Forest. Stone pillars greet you at the entrance as you head down to the fee gate. The recreation area has a full-service campground, a canoe/kayak launch, hiking trails, and an amazing swim area. It's also home to a historic mill house that was built by the Civilian Conservation Corps (CCC) back in the 1930s and to Fern Hammock Springs, a natural spring that rests along the Juniper Springs run. While you're in the area, I highly recommend taking the easy 0.4-mile hike to see this spring as well. For Juniper Springs, an obvious Chattahoochee stone path leads down to the day-use area and spring. There's a camp store/concession area where you can grab a snack or pick up a few things you may have forgotten. A small picnic area sits near the spring, along with a picnic shelter and the remains of some old chimney smoke stacks. Steps lead down to a beautiful circular pool with a working waterwheel at the far end. Brilliant blue water flows by the millions of gallons per day from this second-magnitude spring. It's enough water to keep the waterwheel

A working waterwheel adds to the appeal of Juniper Springs.

moving 24/7. The waterwheel is part of the historic millhouse, which once supplied electricity to the campground. A path leads around the spring to the right where you can go inside the millhouse, but there's not really anything to see but an empty structure and some educational placards.

Beyond the millhouse, a boardwalk and foot trails let you explore more of the recreation area. Around the spring to the left (northeast), another path leads to the canoe launch. Here you can either launch your own canoe or kayak or rent one from the concessioner. No motorboats are allowed in the spring run or in Juniper Creek. The water from Juniper Springs flows through the waterwheel and over a tiny waterfall/spillway before beginning the narrow, crystal-clear spring run that forms the headwaters of Juniper Creek. The shallow run has a sandy bottom, and at times it barely seems deep enough to paddle before it widens and forms Juniper Creek.

A 7-mile paddle trail leads from the canoe launch to a parking area off FL 19. The forest service offers a "haul back" service for a fee so you can make this a one-way trip and not have to paddle against the current, but reservations are required. This is a great way to see portions of the Juniper Prairie Wilderness (JPW) that otherwise wouldn't be accessible. If you prefer to stay on dry land, the Florida National Scenic Trail also cuts through the JPW and can be accessed within the Juniper Springs Recreation Area.

FERN HAMMOCK SPRINGS

GPS coordinates: N29 11.017' / W81 42483'

Several sand boils make up Fern Hammock Springs.

The Spring

An easy 0.4-mile stroll along a boardwalk "trail" leads you to the natural setting of Fern Hammock Springs. The boardwalk is covered in algae and very slippery when wet, so use caution as you make your way out to the spring. The trail begins just past the old millhouse near Juniper Springs. From the millhouse, follow the boardwalk north over a small footbridge and stay left as you shadow the Juniper Springs run in a semicircle through the recreation area. Several platforms and small alcoves overlook the narrow spring run as it flows alongside the wooden path. After nearly 0.4 mile the boardwalk abruptly ends. From here, head left (east) over the footbridge, which affords a perfect vantage point to view Fern Hammock Springs and the sandy boils that create it. This area of the run is environmentally protected, so there is no swimming allowed, but you're welcome to swim in Juniper Springs year-round. You can see the sand boil up from the bottom of the spring as curious fish investigate. It makes you wish you could just reach your hand into the soft sand and touch it, but you know you would disturb the peace in this environmentally sensitive area, so you resist the temptation. Although you could shortcut your way back to the trailhead through the campground, the park service asks that you backtrack the way you came, unless you're a registered camper.

If you wish to see more of the spring run, and Juniper Creek, rent a canoe or launch your own and spend the day exploring the surrounding Juniper Prairie Wilderness. Wildlife is abundant, and you're likely to spy a multitude of turtles and birds, and you may even glimpse an alligator lazily lying in the sun as it reenergizes.

General description: The good news is that Sweetwater Springs is an amazing little slice of heaven where you can sit on a bench, read a good book, and have the spring all to yourself. The downside is that the only way to gain access to the springs is by renting the historic Sweetwater Cabin for the week. There is such a high demand for this pristine location, you can't just pick up the phone and reserve the cabin. Instead, a lottery is held each year to win access and the ability to rent the cabin for a week.

Location: At the western end of FR 76A; about 13 miles south of Salt Springs and 11 miles northwest of Astor; 2.3 miles south of the Silver Glen Recreation Area

Development: Primitive

Best time to visit: Year-round

Restrictions: You must rent the cabin for a week to access the spring. Closed the first week of Apr and the first week of Oct; no pets

Access: Drive to

Fees: $$$

Water temperature: 72°F

Nearby attractions: Silver Glen Recreation Area, Yearling Trail, Juniper Springs Recreation Area, Pats Island Trailhead, Lake George, Lake George State Forest, Salt Springs Recreation Area, Alexander Springs Recreation Area

Services: All services in Astor

Camping: Primitive camping at Hopkins Prairie Campground; full-service at Juniper Springs and Salt Springs Recreation Areas

Management: Ocala National Forest–Lake George Ranger District, Sweetwater Cabin; run by private concessioner

Contact: (352) 625-2520; www.fs.usda.gov/recarea/ocala/recreation/camping-cabins/recarea/?recid=40267&actid=101; for reservation information: (352) 625-0546; http://camprrm.com/2009/09/sweetwater-cabin/

Map: *DeLorme: Florida Atlas & Gazetteer:* Page 73 C2

GPS coordinates: N29 13.133' / W81 39.6'

Finding the spring: From the junction of FL 19 and FL 40 in Healing Waters, drive north on FL 19 for 3.6 miles to a left onto FR 76A. Travel for approximately 0.5 mile to the end of the road and the parking area for the cabin.

From the junction of FL 19 and CR 314 in Salt Springs, drive south on FL 19 for 11.9 miles to a right onto FR 76A and follow directions above.

The Spring

A well-groomed dirt road leads back into the Juniper Prairie Wilderness Area, where you have the opportunity to step back in time alongside your own private springs. That's right; you get these springs all to yourself if you're lucky enough to rent the Sweetwater Cabin for the week. Demand is so high for this historic site that the forest service holds a lotto-type drawing to see who gets to rent the cabin each week throughout the year. This rustic cabin was built by the Civilian Conservation Corps (CCC) back in 1935 and can accommodate up to twelve people. A screened-in porch allows you to view Sweetwater Springs, from the top of a small hill. But for the best view, a set of stairs lead down to a wonderful wooden deck overlooking the springs. Benches built into the deck give you a perfect place to perch alongside this small slice of heaven. Two spring vents feed the creek, and one looks like a tunnel under the water that goes straight back underground, with a current of blue water issuing out against you. A large log stands upright, propping a massive tree limb that overhangs the spring run, and canoes are available for exploring Juniper Creek and the surrounding wilderness.

The property that surrounds the springs and cabin has a small parking area, a barbecue grill, and an outdoor fire pit. Although it's primitive, all you need to bring along are the basics: pillows, linens, food, and a swimsuit. Grab your friends and family and take a step back in time to your own exclusive spring-side sanctuary. To register for the lotto use the contact information above. Entries are accepted between January 1 and May 31. The road leading back to the cabin is gated, and the gate code must be obtained from the forest service prior to your visit. Since the road is gated, this area sees little traffic. As a result, wildlife is abundant in the area. Bring a camera along, and keep a keen eye out for whitetail deer, black bears, wild turkeys, and even alligators if you take the canoes out for a paddle.

An annual lottery is held to gain access to Sweetwater Springs.

General description: This wonderful piece of nature sits on the eastern edge of the Ocala National Forest. The area around the spring seems quite barren, aside from several private hunt camps and the occasional trailhead. But don't be fooled. Silver Glen is worth a visit. Stunning blue water pours from this first-magnitude spring at a rate of 65 million gallons a day. Don your swimsuit, bring a mask and snorkel, and take a dip in this amazing beauty, the highlight of the Silver Glen Recreation Area.

Location: 5271 FL 19, Salt Springs; about 10 miles south of Salt Springs and 14 miles northwest of Astor

Development: Primitive

Best time to visit: Year-round

Restrictions: Open 8 a.m. to sunset; no alcohol, pets, or SCUBA diving

Access: Drive to

Fees: $

Water temperature: 72°F

Nearby attractions: Yearling Trail, Sweetwater Springs Cabin, Juniper Springs Recreation Area, Pats Island Trailhead, Lake George, Lake George State Forest, Salt Springs Recreation Area, Alexander Springs Recreation Area

Services: Restrooms on-site; all services in Astor

Camping: Primitive camping at Hopkins Prairie Campground; full-service at Juniper Springs and Salt Springs Recreation Areas

Management: Ocala National Forest–Lake George Ranger District; run by private concessioner

Contact: (352) 685-2799; www.fs.usda.gov/recarea/ocala/recarea/?recid=37199

Map: *DeLorme: Florida Atlas & Gazetteer:* Page 73 C2

GPS coordinates: N29 14.75' / W81 38.617'

Finding the spring: From the junction of FL 19 and FL 40 in Healing Waters, drive north on FL 19 for approximately 5.9 miles to a right into the Silver Glen Recreation Area.

From the junction of FL 19 and CR 314 in Salt Springs, drive south on FL 19 for 9.6 miles to a left into the Silver Glen Recreation Area.

The Spring

Amazingly blue water greets you in this heavily populated recreation area. As 65 million gallons of water pour out daily from two spring vents, the beauty of Silver Glen Springs easily overshadows the crowds of visitors. In the early morning and late in the day, you may be fortunate enough to spy a deer along the entry road or a manatee in the "Natural Well," the nickname given to the second small spring vent. This little beauty is abundant with both salt- and freshwater species of fish and is closed off to swimming to help protect the natural habitat. You can take a peek at this vent from land though; it sits in the southwest corner of the spring pool.

The recreation area has a large picnic area with picnic tables and charcoal grills scattered about. There's a volleyball net and a nature trail to keep you warmed up in between dips. They also have a small "general store" where you can rent a volleyball and pick up other sundry items, such as ice for your cooler. (*Note:* Don't try to sneak in any alcohol in your cooler. Alcohol is prohibited, and there's a "cooler checkpoint" at the entry to the spring area.) There are no

The head spring at Silver Glen is simply stunning.

lifeguards on duty, so swim at your own risk in the crisp, clean water of Silver Glen. Canoe rentals are available for an additional fee, and the wide spring run sees a lot of traffic, especially on weekends. The run is about 0.75 mile long and leads out to Lake George, which is part of the St. Johns River.

While I'm not a fan of the weekend crowds, during the week, Silver Glen can be a peaceful retreat and is certainly one of my favorites. A pair of hiking trails allow you to further explore the surrounding forest, but quite honestly, the highlight of this wonderful waterway is Silver Glen Springs!

General description: A cement wall wraps around the spring, forming a semicircular walkway from which you can view the clear greenish water. A large picnic area with old oak trees neighbors the extensive swim area, and the water has a slight salinity due to certain minerals it contains, hence the name.

Location: 13851 N Hwy. 19, Salt Springs

Development: Developed

Best time to visit: Year-round

Restrictions: Open 8 a.m. to sunset; no fishing, boating, pets, or bicycles in the swim area; pets and bicycles allowed everywhere else within the recreation area; designated fishing area; boats allowed in the spring run

Access: Drive to

Fees: $

Water temperature: 74°F

Nearby attractions: Salt Springs Marina, Lake George, Lake Kerr, Florida National Recreation Trail, Silver Glen Recreation Area, Juniper Prairie Wilderness, DeLancy OHV trailheads, Great Florida Birding Trail

Services: Restrooms on-site; all services in Astor and Palatka

Camping: On-site

Management: Ocala National Forest— Lake George Ranger District, Salt Springs Recreation Area; run by private concessioner

Contact: (352) 685-2048; www.fs.usda.gov/recarea/ocala/recarea/?recid=32362

Map: DeLorme: Florida Atlas & Gazetteer: Page 73 B2

GPS coordinates: N29 21.033' / W81 43.967'

Finding the spring: From the junction of FL 19 and CR 314 in Salt Springs, drive north on FL 19 for 0.6 mile to the recreation area, on the right.

From the junction of FL 19 and CR 316 in Salt Springs, drive south on FL 19 for 0.3 mile to the recreation area, on the left.

The Spring

As you enter the Salt Springs Recreation Area, the first thing you see is a large gate with a keypad. Don't be intimidated; the gate is simply a way to keep people out after hours. After you pass the gate, there's a small fee booth, and then you immediately come to a T. The left leads to the campground, where there are two separate camping areas. One is a primitive camping area; the other is your basic RV camping area with full-hookup sites. There's not much space between the campsites and little to no privacy, so if you're planning a trip to Salt Springs, don't do it for the camping. To get to the spring and the day-use area, head right at the T and you'll find two parking areas. The north parking lot leads directly to the concession stand and then to the spring; the south lot puts you a bit farther off the beaten path. The concession sells a variety of items from snacks to snorkels, floaties to footwear. A large grassy picnic area surrounds the spring, shaded by enormous oak trees. Picnic tables lie to the right and left of the pathway as you descend the grassy hill toward the spring.

The spring itself is quite impressive as water pours out of a few very active boils, creating the Salt Springs Run. The spring run flows for about 4 miles before feeding into Lake George. A concrete wall surrounds this large spring, and schools of fish congregate at the boil, while anhingas, aka snakebirds, stretch their wings to sun

Salt Springs has a whopping 4-mile spring run.

their feathers on the buoys that block off the swimming area. You may notice that the water is a bit salty. That's due to the presence of sodium, potassium, and magnesium. These elements give the water its salinity, which led to the name Salt Springs. There are showers and a water fountain along the path, if you feel the need to rinse.

Along with swimming in the briny water, you can also fish in designated areas as long as you carry a fishing license, and a 1.5-mile hiking trail loops through the eastern portion of the recreation area. Canoe rentals and a boat ramp are available at the neighboring Salt Springs Marina.

NORTH REGION

Several species of turtles are native to Florida.

Ah, the North—the cream of the crop, spattered with springs along the Santa Fe and Upper Suwannee Rivers. Here you'll find golden gems gathered in groupings, like the spirited Ginnie Springs Outdoors, which houses seven stunning springs on one parcel of land. Or the Ichetucknee River, fed by eight powerhouse springs and many smaller windows into the aquifer below. Within this region you'll find recreational activities to your heart's content. Tube a river, snorkel a spring, SCUBA dive in a cavern, jump from a platform high above the water, or paddle on a perfect and pristine blue-colored river. You'll see an abundance of wildlife and birdlife, so bring a camera, and plan on being blown away by the amazing beauty this region has to offer.

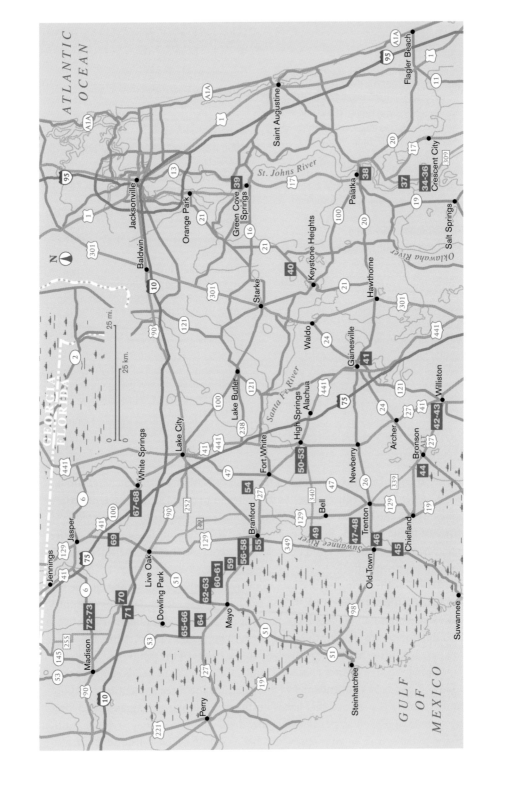

General description: The Beecher Unit of Florida's only national fish hatchery was built in 1926 and is named for the spring that serves as its water supply. The spring, hidden away at the far northeast end of the property, feeds and fills each of the many retention ponds you hike past on your way to see it.

Location: Within the Beecher Unit of the Welaka National Fish Hatchery, about 3 miles south of Welaka and 19 miles south of Palatka

Development: Developed

Best time to visit: Year-round

Restrictions: Open 8 a.m. to 5 p.m.; no vehicles or fishing; designated parking area located just north of the entrance

Access: Hike to; 0.7 mile one way

Fees: No fee

Water temperature: 72°F

Nearby attractions: Welaka National Fish Hatchery Aquarium, Welaka Spring, Welaka State Forest, Mud Spring, Sulfur Spring, 40 Acre Park, Log Cabin Farm, Vineyard & Winery

Services: All services in Welaka

Camping: Dispersed primitive camping at Welaka State Forest; full-service at Welaka Resort Marina (no tents), Salt Springs Recreation Area

Management: Welaka National Fish Hatchery

Contact: (386) 467-2374; www.fws.gov/welaka/aboutus.html

Map: *DeLorme: Florida Atlas & Gazetteer:* Page 73 A2

GPS coordinates: N29 26.928' / W81 38.802'

Finding the spring: From the junction of CR 309 and CR 308B in Welaka, drive south on CR 309 for 3.3 miles to the parking area on the left, just before reaching the entrance to the Welaka National Fish Hatchery.

From the junction of CR 309 and CR 308 in Fruitland, drive north on CR 309 for 1 mile to the parking area on the right, just past the entrance to the Welaka National Fish Hatchery.

The Spring

At the far end of the Beecher Unit of the Welaka National Fish Hatchery, you'll find Beecher Spring, which serves as the water source for the many retention ponds within the hatchery. To reach the spring, park just north of the gated entrance to the hatchery, near the observation tower and trailhead for the nature trail. The nature trail leads you on an interpretive walk through the forest but does not lead to the spring.

To access the spring, walk down to the gated entrance, head through the gate, and hike past the buildings, where you can hear and see several pumps running. Once you get past all the buildings, you'll see a gravel road leading north between the retention ponds. Follow this road north as far as you can go. Along the way you may see turtles sunning themselves on the banks of the ponds and an abundance of bird activity. After about 0.25 mile, the gravel road bends right (east). Follow it, and before it bends right (south) again, you'll see a retention pond on your left and a grassy road that heads northeast. Hike along the grassy road for a bit more than 0.25 mile, passing an empty dried-up pond on your right. Continue hiking to the spring on your left, which has a portion of fence around it and a

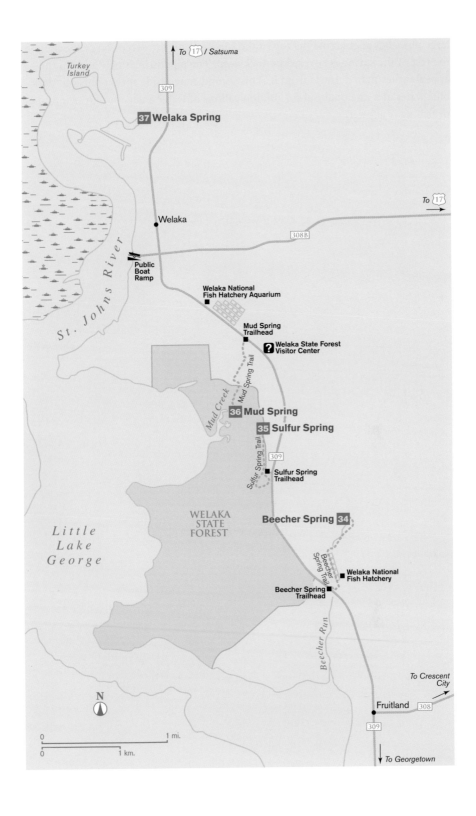

large pipe that goes across the top of the spring. With the exception of the boil, the rest of the spring is covered in duckweed. The pipe surprisingly adds to the appeal rather than detracts from it. This second-magnitude spring puts out dark blue water at a rate of about 5.7 million gallons of water a day, but no swimming or fishing is allowed.

General description: In the middle portion of the Welaka State Forest, you'll find this shallow little spring. A permanent staff gauge measures the depth, which is typically 2 feet or less. A slight smell of sulfur wafts through the air, but not so much as to drive you away before you get a chance to gaze upon the spring.

Location: Within Welaka State Forest; about 2 miles south of Welaka and 18 miles south of Palatka

Development: Primitive

Best time to visit: Year-round

Restrictions: Open sunrise to sunset

Access: Hike to; 0.4 mile one way

Fees: $

Water temperature: 72°F

Nearby attractions: Welaka National Fish Hatchery Aquarium, Welaka Spring, Mud Spring, Beecher Spring

Services: Restrooms on-site; all services in Welaka

Camping: Dispersed primitive camping at Welaka State Forest; full-service camping at Welaka Resort Marina (no tents), Salt Springs Recreation Area

Management: Florida Forest Service

Contact: (386) 467-2388; www.fresh fromflorida.com/Divisions-Offices/Florida -Forest-Service/Our-Forests/State-Forests/ Welaka-State-Forest

Map: DeLorme: Florida Atlas & Gazetteer: Page 73 A2

GPS coordinates: N29 27.533' / W81 39.517'

Finding the spring: From the junction of CR 309 and CR 308B in Welaka, drive south on CR 309 for 2.1 miles to a right into the parking area for the trailhead.

From the junction of CR 309 and CR 308 in Fruitland, drive north on CR 309 for 2.2 miles to a left into the parking area for the trailhead.

The Spring

South of the visitor center for the Welaka State Forest, you'll find the trailhead for the Environmental Education Trail and for Sulfur Spring on the west side of CR 309. You really can't miss the parking area, since a giant fire tower stands tall adjacent to the parking lot. The trails in this area are open to foot and mountain bike traffic, although they are pretty sandy, so it wouldn't be a very enjoyable bike ride. A small picnic area surrounds the parking lot, and there's a vault toilet and some trash cans.

You'll see the main trailhead near a kiosk behind the fire tower. This leads to the Environmental Education Trail, a short but enjoyable interpretive trail that makes a loop and leads back to the parking area but does not lead to Sulfur Spring. Instead, at the northwest end of the picnic area, behind the restrooms, look for a trail wide enough to fit a car through that heads due southwest and back between the trees. Follow it for 200 feet to a fire road; go right (north) on the fire road. As you hike north, you almost immediately make a low-water crossing. Continue north on the wide sandy track and you'll come to an intersection with another fire/service road. Go straight across it, still hiking north; soon after the intersection, the road begins to go downhill and bends a bit west. As you get to the bottom of the hill, just past a small bench, you'll see a small path on your right. Follow this path due east and in less than 100 feet you arrive at Sulfur Spring. If you keep your nose open, you can actually smell the spring before you see it, but the slight sulfur smell isn't as bad as you might expect, given the name. Crystal-clear water boils up from this tiny primitive spring, and there's a staff gauge in the spring. The spring run crosses the main fire road you were following north, so if you get to a water crossing, you've gone too far. The turnoff to the spring is about 100 feet before the spring run crosses the road. Amazingly, this shallow spring run ambles through the forest for another 2.5 miles before it meets up with the St. Johns River.

General description: Mud Spring is probably one of the most pleasant, unexpected surprises in this book. The spring requires an easy hike to reach. You meander through the forest, literally come around a blind corner, and all of a sudden there's a beautiful, almost perfectly circular blue-green spring in front of you. A wooden dock gives you a great viewing platform to see the spring run as well.

Location: Within the Welaka State Forest; about 1 mile south of Welaka and 17 miles south of Palatka

Development: Primitive

Best time to visit: Year-round

Restrictions: Open sunrise to sunset

Access: Hike to; 0.7 mile one way

Fees: $

Water temperature: 72°F

Nearby attractions: Welaka National Fish Hatchery Aquarium, Welaka Spring, Sulfur Spring, Beecher Spring

Services: All services in Welaka

Camping: Dispersed primitive camping at Welaka State Forest; full-service camping at Welaka Resort Marina (no tents), Salt Springs Recreation Area

Management: Florida Forest Service

Contact: (386) 467-2388; www.fresh fromflorida.com/Divisions-Offices/Florida -Forest-Service/Our-Forests/State-Forests/ Welaka-State-Forest

Map: *DeLorme: Florida Atlas & Gazetteer:* Page 73 A2

GPS coordinates: N29 27.667' / W81 39.7'

Finding the spring: From the junction of CR 309 and CR 308B in Welaka, drive south on CR 309 for 1 mile to a right into the parking area for the trailhead.

From the junction of CR 309 and CR 308 in Fruitland, drive north on CR 309 for approximately 3.3 miles to a left into the parking area for the trailhead.

The Spring

A mere 0.1 mile north of the visitor center for the Welaka State Forest, you'll find the parking area for the Mud Spring trailhead on the west side of CR 309. The trailhead is at the southwest corner of the parking lot, near a kiosk with a trail map on it and the self-pay station. Open to foot traffic only, the wide, flat, green-blazed trail heads due south into the Welaka State Forest.

After hiking generally south for about 0.3 mile, you come to an intersection where the main trail you're on heads south and a side trail heads off to the left (east). The left actually leads to the spring as well, since the southern portion of the trail forms a loop that passes the spring and comes back out at this junction. Bypass this trail and continue south on the main green-blazed trail, which is well maintained but covered with pine needles most of the way. A short distance after passing the loop trail, you come to a fork. Go left (southeast) at this fork as you continue to follow the green blazes. After about 0.1 mile the trail crosses a forest service road. Almost immediately after you cross the road, the landscape transforms into a dense, damp, lush green forest, with moss, saw palmetto, and a wide variety of ferns. After hiking about 0.25 mile through this lush forest, you come around a corner and suddenly there's an amazingly brilliant blue-green pool of water in front of you.

At 0.7-mile hike through the Welaka State Forest leads to Mud Spring.

Sitting in the middle of a small open area, deep within the forest, there's a picnic shelter, trash cans, and a bench right alongside this wonderful unexpected spring. A spillway flows underground for a few feet from the spring to form the headwaters of Mud Creek. A dock juts out over the water, so you can watch it as it flows away. Just beyond the picnic shelter, the trail continues past the spring and loops back north and then west before coming back on itself at that first junction I spoke about earlier. Continue on, or go back the way you came. Either way, you're sure to have a smile on your face after the pleasant surprise that just presented itself in the form of Mud Spring.

General description: Reached only by boat, in a small cove on the eastern bank of the wide St. Johns River you'll find the clear running water of Welaka Spring. Although this is only a third-magnitude spring, it's surprisingly pretty. The land around the spring is all private property, so make sure you stay in the water or you will be trespassing.

Location: Within a cove on the east bank of the St. Johns River; about 1.75 miles downstream (north) of the public boat ramp in Welaka

Development: Primitive

Best time to visit: Year-round

Restrictions: Surrounded by private property

Access: Boat to; 1.75 miles downstream

Water temperature: 72°F

Nearby attractions: Welaka National Fish Hatchery & Aquarium; Welaka State Forest; Mud, Sulfur, and Beecher Springs

Services: All services in Welaka

Camping: Welaka Lodge and Resort (no tents), Salt Springs Recreation Area

Management: n/a

Contact: n/a

Map: DeLorme: Florida Atlas & Gazetteer: Page 73 A3

GPS coordinates: Welaka Boat Ramp: N29 28.717' / W81 40.48'; Welaka Spring: N29 29.667' / W81 40.4'

Finding the spring: From the junction of CR 308B (Elm Street) and CR 309 in Welaka, drive west on CR 308B for 0.1 mile to the public boat ramp.

The Spring

Welaka Spring is surrounded by private property, so the only way to reach it is by boat. This portion of the St. Johns River is wide and deep, so you can reach it in almost any type of watercraft. You may choose to take your fishing boat out, hop on a personal watercraft, paddle a kayak, or even stand up on a paddleboard. The public boat ramp is wide and well maintained, but there's not much parking available.

To reach the spring, follow the river north (downstream); after about 1.25 miles you'll pass a highly populated area on the eastern bank. This is known as Stephens Point. Immediately after passing Stephens Point you'll see a few islands in front of you. Before you reach the first island, head due east; in less than 0.5 mile you'll see a small cove right in front of you. Head into that cove, which is actually the wide Welaka Spring Run, and at the head of the run you'll reach Welaka Springs. The spring forms an obvious boil as it issues clear blue water, but the spring run has a slow-moving current.

If you're looking for a place to stay in the area, I highly recommend the Welaka Lodge and Resort off Front Street. They're pet friendly and have a fabulous restaurant and bar right on the edge of the St. Johns River offering stunning sunset views. You can camp in an RV or pop-up or rent a quaint cottage at this wonderful riverside location.

General description: Two tiny spouts of water pop up out of the ground in the middle of a large ravine in Ravine Gardens State Park. The shallow, narrow spring run then continues to flow downstream through the ravine before ending up in what's known as the "reflecting pond." While the spring run is pretty, the rest of the park is far more impressive and worth checking out.

Location: 1600 Twigg St., Palatka

Development: Primitive

Best time to visit: Year-round

Restrictions: Open 8 a.m. to sunset

Access: Hike to; 0.3 mile one way

Fees: $

Water temperature: 72°F

Nearby attractions: Palatka Golf Course, Welaka State Forest, Dunns Creek State Park

Services: All services in Palatka

Camping: Mike Roess Gold Head Branch State Park

Management: Florida Park Service

Contact: (386) 329-3721; www.florida stateparks.org/ravinegardens/default.cfm

Map: *DeLorme: Florida Atlas & Gazetteer:* Page 67 C2

GPS coordinates: N29 38.116' / W81 38.83'

Finding the spring: From the junction of FL 20 (Crill Avenue) and FL 19 in Palatka, drive east on FL 20 for 1.6 miles to a right onto Moseley Avenue. Travel for 0.3 mile to a left onto Twigg Street. Follow Twigg Street for 0.1 mile to the park, on the right.

From the junction of FL 20 and US 17 in Palatka, drive west on FL 20 for 0.9 mile to a left onto Moseley Avenue and follow directions above.

The Spring

The people of Palatka are blessed to have such a lovely state park at their disposal. Stone walls, pillars, and even a suspension bridge that crosses the ravine over the spring run compose this wonderful state park. Birds sing in the background as you sit in the picnic area. Bubbling artesian wells, flowing fountains, and a lovely reflecting pond are just a few of the highlights. A 1.8-mile drive circles the ravine, with overlooks and a handful of tiny parking areas along the way, but you'll find the best way to experience this park is on foot. Local residents walk the ravine drive for exercise on a regular basis.

The Palatka Garden Club has a small building on-site, and within the ravine itself there's an unusual diversity. Bamboo, oak, and maple trees stand side by side, with a multitude of palm trees and an impressive showing of gigantic cala-dium plants (elephant ears). Wooden platforms overlook the ravine, or you can delve deeper along the pleasant hiking trail. Rolling hills and old moss-covered stone lead down into the ravine, and while the trails are well maintained, the trail map isn't that accurate. I found that the best way to see the spring was to head down into the ravine and then follow the Spring Trail as it follows the spring run upstream on both sides. The spring run is unlike most. It's a very shallow, very narrow, swiftly moving creek of crystal-clear water with a white sandy bottom.

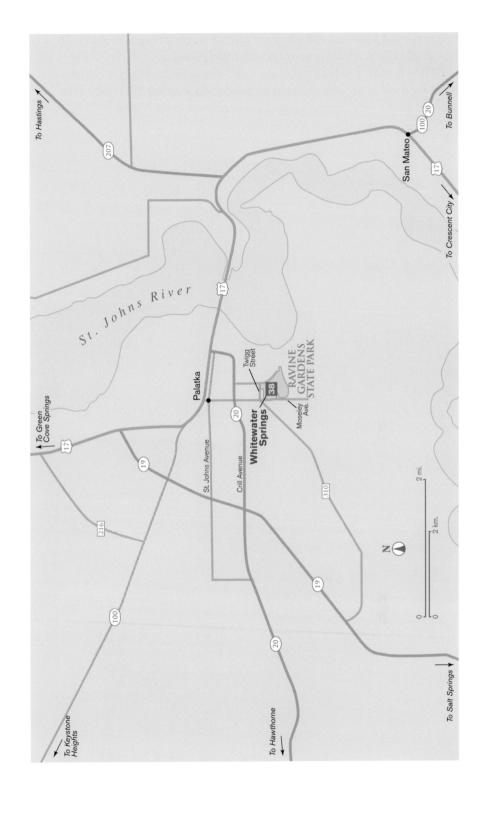

Follow the run upstream and you'll see a bench perched peacefully alongside two very small boils that bubble up from under the ground.

I'll be honest. The park itself is fantastic, but as far as springs go, Whitewater is not the most impressive, which is surprising, since up until the mid-1980s, it supplied all the water for the town of Palatka.

General description: Spring Park lies in the heart of historic downtown Green Cove Springs. The spring itself is on the western end of this small city park and has been contained by a low circular cement wall. You can view the spring by peeking over the wall, and a slight sulfur smell greets you as you do. The crystal-clear water has been routed to fill the adjacent community pool before dropping over a spillway on the opposite end of the pool. It then briskly flows a short distance to its final destination in the wide St. Johns River.

Location: In downtown Green Cove Springs; just east of city hall

Development: Developed

Best time to visit: Year-round

Restrictions: Open dawn to dusk; no swimming in spring but you can swim in the park's spring-fed swimming pool

Access: Drive to

Water temperature: 78°F

Nearby attractions: City Pier, St. Johns River, Bayard Conservation Area, Knights Marina

Services: Restrooms on-site; all services in Green Cove Springs

Camping: Mike Roess Gold Head Branch State Park, Camp Chowenwaw Park

Management: City of Green Cove Springs Parks and Recreation

Contact: (904) 297-7500, ext. 3307; www .greencovesprings.com/departments/spring _park.php

Map: *DeLorme: Florida Atlas & Gazetteer:* Page 67 A2

GPS coordinates: N29 59.6' / W81 40.683'

Finding the spring: From the junction of US 17 and FL 16 West (Ferris Street) in Green Cove Springs, drive north on US 17 for less than 0.1 mile to a right onto Spring Street (right before reaching city hall). Travel for less than 0.1 mile to a stop sign at Magnolia Avenue. Go straight across to the park.

From the junction of US 17 and CR 315, drive south on US 17 for 2.7 miles to a left onto Walnut Street. Travel for less than 0.1 mile to a stop sign at Magnolia Avenue. Go straight across to the park.

The Spring

Whether you park on Spring Street or Walnut Street, Green Cove Springs is easy to reach. Resting in a small grassy field at the western end of Spring Park, the circular spring is surrounded by a low cement wall. Peek inside, and beyond the concrete wall lies a perfect specimen of a small, natural Florida spring. The town has routed the flow of water to constantly feed the community swimming pool. From the pool the water then flows out the other side over a small spillway before ending up a short distance away in the St. Johns River. The river is wide at many parts, and if you didn't know better, you would think it was a large lake. A slight smell of sulfur wafts through the air as you stand near the spring, but you don't seem to smell it anywhere else in the park.

The park has a playground and a small walkway that crosses over the spring run. Picnic shelters line the banks of the river and are heavily used by the community. The shelters and gazebo can be reserved for special events by contacting the number above. There is no swimming allowed in the spring, but the community pool is open to the public. Hours vary, so call ahead if you plan on taking a dip.

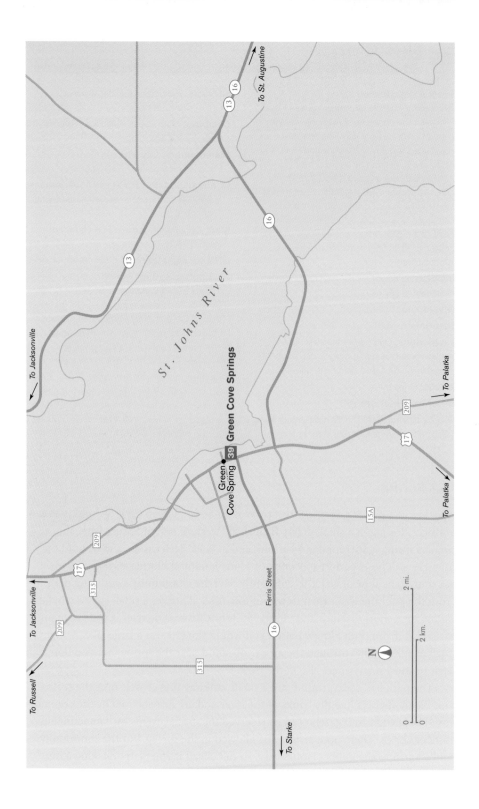

Green Cove Springs sits isolated behind its concrete confines.

The town of Green Cove Springs is rich in history. While you're in the area, consider visiting one or more of the town's landmarks, which create what is known as "The Historical Triangle" of Green Cove Springs. The "triangle" consists of the Clay County Historic Courthouse, the 1884 County Jail, and the Clay County Historical Society's History and Railroad Museums. For more information call (904) 278-4780.

General description: At the far north end of a ravine that's found within Mike Roess Gold Head Branch State Park, two tiny springs form the beginning of Gold Head Branch. A pleasant nature trail follows the shallow spring run as it flows through the ravine. There's no place to swim within the springs, but the park does have a large swim area at the western end of Little Lake Johnson.

Location: 6239 SR 21, Keystone Heights

Development: Primitive

Best time to visit: Year-round

Restrictions: Open 8 a.m. to sundown

Access: Hike to; 0.2 mile one way

Fees: $

Water temperature: 72°F

Nearby attractions: Florida National Recreation Trail, Camp Blanding Wildlife Management Area, Little Rain Lake County Park, Belmore State Forest, Palatka–Lake Butler Trail

Services: Restrooms on-site; all services in Keystone Heights

Camping: On-site

Management: Florida Park Service

Contact: (352) 473-4701; www.florida stateparks.org/mikeroess/default.cfm

Map: *DeLorme: Florida Atlas & Gazetteer:* Page 66 B3

GPS coordinates: N29 50.485' / W81 57.234'

Finding the spring: From the junction of FL 21 and FL 100 in Keystone Heights, drive northeast on FL 21 for 6 miles to the park, on the right.

From the junction of FL 21 and CR 315C near Belmore, drive southwest on FL 21 for 2.9 miles to the park, on the left.

The Spring

As you enter Mike Roess Gold Head Branch State Park, immediately after you pass through the entrance gate you'll see a small parking area for the Florida National Scenic Trail. The trail, open to hikers only, is a nice way to stretch your legs and see a variety of Florida's native flora and fauna. But you won't find the Gold Head Branch Springs off of the Florida Trail. The springs are actually at the base of a ravine that sits in the middle of this 2,000-acre park and seem disproportionately small for such an enormous park. The park is extremely spread out, with rolling hills dotted with stands of longleaf pine trees. The park rangers will give you a well-marked map when you enter the park. The first stop as you drive through the park comes at 0.7 mile, where you can park and get a so-so view of the ravine from above. The ravine is certainly an unusually deep hole in the ground for the primarily flat state of Florida.

To hike down into the ravine and see the springs, follow the main park road for another 0.2 mile to another small parking area on the left with about ten parking spaces. You have to descend more than eighty steps to get down into the ravine. When you reach the floor of the ravine, you'll come to a T junction. If you want to explore the ravine, go right (south); the nature trail follows the spring run through the ravine. To see the springs, head left (north) at the T and you'll come to a fork that begins the Fern Loop trail. The trail makes a 0.15-mile loop around the northern part of the ravine before bringing you back to this fork. You can go either way on this tiny loop to view the springs. One of the spring heads is masked by dense vegetation, so you can't really see the source of the water, but it seems to come from two separate outlets. A footbridge crosses over one of them, giving you a better view, but again, it's difficult to see through the thick vegetation. Flora and ferns cover the damp ravine floor, so all you can really see is the narrow, shallow, crystal-clear spring run as it passes by.

This is easily one of the smallest springs in this book, so don't expect to swim here. But don't despair. The park does have a designated swimming area along the western banks of Little Lake Johnson. A beautiful picnic area overlooks the lake, and there are playgrounds, picnic shelters, volleyball nets, and a large sandy beach by the swim area. Several lakes are located within the park boundaries, and fishing is allowed. They also rent canoes and have an equestrian trail that stretches more than 7 miles. At first glance, it may seem that there's not much to do here, but as you travel through the park and the activities slowly unfold, you realize it's quite the contrary. They offer backcountry camping and have three separate full-service campgrounds, as well as lakefront cabin rentals if camping's not your thing. It seems the only thing this park is missing is some mountain bike trails.

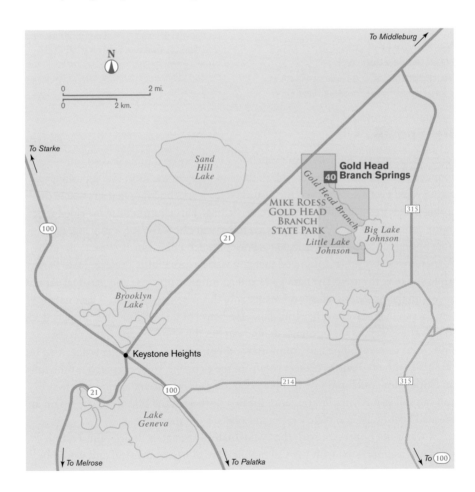

General description: Boulware Spring is not much to see, but the old waterworks building is pretty cool and adds to the scenery. I recommend bringing a bike along and taking a ride on the Gainesville-Hawthorne Trail. Also, a visit to Paynes Prairie, right down the road, is a *must*. A short hike over the boardwalk in Paynes Prairie leads you to a place where you can view hundreds of alligators as they lay on the banks soaking in the sun as they reenergize.

Location: 3300 SE 15th St., Gainesville

Development: Developed

Best time to visit: Year-round

Restrictions: Open 7 a.m. to 6 p.m. Nov–Apr, 7 a.m. to 8 p.m. May–Oct; no swimming or fishing

Access: Drive to

Water temperature: 72°F

Nearby attractions: Gainesville-Hawthorne Trail, Paynes Prairie Preserve State Park

Services: Restrooms on-site; all services in Gainesville

Camping: Paynes Prairie Preserve State Park

Management: City of Gainesville Parks, Recreation and Cultural Affairs

Contact: (352) 334-2231; www.cityofgainesville.org/GOVERNMENT/CityDepartmentsNZ/NatureOperationsDivision/ParksFacilities/tabid/182/Default.aspx

Map: *DeLorme: Florida Atlas & Gazetteer:* Page 65 D3

GPS coordinates: N29 37.25' / W82 18.433'

Finding the spring: From the junction of FL 20 (SE Hawthorne Road) and FL 26 in Gainesville, drive southeast on FL 20 for less than 0.1 mile to a right onto SE 15th Street. Travel for approximately 2 miles to the second (southernmost) entrance to the park, on the right.

The Spring

As far as springs go, Boulware isn't much to see. It's covered in duckweed, surrounded by brick and concrete, and, simply put, just not the most eye-appealing spring you'll ever see. However, the historic waterworks building that sits beside the spring makes this a unique location worth visiting. This location once provided water to the entire city of Gainesville. Although today you can barely see it moving, Boulware Spring produces nearly 200,000 gallons of water a day, which flows south into Paynes Prairie. I *highly* recommend that you visit Paynes Prairie Preserve State Park while you're in the area. The park gives you an intimate up-close and personal experience with the American alligator. I assure you, this is *no* exaggeration. These native reptiles sun themselves by the score along the banks of the Alachua Sink. Birders flock to the area as well, as the birdlife is as abundant as the alligators and quite diverse. Bring your camera, binoculars, comfortable shoes, and *lots* of drinking water. It's a bit of a hike, with no shade to protect you from the elements, so be prepared for the full-on Florida heat and humidity. If you're a bit leery of the extreme nature experience, you can still visit Paynes Prairie, since the first portion of the trail keeps you up on an elevated boardwalk, completely safe and isolated from the wetlands below.

I was quite impressed with the "wild" nature at Paynes Prairie. But I admit I was just as impressed with the Gainesville-Hawthorne State Trail and would be

Hundreds of alligators bask in the sun at Paynes Prairie.

remiss in my duties if I did not boast about it as well. The trail can be accessed from Boulware Springs Park and is a fantastic "rails to trail" paved path that covers a full 17 miles from Gainesville to Hawthorne. The trail suits any fancy and is open to hikers, bikers, and horseback riders. Boulware Springs Park itself is surprisingly hilly, with big shade trees with Spanish moss hanging from their large limbs. This is a refreshing change from its neighbor, Paynes Prairie, which is a flat grassy wilderness with no shade and no topography.

Enjoy the picnic area and playground amid the shade trees as you visit the waterworks, the spring, the trail, and the prairie—all within minutes of one another. In the near future, the face of Boulware Springs Nature Park will be drastically changing. The county is in the process of restoring the park to its former habitat. At first it won't look like much, but over time, a longleaf pine canopy will emerge, with an understory of native sandhill grasses and flowers. Hopefully, the native creatures, such as gopher tortoises will soon follow.

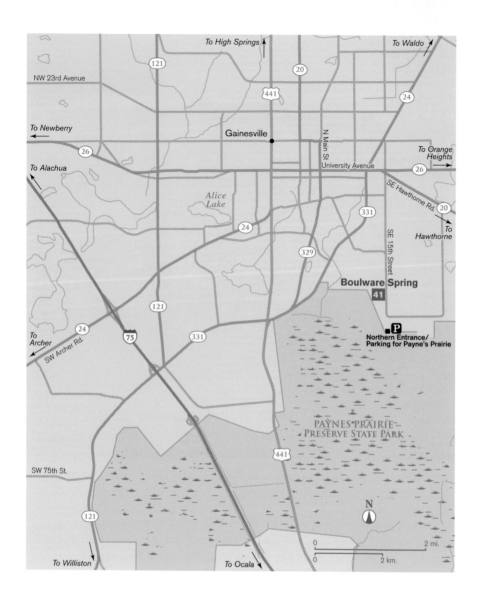

General description: Blue Grotto is absolutely gorgeous, from above the water and below. The grotto is primarily a SCUBA diving destination, but snorkelers can float about on the surface too, provided they are accompanied by a diver. Whether you're open-water, cavern, or cave certified, there's a place for you to explore at Blue Grotto.

Location: 3852 Northeast 172nd Ct., Williston

Development: Developed

Best time to visit: Year-round

Restrictions: Open 8 a.m. to 6 p.m. in summer; 8 a.m. to 5 p.m. in winter; night dives by appointment only; snorkeling and swimming only when accompanied by divers

Access: Drive to

Fees: $–$$$

Water temperature: 72°F

Nearby attractions: Devil's Den Spring, Cedar Lake Ranch and Reserve

Services: Restrooms on-site; all services in Williston

Camping: On-site

Management: Blue Grotto Dive Resort

Contact: (352) 528-5770; www.dive bluegrotto.com

Map: *DeLorme: Florida Atlas & Gazetteer:* Page 71 A2

GPS coordinates: N29 23.283' / W82 29.183'

Finding the spring: From the junction of US Alt 27 and US 41 in Williston, drive west on US Alt 27 for 1.9 miles to a left onto NE 172nd Court. Travel for 0.4 mile to Blue Grotto, on the right. ***Note:*** NE 172nd Court is a bumpy dirt road.

From the junction of US Alt 27 and CR 335A near Williston, drive east on US Alt 27 for 0.5 mile to a right onto NE 172nd Court and follow directions above.

The Spring

Blue Grotto is easily one of my favorites—not only because there's a waterfall plummeting into the depths of the grotto but also because the rich blue color of the water simply mesmerizes you. Mother Nature, with a little help from mankind, has created a jaw-dropping setting at this well-managed facility. Tall limestone walls form the backdrop to the brilliant blue natural pool, and the waterfall adds to the picturesque setting. The deck almost splits the water into two separate sections. On one side of the deck is the cave-diving entrance, where cave-certified divers can explore the cave system. The other side of the deck, where the waterfall flows into, is much larger. This is where snorkelers, open-water divers, and cavern divers are welcome to explore the grotto, which extends to a depth of 100 feet.

The property is in the process of development, but when finished, this will certainly be a SCUBA diving mecca. The people at Blue Grotto have a vision, and they are rapidly bringing it to fruition. So if you haven't been here lately, go back! They've built a large new deck near the spring, with benches and bungees to keep your tanks in place while you do your last-minute gear check before taking the plunge. On the land surrounding the grotto, there are shelters with picnic tables where you can prep your gear in the shade or simply enjoy a picnic. The shelters even have a place to hang your equipment to dry. There are wash sinks on the side

A peaceful waterfall adds to the scenery at Blue Grotto.

of the bathhouse and nice hot showers, which is a welcome treat after you emerge from the 72°F water and peel off your wet suit. They have cabins and camping right on-site, so you can stay on the premises. They even have a swimming pool, which seems silly when you have that beautiful grotto to dip into, but the grotto is only open to divers (and snorkelers and swimmers when accompanied by divers), so if you just want to swim and are not with a diver, you can do so in the pool. The pool also comes in handy when they are teaching people to dive. That's right; this is one of only a handful of springs where you can get Scuba certified on-site. As a matter of fact, they not only offer basic certifications, they have a full service dive school that offers all levels of training. With all this to offer, it's clear to see why this location stays busy year-round.

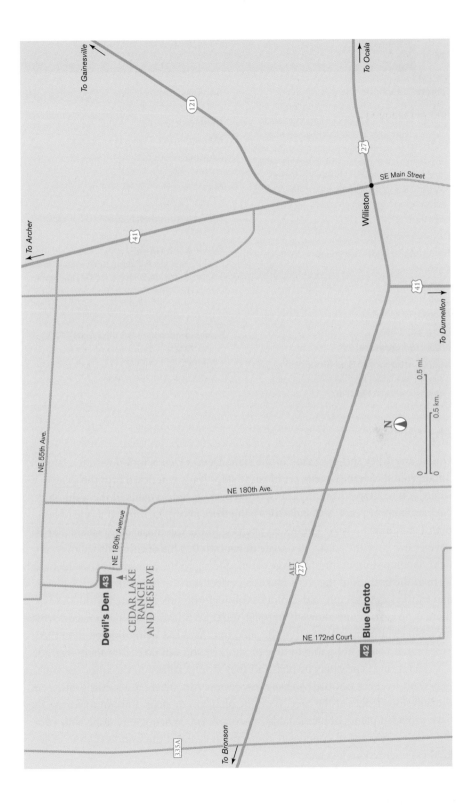

General description: In a word, unique! Devil's Den is found within an underground cavern with a hole in the ceiling that lets in just enough light to add to the ambience. SCUBA divers and snorkelers enjoy the rare experience of exploring the limestone walls that lie both above and below the water. Without a doubt, this one makes the Author's Favorites list with flying colors!

Location: 5390 NE 180th Ave., Williston

Development: Developed

Best time to visit: Year-round

Restrictions: Open 9 a.m. to 6 p.m. Mon–Thurs, 8 a.m. to 6 p.m. Fri–Sun; night dives by appointment only

Access: Drive to

Fees: $$–$$$

Water temperature: 72°F

Nearby attractions: Blue Grotto Spring, Two Hawk Hammock, Two Tails Ranch, Cedar Lake Ranch and Reserve

Services: Restrooms and limited food on-site; all services in Williston

Camping: On-site

Management: Devil's Den Springs

Contact: (352) 528-3344; www.devilsden .com

Map: *DeLorme: Florida Atlas & Gazetteer:* Page 71 A2

GPS coordinates: N29 24.467' / W82 28.817'

Finding the spring: From the junction of US Alt 27 and US 41 South in Williston, drive north on US Alt 27 for 1.1 miles to a right onto NE 180th Avenue. Travel for 1 mile to a left onto NE 180th Avenue and drive for another 0.3 mile to Devil's Den, on the left.

From the junction of US Alt 27 and CR 335A near Williston, drive south on US Alt 27 for 1.4 miles to a left onto NE 180th Avenue and follow directions above.

The Spring

Unlike any other spring or sink in the state, Devil's Den is found within a large underground cavern. A steep set of stone steps leads you down into the cavern, where you're almost instantly transported back in time. Fossils in the walls date back millions of years, and stalactites hang from above, growing at a rate of less than 1 millimeter a year. There's an opening in the top of the cave, where plants have grown over the edge and dangle down into it. This opening also allows sunlight to come shining into the large room, adding to the ambience. A wooden platform at the bottom of the steps makes a perfect starting point for SCUBA divers and snorkelers to set out and explore. Although the sink is located within a cave, there is no cave diving allowed; an open-water certification is all you need to dive here. No swimming is allowed in the sink, but there is a swimming pool on the property. If you're not going to dive or snorkel, you can take a dip there instead.

The spring is privately owned, and they strictly adhere to the rules, so you may want to check out their website before you visit. There is no sitting either on the limestone ledges of the cave or on the platform or steps. But not to worry; they have provided plenty of picnic tables aboveground. When you're done with your dip, you're welcome to congregate there and talk about the wonderful one-of-a-kind experience you just had.

Devil's Den is found within an underground cavern.

Beyond the picnic area is a pair of funky, shallow, concrete "grottos." These grottos were covered in hydrilla and lyngbya at the time of my visit, and the owners had recently introduced carp to eat away at these invasive intruders. The area eventually will be used for beginner divers and dive instruction. There's a campground and cabins on the property as well, so you can easily extend your stay if you wanted to.

Adjacent to the property on one side is Two Hawks Hammock, where you can go horseback riding; on the other side is Cedar Lake Ranch and Reserve, where they have stunning botanical gardens. Both are a fun addition while you're in the area, as is a visit to the nearby Blue Grotto (#42).

General description: There's plenty of fun to be had at this small county-run park, but unfortunately it's closed during the winter months. The spring is by far the highlight, and the whole family will enjoy splashing around in the clear blue water.

Location: 4550 NE 94th Place, Bronson

Development: Developed

Best time to visit: Open Apr 1—Oct 1

Restrictions: Open 10 a.m. to 7:30 p.m.; no alcohol, pets, fishing, or SCUBA diving

Access: Drive to

Fees: $

Water temperature: 72°F

Nearby attractions: Devil's Hammock Wildlife Management Area

Services: Restrooms on-site; all services in Bronson

Camping: Devil's Den, Blue Grotto, Breezy Acres RV Park

Management: Levy County Parks and Recreation

Contact: (352) 486-3303; www.levycounty .org/cd_parks.aspx

Map: *DeLorme: Florida Atlas & Gazetteer:* Page 70 A3

GPS coordinates: N29 27.05' / W82 41.933'

Finding the spring: From the junction of CR 339A and CR 339 near Bronson, drive south on CR 339A for 2 miles to the park, at the end of the road.

The Spring

What a fun little park this is! Blue Springs is the center of attention, but surrounding the spring in this 30-acre park is a playground, swing set, sand volleyball court, and picnic area. Clear blue water flows from the spring, and there are several spots around it where you can hop in. There's even an elevated platform where you can grab a little air as you leap into the crisp water from a few feet up. A nominal fee is charged for entry, or you can buy an annual pass that gets you in all season long. The only downfall I see here is that the park is closed for an extended period during winter. If you're looking for a little more outdoor adventure, the neighboring Devil's Hammock Wildlife Management Area allows hiking, mountain biking, and horseback riding and has two access points for paddling the Waccasassa River, whose headwaters happen to be Levy Blue Spring.

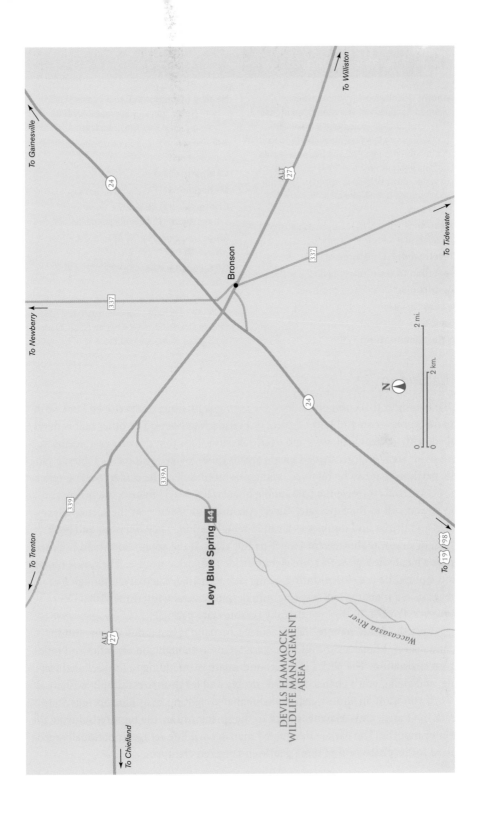

General description: Within the densely wooded floodplain of Manatee Springs State Park, crystal-clear water with a greenish hue flows from this first-magnitude spring. A strong boil is present, and this spring puts out anywhere from 71 to 173 million gallons of water a day. Wildlife is abundant, and the campground is well spaced in this wonderful state park.

Location: 11650 NW 115th St., Chiefland; about 6 miles west of Chiefland

Development: Partially developed

Best time to visit: Year-round

Restrictions: Open 8 a.m. to sunset

Access: Drive to

Fees: $

Water temperature: 72°F

Nearby attractions: Camp Azalea Public Boat Ramp, Fanning Springs, Levy Blue Spring, Cedar Key, Clay Landing

Services: Food, restrooms on-site; all services in Chiefland

Camping: On-site

Management: Florida Park Service

Contact: (352) 493-6072; www.florida stateparks.org/manateesprings/default.cfm

Map: *DeLorme: Florida Atlas & Gazetteer:* Page 70 A1

GPS coordinates: N29 29.367' / W82 58.617'

Finding the spring: From the junction of CR 320 (Manatee Springs Road) and US 19 in Chiefland, drive west on CR 320 for 5.8 miles to the park, at the end of the road.

The Spring

Like two sides to a coin, one side of the spring is pristine, undeveloped land, with many cypress trees and knees typical of Florida waterways. The other half is developed, with cement walkways and overlooks and steps that provide easy access to the swim area. A large, shaded picnic area is quite lovely, with picnic tables, a picnic pavilion that can be reserved, and a playground near the center. Several miles of nature trails traverse the park, and a boardwalk closely follows the spring run on its way out to the Suwannee River. A concession stand near the spring offers food and drinks and doubles as a canoe rental station. They offer out and back trips, or one-way shuttles for longer paddle trips. If the concession stand is closed, there's a cute little general store right outside the park entrance. The canoe rental and launch site are closed during winter due to manatee activity, although I've never seen a manatee in the spring run, despite several wintertime visits. Deer, however, flourish in this wonderfully remote state park.

I use the term "remote" lightly, since Chiefland is just 6 miles away. But for some reason, Manatee Springs State Park seems as though you are miles and miles from civilization. The park's campground is fantastic, adding to the secluded feeling, and giving you a chance to exhale deeply and let your stress simply wash away.

If you want an almost guaranteed manatee sighting, visit Blue Springs State Park in Orange City. Manatees flock to the spring run by the hundreds during the winter months. The park, a designated manatee wildlife refuge, is nationally recognized for its protection of these gentle endangered creatures.

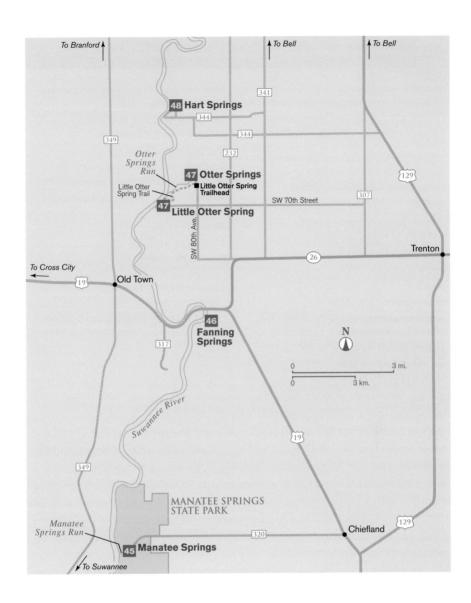

To Branford↑

↑To Bell

↑To Bell

341

48 Hart Springs

344

344

349

232

Otter Springs Run

47 Otter Springs

■ Little Otter Spring Trailhead

Little Otter Spring Trail

129

307

SW 70th Street

47 Little Otter Spring

SW 80th Ave.

Trenton

26

To Cross City
←

19

Old Town

N

317

46 Fanning Springs

0   3 mi.

0   3 km.

Suwannee River

19

349

MANATEE SPRINGS STATE PARK

Chiefland

320

129

Manatee Springs Run

45 Manatee Springs

↙ To Suwannee

General description: Some of the brightest blue water I've ever seen flows from a conical depression in the floor of Fanning Springs, which is found within Fanning Springs State Park. The park is relatively small, but the color of the water really is spectacular. Make sure you bring a snorkel so that you can enjoy the many facets of the limestone below.

Location: 18020 NW US 19, Fanning Springs

Development: Developed

Best time to visit: Year-round

Restrictions: Open 8 a.m. to sunset

Access: Drive to

Fees: $

Water temperature: 72°F

Nearby attractions: Nature Coast State Trail, Fort Fanning Historical Park, Lower Suwannee National Wildlife Refuge, Otter Springs, Hart Springs, Manatee Springs State Park

Services: Restrooms on-site; all services in Fanning Springs

Camping: Suwannee River Campground, Manatee Springs State Park

Management: Florida Park Service

Contact: (352) 463-3420; www.florida stateparks.org/fanningsprings/default.cfm

Map: DeLorme: Florida Atlas & Gazetteer: Page 64 D1

GPS coordinates: N29 35.25' / W82 56.117'

Finding the spring: From the junction of US 19 and CR 317 near Old Town, drive south on US 19 for 1.6 miles to the park, on the right.

From the junction of US 19 and FL 26 in Fanning Springs, drive north on US 19 for 0.4 mile to the park, on the left.

The Spring

Don't be fooled by the size of this small state park. The spring that makes its home here is simply spectacular! Deep, clear, blue-colored water makes Fanning Springs an ideal snorkel spot and swim hole. It also gives it a solid position among the Author's Favorites. The park is small for a Florida State Park, but there's still plenty to do. The spring is phenomenal, and the Suwannee River is right there as well. The park now has a canoe/kayak rental concession on-site, so once you've explored the spring, you can sightsee on the river as well. If you have your own canoe or kayak, a path leads to the launch site, but you may want to bring some portage wheels along to make the descent a little easier. The spring area is blocked off from the river, so it can only be accessed on foot. If you paddle in from elsewhere, you must tie off, hop out of the canoe, and take the short walk over to the boil. A well-groomed picnic area sits high above the spring, but I must say that the tables are a bit too close together. Hefty size oak trees bent over by time are scattered throughout the park, and Spanish moss dangles from their large limbs. A unique natural archway big enough to drive a car through is created by two such trees intertwined overhead.

Paths lead to almost all sides of the spring, so access and photo opportunities are plentiful. A playground and sand volleyball court add to the fun, and a 0.75-mile nature trail leads you out into the forest and past some sinkholes. If you want to experience this park at its best, you can paddle to their primitive campsite or stay in one of five cabin rentals. The cabins sleep up to six people, and reservations are required.

Grass carp is often used to help control the growth of algae such as lyngbya.

General description: You can practically drive right up to Otter Springs, but Little Otter requires a 1.0-mile hike to reach. I recommend taking the time to hike out to Little Otter, especially if the river levels are within normal limits. You'll find it quite peaceful and pretty. The main body of the park is packed with activities, but the camping lacks privacy, although it's well shaded with large live oak and pine trees.

Location: 6470 SW 80th Ave., Trenton; about 4.5 miles north of Fanning Springs

Development: Developed

Best time to visit: Year-round

Restrictions: Open 9 a.m. to 5 p.m.; no fishing the spring

Access: Otter: Drive to; Little Otter: Hike to; an easy 1.0-mile hike one way

Fees: $

Water temperature: 73°F

Nearby attractions: Hart Springs, Fanning Springs, Nature Coast State Trail

Services: Food, restrooms, wi-fi, and laundry facility on-site; all services in Fanning Springs

Camping: On-site

Management: Privately owned; run by ForVets Inc.

Contact: (352) 463-0800 or (800) 883-9107; www.ottersprings.com

Map: DeLorme: Florida Atlas & Gazetteer: Page 64 C1

GPS coordinates: Otter Spring: N29 38.683' / W82 56.567'; Little Otter Spring: N29 38.183' / W82 57.5'

Finding the spring: From the junction of CR 232 and CR 344 East near Hart Springs, drive south on CR 232 for 2 miles to a right onto SW 70th Street. Travel for 1 mile to a right onto SW 80th Avenue and follow it north for 0.5 mile to the park, at the end of the road.

From the junction of CR 232 and FL 26 in Wilcox, drive north on CR 232 for 1.7 miles to a left onto SW 70th Street and follow directions above.

The Spring

Otter Springs Resort has changed hands a few times over the past years, and it is once again privately owned and under new management. Upon arrival you must check in at the office, which is a good idea anyway, since they'll give you a map of the property and directions to the springs. Dirt roads crisscross throughout this large plot of land, so it can get confusing without a map. The surprisingly busy full-service campground covers most of the property. There's also group camping, tent camping, cabins, and a stilt house available for lodging. A swim area is roped off from the spring run, but there are no lifeguards on duty, so swim at your own risk. An abundance of fish steadily leap from the springs, almost taunting you, since there is no fishing from the banks, license or not.

The spring run flows for a solid mile before reaching the Suwannee River. Canoe rentals are available, and there's a canoe launch on-site if you have your own canoe/kayak. If the greenish hue of the spring intimidates you, the park also has a heated swimming pool, which is open year round. On top of that, there's a playground and basketball and volleyball nets to keep the entire family entertained. Over 4.5 miles of hiking trails allow you to explore on foot, and deer, wild turkey, and peacocks tend to frequent the Sand Pine Trail loop, although this is not the most scenic trail in the park.

You can either hike or paddle out to see Little Otter Spring. Like many springs that sit near the river's edge, Little Otter is dependent on river levels. Sometimes it's flooded over and not worth the 1.0-mile hike; but when it's not flooded, you have the pleasure of seeing a crystal-clear spring pool. By far, the best time of day to see Little Otter Spring is at high noon. The sun's rays make it through the tree cover and shine down upon the spring pool, giving you perfect clarity to see the cave below.

This snapping turtle seems friendly, but it could easily take a finger off with one bite.

General description: Hart Springs has lots of facets that add to the scenery. The remains of a large cypress tree sit near the head of the spring, and a small peninsula juts out into the spring with two tall living cypress trees. A footbridge over the spring run gives visitors a good vantage point, as well as an easy way to get from one side of the spring to the other.

Location: 4240 SW 86th Ave., Bell; about 6.5 miles northwest of Fanning Springs

Development: Primitive

Best time to visit: Year-round

Restrictions: Open 9 a.m. to dusk Apr 1—Oct 31, 9 a.m. to 5 p.m. Nov 1—Mar 31; no pets allowed in the day-use area

Access: Drive to

Fees: $

Water temperature: 72°F

Nearby attractions: Otter Springs, Fanning Springs, Florida Greenway

Services: Food, lodging, restrooms on-site; all services in Fanning Springs

Camping: On-site

Management: Gilchrist County Parks Department

Contact: (352) 463-3444; www.hartsprings.com

Map: *DeLorme: Florida Atlas & Gazetteer:* Page 64 C1

GPS coordinates: N29 40.55' / W82 57.1'

Finding the spring: From the junction of CR 344 West and CR 232 north of Wilcox, drive west on CR 344 for 1.6 miles to the park, on the right.

The Spring

Hart Springs is composed of several spring vents, and the remains of an old cypress tree can be seen at the head of the run. Two large living cypress trees really seem to stand out in the center of the swim area. A peaceful footbridge passes over the spring, and manatees occasionally seek the warmer waters in winter. A ramp gives SCUBA divers easy access to dive in what's known as Little Hart Springs. *Note:* Divers *must* be cave certified and accompanied by an approved Hart Springs guide.

Surrounding the springs are a playground, volleyball nets, and a large picnic area. Cement picnic shelters with cement tables make it seem as though the park has been here for a long time. A wonderful boardwalk follows the spring run all the way out to the Suwannee River before looping back on itself, forming a pleasant 0.5-mile hike. If you'd rather explore by bike, you can access the Florida Greenway from Hart Springs Park. The park office doubles as a camp store, and there's a full-service campground on-site. Pets are allowed in the campground but not in the day-use area, so plan accordingly.

General description: Seemingly in the middle of nowhere, down a dirt road that zigzags through a barren countryside, is this surprisingly pretty spring with a great swim area. Dark green water pours out, and you can access the spring from either side. A small land bridge and chain-link fence separate the spring from the river, but another section of the park, right next door, has a boat ramp where you can reach the river if you wanted to.

Location: 2463 NE 816 Ave., Old Town; about 12.5 miles south of Branford

Development: Primitive

Best time to visit: Year-round

Restrictions: Open 8 a.m. to dusk; no alcohol

Access: Drive to

Fees: No fee

Water temperature: 72°F

Nearby attractions: Guaranto Springs Tract Log Landing Wildlife Management Area, Lower Suwannee National Wildlife Refuge

Services: Restrooms on-site; all services in Fanning Springs

Camping: Suwannee River Campground

Management: Dixie County Parks and Recreation

Contact: http://parks.dixie.fl.gov/?page_id=5

Maps: *DeLorme: Florida Atlas & Gazetteer:* Page 64 B1

GPS coordinates: N29 46.783' / W82 56.4'

Finding the spring: From the junction of CR 353 (NE 816th Avenue) and FL 349 near Fletcher, drive east on CR 353 for 2.4 miles to the park, on the right. ***Note:*** CR 353 makes several bends along the way.

The Spring

A chain-link fence and a narrow culvert are all that separate Gornto Park from the Suwannee River. An RV sitting outside this tiny county-run park houses the park manager. The spring is a hidden gem with two swim platforms, one on each side. Clear green water pours out from the spring vents before passing through the pipe at the culvert and ending up in the tannic water of the Suwannee River. This very peaceful park is well off the beaten path, but it can be quite entertaining. They have a playground, volleyball net, picnic shelter, and restrooms. The fence blocks you from getting to the river where the spring is located, but if you drive just past the spring, there's a small boat ramp where you could launch a kayak, canoe, or small boat.

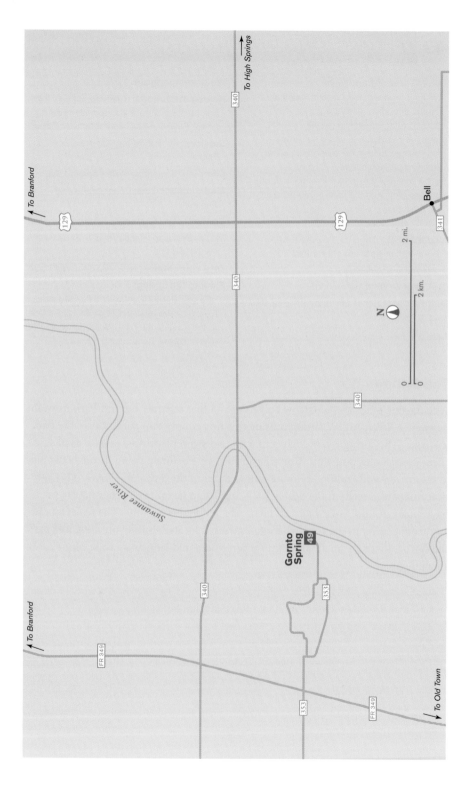

White-tailed deer can be found throughout the state.

General description: Poe Springs has some tough competition within this corridor of the Santa Fe River, and although it's not as blue as the other springs, it has merits of its own. In the first place, it's free. But that's just a bonus. The spring is isolated from the main body of the park, and an elevated boardwalk leads you through beautiful wetlands where cypress knees and trees stand out above all else. At the end of the boardwalk, clear water with a golden hue greets you at the spring, and a large shaded picnic ground lies beyond.

Location: 28800 NW 182nd Ave., High Springs; about 3 miles west of High Springs

Development: Developed

Best time to visit: Year-round

Restrictions: Open 8 a.m. to 6 p.m. Thurs–Sun; closed Mon–Wed and Dec 25 and 26; no pets allowed in the spring area; no SCUBA diving

Access: Hike to; 0.3 mile one way

Water temperature: 72°F

Fees: No fee

Nearby attractions: Big Blue Spring, Ginnie Springs Outdoors, Rum Island Park, Ichetucknee Springs State Park

Services: Restrooms on-site; all services in High Springs

Camping: Gilchrist Blue Springs, Ginnie Springs Outdoors

Management: Alachua County Parks and Recreation

Contact: (352) 374-5245; www.alachua county.us/Depts/PW/parksAndRecreation/ Pages/ParksandRecreation.aspx

Map: DeLorme: Florida Atlas & Gazetteer: Page 64 B3

GPS coordinates: N29 49.55' / W82 38.933'

Finding the spring: From the junction of CR 340 and US 41 in High Springs, drive west on CR 340 for 3.2 miles to a right into the park.

From the junction of CR 340 and FL 47 near Craggs, drive east on CR 340 for 5.3 miles to a left into the park.

The Spring

In a county teeming with water, Poe Springs is the only Alachua County–run park that allows swimming. Luckily, there are many other privately run springs within the county that also allow swimming, snorkeling, and even SCUBA diving. An obvious path leads northwest from the parking area, and you soon come to a fork near picnic pavilion #1. Head right from the fork and the paved path takes you alongside the Watermelon Spring Run. Because the area is environmentally sensitive and protected, you can't really see Watermelon Spring itself. But don't despair; you're in for a nice treat when you reach Poe Springs. A slightly raised wooden boardwalk leads to an observation deck and then onto the swimming area at Poe Springs. An average of 45 million gallons of fresh golden-colored springwater pours from the limestone crevices each day, before swiftly making its way out to the Santa Fe River.

Isolated from the main body of the park, this section has a large picnic area, picnic pavilions, fitness equipment, and restrooms. You'll have to carry anything you bring with you just over 0.25 mile to reach this portion of the park, so you may want to bring a cooler with wheels or a wagon to cart your belongings. Wide cement steps lead to the inviting spring pool, which is ideal for swimming and snorkeling. SCUBA diving is not allowed within the park, but Ginnie Springs Outdoors, just up the road, is a perfect place for both beginner and advanced divers.

Poe Springs Park comprises more than 200 acres. Along with the spring, the park borders the Santa Fe River. You can paddle on the river or use their boat ramp to explore even farther in a motor boat. If you choose to keep your feet on dry land, the park has a nature trail as well. Playgrounds, a volleyball net, and ball fields make this place popular among the locals, especially during the summer months. While you're in the area, I highly recommend spring hopping your way west along CR 340 and visiting Big Blue Springs (#52) and Ginnie Springs Outdoors (#53) as well.

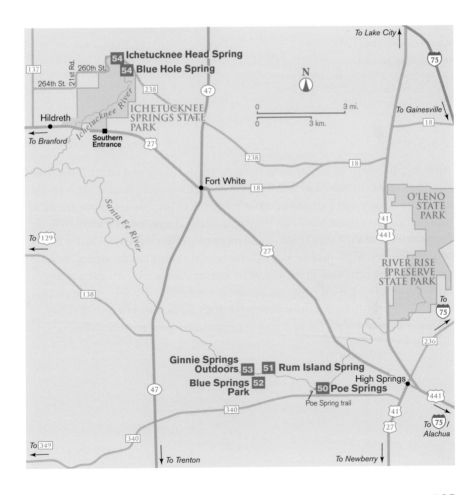

General description: The spring is found just west of the parking lot in a perfect little cove off the Santa Fe River. Sandy banks surround the spring, giving visitors a perfect place to lie out while they stay cool in the shallow edges of the spring. Rum Island is a very popular local swim hole, and this small county-run park fills up quickly on the weekends.

Location: 1246 SW Rum Island Ter.; about 6 miles northwest of High Springs and 10 miles southeast of Fort White

Development: Primitive

Best time to visit: Year-round

Restrictions: Open sunrise to sunset; closed on Tues until noon; no pets or alcohol

Access: Drive to

Fees: No fee

Water temperature: 72°F

Nearby attractions: Gatorback Cycle Park (motorcycles), Ichetucknee Springs State Park, Ginnie Springs Outdoors, Big Blue Spring, Poe Springs Park

Services: Restrooms on-site; all services in High Springs

Camping: Ginnie Springs Outdoors, Ellie Ray's River Campground

Management: Columbia County Parks and Recreation

Contact: (386) 719-7545

Map: *DeLorme: Florida Atlas & Gazetteer:* Page 64 B3

GPS coordinates: N29 50.04' / W82 40.644'

Finding the spring: From the junction of CR 138 and US 27 near High Springs, drive west on CR 138 for 2 miles to a left onto SW Rum Island Terrace. Travel for 1.2 miles as the road bends to the right and then left before ending at the park.

From the junction of CR 138 and FL 47 near Fort White, drive east on CR 138 for 4.4 miles to a right onto SW Rum Island Terrace and follow directions above.

The Spring

Often overshadowed by neighboring springs such as Ginnie and Ichetucknee, Rum Island Spring has its merits as well. For one, the price is right, since there is no fee to visit this county-run park. Although it's dependent on river levels, the spring at Rum Island can be quite nice. This third-magnitude spring sits in a small cove on the north bank of the Santa Fe River and more often than not has an active boil. If the river isn't too high, shallow sloping, sandy banks surround the spring, making this a perfect place to bask in the sun while staying cool in the refreshing spring-water. Because this park is fairly small, with limited parking, it fills up fast on the weekends. A heavily used narrow boat ramp gives locals easy access to the river. Fishing is allowed within the park and is a popular pastime for many visitors.

General description: Four springs are found on this wonderful piece of property, but Big Blue is without a doubt the highlight of this privately owned park. It's also the only one that's "developed." The other three are primitive and surrounded by forest. There's a campground, volleyball, and horseshoes on-site. They rent canoes, kayaks, and tubes. A large picnic area overlooks the main spring, and a concession stand sells drinks and snacks. With all this, you can stay and make a day or an enjoyable weekend of it.

Location: 7450 NE 60th St., High Springs; about 4 miles west of High Springs

Development: Big Blue: developed; Little Blue, Naked, and Johnson: primitive

Best time to visit: Year-round; closed for three weeks during the Christmas and New Year's holidays

Restrictions: Open Apr–Sept 9 a.m. to 7 p.m., Oct–Mar 9 a.m. to 5 p.m.; no pets or glass bottles

Access: Drive to

Fees: $$

Water temperature: 72°F

Nearby attractions: Ginnie Springs Outdoors, Poe Springs Park, Rum Island Park, Ichetucknee Springs State Park

Services: Food on-site; all services in High Springs

Camping: On-site

Management: Blue Springs Park

Contact: (386) 454-1369; www.blue springspark.com

Map: DeLorme: Florida Atlas & Gazetteer: Page 64 B3

Finding the spring: From the junction of CR 340 (Poe Springs Road) and US 41 near High Springs, drive west on CR 340 for 4.0 miles to a right onto an unmarked private road (NE 80th Avenue). Travel for 0.5 mile and the road bends left onto NE 60th Street. Follow this for 0.4 mile to the park, at the end of the road.

From the junction of CR 340 (Poe Springs Road) and FL 47 near Craggs, drive east on CR 340 for 4.1 miles to a left onto Blue Springs Road and follow directions above.

BIG BLUE SPRING

GPS coordinates: N29 49.784' / W82 40.976'

The Spring

Although there are four springs on the property, Big Blue is by far the main attraction; it's also the biggest spring. It's hard to believe that this gorgeous body of water is only a second-magnitude spring, pushing out about 55 million gallons of baby blue water a day. Overlooking the spring is a large grassy hill. Picnic tables and charcoal grills are scattered about, so you can claim your spot and enjoy an entire day in the park. To the left of the spring you'll see a large platform where you can get a running start and jump out into the spring. The platform sits about 10 feet above the surface of the water—high enough that you catch a little bit of air on the way down. You don't have to jump though. You can also wade into the spring from the sandy banks near the shallow outskirts of the spring. To the right of the spring you'll see a boardwalk that follows the spring run for 0.25 mile all the way out to the Santa Fe River. While the entire property and other springs are nice, Big Blue is why this place is listed among the Author's Favorites. The spring

The long claws are a telltale sign that this is a male.

is home to nine different species of turtle, which mate and form a nursery in Big Blue Spring a few months out of the year. The turtles eat any invasive hydrilla, and snails help filter the water. With these helpful critters around, the spring will stay as pristine as it is now for years to come.

LITTLE BLUE SPRING

GPS coordinates: N29 49.822' / W82 41.024'

The Spring

To the left (west) of Big Blue Spring, you'll see a short boardwalk. It leads to a small platform overlooking Little Blue Spring. The tall trees surrounding this circular spring reflect off the dark blue water. Unfortunately there's quite a bit of hydrilla in this spring, but the fish seem to like it.

Aquatic vegetation such as hydrilla is an invasive threat to the Florida springs.

NAKED SPRING

GPS coordinates: N29 49.799' / W82 40.868'

The Spring

On the east side of Big Blue Spring, beyond the boardwalk that follows the spring run out to the river and about 0.1 mile from Big Blue, you'll see another much smaller boardwalk that quickly leads to a platform over the spring. Much like Little Blue, this primitive spring is also surrounded by trees. You can see the remains of a large cypress tree beneath the clear blue water; hydrilla was present in this spring at the time of my last visit as well.

JOHNSON SPRING

GPS coordinates: N29 49.862' / W82 40.776'

The Spring

From Naked Spring, a wide sandy nature trail leads farther east, and after 0.1 mile you'll see a small open area with a few picnic tables, a charcoal grill, and a trash can. Beyond the tables a rustic sign leaning against a tree says "Johnson Spring." This is by far the most primitive spring on the property. There is no boardwalk or platform over the spring, but you're allowed to swim here. The spring run flows through a swampy area before reaching the river. At first glance the spring looks brown and tannic, but when you take closer peek, you see that it's clear and blue. Again, hydrilla and algae are taking over the spring, making it appear darker than it really is.

General description: This entire property is a natural wonder. Nine springs can be found here, although two sit right across the river and must be reached by boat. The only downside of Ginnie Springs is how extremely popular it is. On any given weekend, especially in the summertime, hundreds of people pass through the property to tube on the Santa Fe River or swim, snorkel, and SCUBA dive in the springs. The camp store/office doubles as a dive shop, and you can rent gear, fill bottles, and even take SCUBA lessons on-site. Rent a tube, canoe, or kayak and explore the lovely Santa Fe River. Spring hop on foot and snorkel in any or all of the seven springs on this side of the river. On top of it all, you can camp right along the river's edge or rent a cabin and spend the weekend. If my listing this with the Author's Favorites isn't enough to convince you, the enormous number of people who pass through this property should be a testament to the sheer beauty that Mother Nature has created here at Ginnie Springs. Along with other visitors, birdlife is also abundant, so keep your eyes peeled for pileated woodpeckers, hawks, owls, and cardinals, to name a few. Be sure to bring a camera for both above and below the water.

Location: 7300 NE Ginnie Springs Rd., High Springs; about 6.5 miles northwest of High Springs

Development: Primitive

Best time to visit: Year-round

Restrictions: Open summer hours: 8 a.m. to 7 p.m. Mon–Thurs, 8 a.m. to 7 p.m. Fri–Sat, 8 a.m. to 8 p.m. Sun; winter hours: 8 a.m. to 4 p.m. Mon–Thurs, 8 a.m. to 8 p.m. Fri–Sat, 8 a.m. to 6 p.m. Sunday; no pets

Access: Drive to; July and Sawdust Springs by boat only

Water temperature: 72°F

Fees: $$

Nearby attractions: Big Blue Springs, Poe Springs Park, Ichetucknee Springs State Park

Services: Food, restrooms, cabin rentals available; all services in High Springs

Camping: On-site

Management: Ginnie Springs Outdoors

Contact: (386) 454-7188; www.ginnie springsoutdoors.com

Map: *DeLorme: Florida Atlas & Gazetteer:* Page 64 B3

Finding the spring: From the junction of CR 340 and US 41 in High Springs, drive west on CR 340 for 6.4 miles to a right onto NE 60th Avenue. Travel for 1 mile to a right onto NE 62nd Place. Travel for 0.4 mile as the road bends left and leads to the entrance.

From the junction of CR 340 and FL 47 near Craggs, drive east on CR340 for 2.1 miles to a left onto NE 60th Avenue and follow directions above.

From the junction of FL 47 and CR 138 West near Fort White, drive south on FL 47 for approximately 1.3 miles to a left onto NE 65th Street. Travel for approximately 1.5 miles to a right onto NE 62nd Place. Follow NE 62nd Place for approximately 1.2 miles as it bends left and then bends left again, leading to the entrance.

GINNIE SPRING

GPS coordinates: N29 50.163' / W82 42.009'

The Spring

From the moment I set eyes on Ginnie Spring it captured my heart, and it has held my affection ever since. This entire outdoor complex is on the Author's Favorites list, and when you see it for yourself, you'll know why. Blue green water forms a perfect pool with limestone rock covering the floor, so you can stand in several spots within the spring without disturbing the vegetation or stirring up silt. A large cavern lies below the limestone ledges, making this an ideal snorkel site. SCUBA divers also enjoy exploring the cavern, and you can do so with an open-water dive certification. They also teach diving in this cavern, which is a unique place to say you earned your certification.

Ginnie Spring is a perfect swimming hole.

One side of the spring is rustic and undeveloped, with cypress knees and trees lining the bank. The other side has a large deck lined with benches and several sets of steps leading down into the water. The canoe/kayak launch site sits at the far end of the spring run near the river, and picnic tables are scattered throughout the grassy field alongside the spring. Several sand volleyball courts are found on this large parcel of land, including one near Ginnie Spring.

LITTLE DEVIL SPRING

GPS coordinates: N29 50.079' / W82 41.827'

The Spring

As you drive or walk upstream from Ginnie Spring, you'll come to a parking area that gives you access to three springs: Little Devil, Devil's Ear, and Devil's Eye. Little Devil is the most inland of the three and sits at the head of the spring run. A distinct and visible crack in the limestone rock under the water is where Little Devil issues out bright blue water. The run is almost 400 feet long; it starts out fairly shallow but gets a bit deeper as you approach the mouth of the river. A set of steps leads down to the spring, and it's fun to snorkel down the spring run out to Devil's Eye and Ear, which are found near the river at the mouth of the run.

DEVIL'S EYE & DEVIL'S EAR SPRINGS

GPS coordinates: N29 50.107' / W82 41.809'

The Spring

At the end of the Little Devil spring run, two springs lie in wait, and a double set of steps leads down into the water. One set of steps is dedicated to SCUBA divers; the other is for tubers, swimmers, and snorkelers. Devil's Eye is a narrow, almost-perfect circle in the ground where the water flows out with an immense force. You can see the spring not far from the staircase that leads into the beautiful blue water. Devil's Ear sits out in the Santa Fe River, but you can easily swim to it from the staircase. A bright orange buoy marks the entrance to the spring. Both Devil's Eye and Ear lead to a far-reaching cave system that extends for thousands of feet below the river and beyond. Cave diving certification is required to dive here.

DOGWOOD SPRING

GPS coordinates: N29 50.285' / W82 42.104'

The Spring

As you work your way downstream from Ginnie Spring, Dogwood is the first spring you'll come to. I'm not sure why, but I am drawn to this spring. It's a much smaller

This Suwannee bass swims where the clear blue spring run meets the river.

pool than Ginnie, but the water is just as clear. Limestone walls create a perfectly circular opening in the floor of the pool, and you can see straight down into the depths of the earth as you snorkel on the surface. The spring is particularly pretty when the midday sun shines directly down upon it and at night, when they light it up. A small wooden deck with steps leading into the spring gives visitors easy access to this bright blue beauty. Often you'll see groups of friends playing volleyball on the sand court near the spring or lying out on the grassy fields that surround it.

TWIN SPRINGS

GPS coordinates: N29 50.430' / W82 42.353'

The Springs

Downstream from Dogwood Spring you'll find Twin Springs. It too has a small deck with benches, giving swimmers easy access to the spring. At one time there was a rope swing near Twin where you could get a running start and leap out into the water, but it was not there on my last visit. Twin, along with Ginnie Spring, is where you'll see lots of families with smaller children swimming. Perhaps it's because the spring and run are very narrow, so parents can keep a closer eye on the little ones. Regardless, this one is another fun swim hole, where crystal-clear water flows from a pair of cracks in the limestone rock below the surface.

DEER SPRING

GPS coordinates: N29 50.467' / W82 42.433'

The Spring

Deer Spring is by far the least-populated spring on the property—well, at least of those reached by land. It sits just downstream from Twin Springs and has a bit longer spring run. It too is on the narrow side, and steps on both sides of the spring give visitors easy access. Perhaps because the spring has a bit more aquatic vegetation and algae growing in it, people are a bit more leery of this one despite the clear blue water that flows from it.

JULY AND SAWDUST SPRINGS

GPS coordinates: July: N29 50.186' / W82 41.777'; Sawdust: N29 50.333' / W82 42.2'

The Springs

Both July and Sawdust Springs sit on the opposite side of the river from the Ginnie Springs property and are reached by boat only. You can rent a canoe or kayak on-site or launch your own. A quick and easy paddle will take you to both springs. July sits about 0.2 mile upstream from the canoe launch and is on the north side of the river, directly across from Devil's Ear. Look for the orange buoy out in the river that marks Devil's Ear; then head to the opposite bank, where you'll see a perfect little clear blue pool occupying a small cove along the river's edge. This is July Spring. From here let the river do the work as you float downstream to Sawdust Spring. This one is also on the north bank of the river, about 0.5 mile downstream from Ginnie Spring. Paddle downstream from Ginnie; the second spring run entering the river is the Twin Spring run. Sawdust Spring is found across and a little upstream from the mouth of this run. There's a small boil, and clear water flows from the spring. *Note:* The land adjacent to the spring is private property.

General description: Several large springs feed and form the Ichetucknee River, and it's best known for its tubing opportunities. The park is split into two sections. Within the northern portion of the park, you can gain access to two of the springs, as well as swim, snorkel, or cave dive. You can also tube or paddle from here. The southern portion of the park is primarily a tubing destination, and you have several options and routes to choose from. The river is crystal clear over its entire length, which is understandable, since the springs put forth an average 233 million gallons of water each day.

Location: 12087 SW US 27, Fort White; about 10 miles northeast of Branford and 5.5 miles northwest of Fort White

Development: Primitive

Best time to visit: Year-round

Restrictions: Open 8 a.m. to sunset; no fishing, tobacco products; SCUBA permitted from Oct–Mar; food and drink permitted on the river in non-disposable containers only. Canoes/kayaks must be on the river by 3 p.m.

Access: Drive to

Fees: $

Water temperature: 72°F

Nearby attractions: Ginnie Springs Outdoors, Big Blue Springs, Poe Springs Park, O'Leno State Park, Rum Island Park, Branford Spring, Little River Spring, Ruth Spring, Troy Springs State Park

Services: Restrooms on-site; all services in Branford and Fort White

Camping: O'Leno State Park, Ginnie Springs Outdoors

Management: Florida Park Service

Contact: (386) 497-4690; www.florida stateparks.org/ichetuckneesprings/default .cfm

Map: *DeLorme: Florida Atlas & Gazetteer:* Page 64 A2

GPS coordinates: Head spring: N29 59.045' / W82 45.726'; Blue Hole Spring: N29 58.836' / W82 45.515'

Finding the springs:

Northern entrance: From the junction of CR 238 and FL 47 near Fort White, drive west on CR 238 for approximately 3.7 miles to the park, on the left.

From the junction of CR 137 and US 27 near Hildreth, drive north on CR 137 for 1.2 miles to a right onto 264th Street. Travel for 1.5 miles to a left onto 21st Road. Travel for 0.5 mile to a right onto 260th Street. Follow 260th Street for 2 miles the park, on the right.

Southern entrance: From the junction of US 27 and CR 137 near Hildreth, drive east on US 27 for 2 miles to the entrance, on the left.

From the junction of US 27 and FL 47, drive west on US 27 for approximately 4.4 miles to the entrance, on the right.

The Springs

Rich in history, Ichetucknee Springs and River have endured through time. A Spanish mission, a gristmill, phosphate mines, and turpentine production have all intruded on her banks. Fortunately, today the springs are protected and the river is designated as a National Natural Landmark. It earned this designation in 1972, shortly after being purchased by the State of Florida for development into the state park you now enjoy. The minute you cast your gaze upon any of the many springs that form this river, you'll instantly see why it rightfully earned this privilege.

The park is broken into two separate sections, with two distinct entrances, a north and a south. The north entrance is where you'll find the glorious headwaters

Ichetucknee's head spring is one of a kind.

of the river. This portion of the park has two separate swim areas. One is at the head spring, which is pure tranquility. A stone staircase leads down to the spring, and the blue-green color of the water is absolutely divine. You may find yourself sitting and staring in disbelief of the beauty before you. I know I do, every time I see this spring.

The second swim area requires a short hike of about 0.25 mile. This is Blue Hole Spring, and it is the largest of all the springs on the river. Blue Hole is just that. A rich deep blue-colored hole at the far end of the spring pool is ideal for snorkeling. This is also the only place in the park where SCUBA divers are welcome, but only from October through March. A cave system lies below, so you must be a certified cave diver to dive here.

Blue Hole sees less traffic than any other place in this park, so enjoy the solitude while you can. Picnic areas are scattered near the head spring, and two other hiking trails also originate from here. One follows a portion of the river, and to help protect the springshed, no pets are allowed on this trail. The second trail does allow pets. It's a 2.0-mile loop trail that provides insight into the park's diverse terrain.

If you drive beyond the head spring, you'll find a canoe/kayak and tube launch. The park does not rent boats or tubes, but several concessioners outside the park offer tube rentals and a shuttle service. You're also welcome to bring your own. A nominal launch fee ($) is required, and to ease the impact on the upper portion of the river, tubing from the northern entrance is allowed only from the Saturday before Memorial Day through Labor Day. (**Note:** The tubing trip from here takes a full three hours to reach the last takeout point.)

The southern entrance to the park has a massive parking lot with a multitude of picnic tables dispersed between the parking aisles. A wildlife education center gives visitors a wonderful lesson on the aquifer and the water cycle that occurs to form such an amazing collection of springs along the river. A concession stand where you can get sodas and snacks is on the premises, but they do not rent tubes, so you must bring your own or visit an outside vendor prior to arrival. Remember, *no* alcohol, tobacco, or pets are allowed anywhere on the river, and food and drink must be in non-disposable containers. So plan your mealtime accordingly.

The southern portion of the park is open for tubing year-round and is primarily designed to accommodate the thousands of tubers the park sees each year. They have two launch sites, and each is reached by trail and by tram. The amount of time you want to float on the river should dictate which you take. You can take the tram up to the short trail that leads to the Midpoint launch and float for up to 1.5 hours down to the last takeout, or you can shorten the trip by hopping out at Dampiers Landing Dock. You can also put in at Dampiers Landing and float downstream for about 45 minutes to the last takeout. In season, a tram takes tubers back to the parking area, or back up to the Midpoint launch if they want to have another go. In the off-season, tubers must walk back, with their tube in tow. There is a nominal fee to launch at any location in the park, and during the off-season they may have a self-pay station, where visitors pay using the honor system. Every penny goes back into the park, so please keep your karma intact and pay the fee.

During the summer months, people visit this park by the bus load. It's often chaotic in the river, with hundreds of tubes floating at time. If you plan to paddle, the park offers a shuttle service in season. But you must yield to tubers. For this reason, I *highly* recommend that you only canoe or kayak on weekdays, when the river is a bit less crowded. All the rules and limitations as to what you can bring on the river apply to paddlers as well. Please do your part to preserve this astounding natural treasure.

General description: Right in the heart of the town of Branford you'll find the brackish Branford Spring. The spring is a popular local swimming hole and is located in a small city park that also has two busy boat ramps. The park butts up against the Suwannee River, making it a nice spot to sit and read a book or have a picnic lunch.

Location: Within Ivey Memorial Park in Branford

Development: Developed

Best time to visit: Year-round

Restrictions: Open sunrise to sunset; no alcohol or tobacco

Access: Drive to

Water temperature: 72°F

Nearby attractions: Suwannee River Greenway, Troy Springs State Park

Services: All services in Branford

Camping: Suwannee River Rendezvous River Resort & Campground, Ellie Ray's River Campground

Management: Town of Branford Parks

Contact: (386) 935-1146; www.townof branford.net/parks-and-recreation.html

Map: DeLorme: Florida Atlas & Gazetteer: Page 64 A1

GPS coordinates: N29 57.297' / W82 55.711'

Finding the spring: From the junction of US 27 and US 129 North in Branford, drive north on US 27 for less than 0.1 mile to a left into the park, before crossing the bridge.

From the junction of US 27 and CR 349 near Branford, drive south on US 27 for 1.2 miles to a right into the park, after crossing the bridge.

The Spring

A horseshoe-shaped wooden boardwalk encircles the brackish spring that's found in a small local park in the heart of Branford. Along with the spring, the park houses two boat ramps and a decent-size parking area that includes an area for boat trailers as well. Jiffy John porta-potties are on-site, and old-time picnic shelters with charcoal grills sit along the banks of the river. As the Suwannee rushes by, the spring nearly goes unnoticed.

Although the spring is a popular swimming hole, at certain times of year the river level can rapidly fluctuate anywhere from 20 to 40 feet, literally drowning out the spring. The wooden crosses near the picnic area are not a religious testament but convenient canoe racks that can also double as a good place to hang your BC, regulator, and wet suit after SCUBA diving in the spring. The water is brown and brackish due to the spring's low flow and close proximity to the river. This lack of visibility makes the spring more popular with divers than with snorkelers.

Historic flood levels are indicated by this pole sitting alongside the Suwannee River.

General description: A large swim area can be accessed from both sides of the spring, and beautiful views of the Suwannee River can be seen from two observation platforms. The park is mostly used as a local swimming hole, but cave divers also delve through a crack and explore the extensive cave system beyond.

Location: 2489 105th Ln., O'Brien; about 4 miles north of Branford

Development: Developed

Best time to visit: Year-round

Restrictions: Open 7 a.m. to 7 p.m. Apr–Oct, 7 a.m. to 6 p.m. Nov–Mar; closed Tuesday from sunrise to 11 a.m.; no alcohol or pets

Access: Drive to

Fees: No fee

Water temperature: 72°F

Nearby attractions: Paved bike path along US 129, Ruth Spring, Troy Springs State Park, Ichetucknee Springs State Park

Services: Restrooms on-site; all services in Branford

Camping: Ellie Ray's River Campground, Ginnie Springs Outdoors

Management: Suwannee County Parks and Recreation; Suwannee River Water Management District

Contact: (386) 362-3004; http://suwanneeparks.com/little-river-springs-2/

Map: DeLorme: Florida Atlas & Gazetteer: Page 64 A1

GPS coordinates: N29 59.817' / W82 57.983'

Finding the spring: From the junction of US 129 and CR 248 near Branford, drive west on CR 248 for 1.7 miles to the park, at the end of the road.

The Spring

I'm not exactly sure why they call this Little River Spring; it's not little, nor is the Suwannee River, which it butts up against. In fact, the spring pool takes up nearly 10,000 square feet before narrowing just a bit as it heads out to merge with the river. Blue-green water forms a strong boil on the surface as the spring flows out through a large crack in the limestone. However, if the Suwannee River is at high levels, the spring loses some of its brighter color to the tannic brown of the river. An extensive cave system lures cave divers on a regular basis, but in general this is a local swimming hole.

The area surrounding the spring has had an extreme makeover in the past decade and really looks great. They've added picnic tables with charcoal grills and benches designed to help SCUBA divers easily don and doff their gear. A staircase leads to the water at one end of the spring; at the opposite end is a ramp that leads all the way down to the water. A pair of overlooks afford perfect views of both the spring and the river. To enhance the outdoor entertainment, they've even added a nature trail.

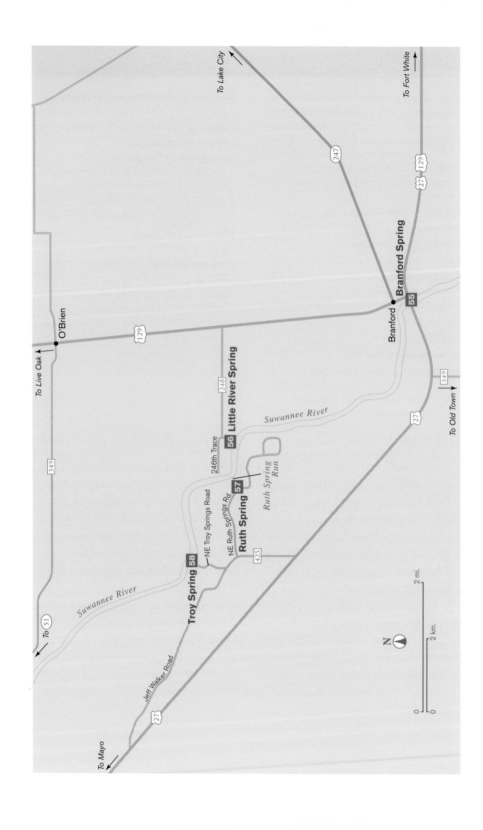

General description: Although it's only 4 miles northwest of Branford, Ruth Spring seems remote—down a dirt road in the middle of nowhere. Whether you jump from the limestone ledge or simply sit on it, the ledge is perfectly placed, slightly submerged along the edge of this dark green spring.

Location: Within Ruth Springs Park; about 4 miles northwest of Branford

Development: Primitive

Best time to visit: Year-round

Restrictions: Open sunrise to sunset

Access: Drive to

Fees: No fee

Water temperature: 72°F

Nearby attractions: Troy Springs State Park, Suwannee River Water Management District—Walker Tract

Services: All services in Branford

Camping: Suwannee River Rendezvous River Resort & Campground, Ellie Ray's River Campground

Management: Suwannee River Water Management District; Lafayette County Parks

Contact: www.srwmd.state.fl.us/index .aspx?nid=234

Map: *DeLorme: Florida Atlas & Gazetteer:* Page 64 A1

GPS coordinates: N29 59.75' / W82 58.6'

Finding the spring: From the junction of US 27 and CR 425 near Branford, drive north on CR 425 for 0.9 mile to a right onto NE Ruth Springs Road (a dirt road that leads into the Troy Springs Conservation Area). Travel for 1.1 miles to a left onto an unmarked dirt road (just past the entrance to the "Son-rise," which is on the right). Follow the unmarked dirt road for 0.1 mile to the bottom of the hill.

The Spring

Ruth Spring is well off the beaten path, tucked away in the Ruth Springs Tract of the Troy Springs Wildlife Management Area (WMA). As remote as it may seem, the spring sees a surprising amount of traffic on the weekends. However, if you can make it out during the week, you're certain to have it to yourself. At first glance the water seems brackish and brown. But as you get a little closer and take a better look, you see that although it's tannic, the water coming from the spring is actually clear. A wide set of slightly dilapidated wooden steps lead down to a limestone ledge that rests just beneath the surface. This ledge makes a good entry point into the chilling water. The spring and spring run appear to be deep as the run flows out to the Suwannee River.

Aside from the spring and a small dirt parking area, there is nothing else here—just trees, saw palmetto, and the untamed forest, with the occasional woodpecker laughing at you from the distance. Right around the corner though, the WMA has trails for hiking, biking, and horseback riding. You can also launch a canoe or go fishing, as long as you have a Florida state fishing license.

Brown water snakes are often misidentified as venomous water moccasins.

General description: By far, the most unusual thing about this remotely located spring is that below the surface of the spring run lies the remains of a Civil War–era steamship, the *Madison*. Visitors can snorkel and SCUBA dive to get a better view of the wreckage.

Location: 674 NE Troy Springs Rd., Branford; about 5.5 miles northwest of Branford

Development: Developed

Best time to visit: Year-round

Restrictions: Open 8 a.m. to sundown; no alcohol; no pets in the swim area

Access: Drive to

Water temperature: 72°F

Nearby attractions: Ruth Spring, Troy Springs Conservation Area, Suwannee River Water Management District–Walker Tract

Services: Restrooms on-site; all services in Branford

Camping: Suwannee River Rendezvous River Resort & Campground, Ellie Ray's River Campground

Management: Florida Park Service

Contact: (386) 935-4835; www.florida stateparks.org/troyspring/

Map: *DeLorme: Florida Atlas & Gazetteer:* Page 54 D1

GPS coordinates: N30 00.367' / W82 59.85'

Finding the spring: From the junction of CR 425 and US 27 near Branford, drive north on CR 425 for 1.1 miles to a right onto NE Troy Springs Road. Travel for 0.1 mile to the park, at the end of the road.

The Spring

Since the opening of Troy Springs State Park in 1983, the park service has done quite a commendable job of developing the park without tainting its natural state. There's a wonderful picnic area, with tables and charcoal grills scattered amid the trees. A ramp-like footpath zigzags down a steep hillside to a platform near the spring. From here steps lead down into the emerald-green water where you can swim, snorkel, or SCUBA dive in the 70-foot deep spring. A shipwreck lies below the surface of the spring run, and divers and snorkelers alike enjoy getting a closer look as they step back in time. The shipwreck is a Civil War–era steamboat named the *Madison*, which ended up in the spring back in 1863. Proof of open-water certification is all that's required to dive here. Benches line the parking lot for SCUBA divers to prep their gear; there's a dive gear rinsing station and outdoor shower on-site as well.

Although the spring is first magnitude, at times when the Suwannee River runs unusually high, the river overpowers the spring. During these times, "brownout" conditions occur, and the spring takes on the tannic brown color of the river. Unfortunately, under these conditions the swim area is closed; since this state park is quite remote, you may want to call ahead or check the park's website before heading out.

Other than Suwannee River Water Management District (SRWMD) land, there's really nothing out here but farms and cows, fields and grass, and the occasional house. If the swimming area is closed, you can still fish from the banks of the river or take a stroll on the 0.5-mile nature trail. The park is in the process of developing equestrian trails, a barn, and a horse washing station, but in the meantime you can use the trails at the SRWMD Ruth Springs Tract.

General description: A perfect hideaway within the Owens Spring Tract of the Suwannee River Water Management District, this untouched area is a great place to bring a picnic lunch or simply enjoy the fresh air. As the sunlight hits the water, the color begins to pop in the spring run and you begin to notice blue and green hues standing out in the water amid the reflection of the trees.

Location: About 8 miles east of Mayo

Development: Primitive

Best time to visit: Year-round

Restrictions: Open sunrise to sunset

Access: Hike to; 0.6 mile one way

Water temperature: 72°F

Nearby attractions: Ft. Macomb boat ramp at the end of NE CR 410, Peacock Springs State Park, Royal Spring, Ruth Spring, Troy Spring State Park

Services: All services are available in Mayo

Camping: Full-service at Suwannee River Rendezvous Resort & Campground, Suwannee River State Park; primitive at Lafayette Blue Springs State Park

Management: Suwannee River Water Management District–Owens Springs Tract

Contact: (386) 362-1001; www.srwmd.state .fl.us/index.aspx?nid=177

Map: *DeLorme: Florida Atlas & Gazetteer:* Page 53 D3

GPS coordinates: N30 02.763' / W83 02.466'

Finding the spring: From the junction of NE CR 411 and US 27 near Mayo, drive north on NE CR 411 for 1 mile to a T at NE CR 410. Turn right here and follow NE CR 410 for 0.7 mile to the parking area, on the left. *Note:* When you reach the T at CR 411 and CR 410, if the gate on the north side of CR 410 is open, continue straight across and follow the forest road to the small parking area at the end of the road. Then follow the trail directions from the small parking area.

The Spring

While the hike to Owens Spring is an easy one, even the locals complain about how bad the trail maps are for this area, so be sure to pay careful attention to my trail directions. In general, the trick is to stay with the silver blazes until you reach the T. To begin, make sure you take the trailhead at the northwest corner of the parking area and ignore the "Boat Ramp Loop" trailhead at the northeast corner. The silver-blazed trail is littered with tree branches as it heads northwest amid a multitude of longleaf pine trees, standing tall and straight above the dense brush below. After 0.1 mile the trail bends right, leaving the openness of the pine trees and heading into the dense cover of the forest. Continue to follow the silver blazes due north along the wide leaf-covered path. You'll notice that you're now hiking through a much wider variety of trees, from oaks to magnolias and saw palmetto to strangler fig.

After about 0.1 mile in the forest, the trail begins a slight descent, and you may see a barely discernible blue-blazed trail that heads off to the right (north-east). Ignore the blue-blazed trail and continue on the wide silver-blazed path as it follows a subtle downhill grade northwest. After hiking about 0.2 mile you'll come to a T junction with another wide, road-like path. Go right (northeast) here and in less than 0.1 mile arrive at a small parking area with a split-rail fence around it and a large gate (this is the parking area at the end of the forest road described above at the end of the driving directions). An obvious trail leads beyond the gate. Follow the narrow trail as it heads north-northeast and downhill. Less than 0.1 mile from the gate, you arrive at the pristine Owens Spring. A rope swing hangs overhead from a giant solitary oak tree limb that dips down over the spring. The tree limb looks as though it's about to die; I certainly wouldn't trust it to swing from, no matter how tempting it may be.

The spring is otherwise seemingly untouched and undeveloped. Birds singing and the wind blowing are all you hear at this peaceful retreat. Clear water with greenish hues allows you see the details in the rocks below the surface. Although there's no obvious boil, the wind makes the water ripple, bringing it to life. A small shelf-like ledge gives you a perfect access point to jump off and snorkel, affording you an even better view of the rocks below.

Alligators primarily feed on fish, snakes, turtles, birds, and small mammals.

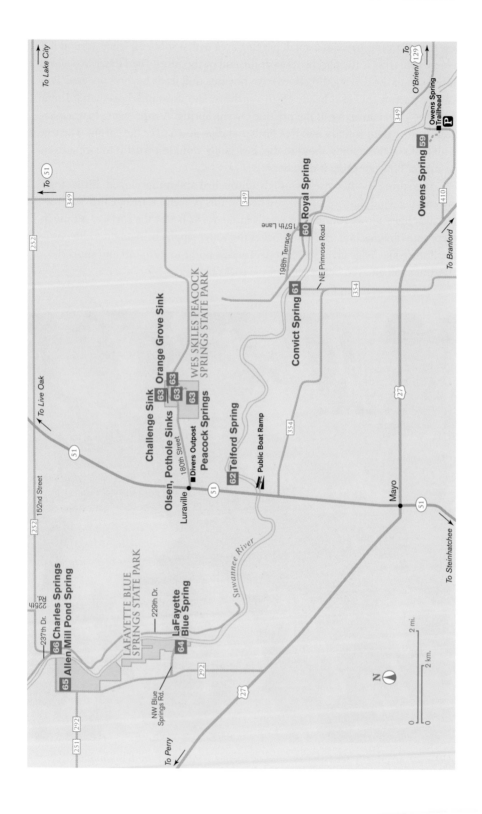

To Lake City

To 51

252

349

252

152nd Street

To Live Oak

51

349

349

198th Terrace

Challenge Sink

Orange Grove Sink

Olsen, Pothole Sinks

180th Street

63

63

63

63

WES SKILES PEACOCK
SPRINGS STATE PARK

Peacock Springs

■ Divers Outpost

Luraville

51

62 Telford Spring

Public Boat Ramp

Suwannee River

354

354

60 Royal Spring

157th Lane

61 Convict Spring

NE Primrose Road

27

Mayo

51

To Steinhatchee

237th Dr.

225th Rd.

251 292

66 Charles Springs

Allen Mill Pond Spring

LAFAYETTE BLUE
SPRINGS STATE PARK

229th Dr.

**64 LaFayette
Blue Spring**

65

NW Blue
Springs Rd.

292

27

To Perry

N

0 ⊢ 2 mi.

0 ⊢ 2 km.

To
O'Brien/ 129

Owens Spring 59

Owens Spring
Trailhead

P

410

To Branford

General description: Royal Spring is the main attraction of a small county-run park. A staircase leads all the way down to the dark blue water of the spring, or you can take the shortcut and jump from a platform that sits about 10 feet above the water. The second option is much more fun!

Location: 20051 157th Ln., O'Brien; about 14 miles northwest of Branford

Development: Developed

Best time to visit: Year-round

Restrictions: Open 7 a.m. to 7 p.m. Apr–Oct, 7 a.m. to 6 p.m. Nov–Mar; closed Wed sunrise to 11 a.m.; no alcohol or pets

Access: Drive to

Fees: No fee

Water temperature: 72°F

Nearby attractions: Peacock Springs State Park, Owens Spring, Little River County Park and Conservation Area, Troy Springs State Park, Convict Spring

Services: Restrooms on-site; all services in Mayo and Branford

Camping: Full-service camping at Suwannee River Rendezvous Resort & Campground; primitive at Lafayette Blue Springs State Park

Management: Suwannee County Parks and Recreation

Contact: (386) 362-3004; http://suwanneeparks.com/royal-springs-2/

Map: *DeLorme: Florida Atlas & Gazetteer:* Page 53 D3

GPS coordinates: N30 05.078' / W83 04.502'

Finding the spring: From the junction of CR 349 and US 129 in Obrien, drive west on CR 349 for 8.9 miles to a left onto 198th Terrace. Travel for 0.7 mile to a left onto 157th Lane. Follow 157th Lane for 0.15 mile to the park, at the end of the road.

From the junction of CR 349 and CR 252 near Mayo, drive south on CR 349 for approximately 6 miles to a right onto 198th Terrace and follow directions above.

The Spring

Space-wise, this is one of the biggest springs in the area. When I was here some fifteen-plus years ago, the spring had nothing but raw earthen banks and some boards nailed to a tree. Locals used these boards to climb up to one of two tiny platforms. One sat about 25 feet above the water; the other was nearly 70 feet high, and only the bravest climbed to take the plunge into the chilling water below. I admit I leapt from the lower platform a time or two, but I never did find my way up to the treetop.

Today Royal Springs looks quite different. Within this wonderful park are observation decks alongside the spring, stairways that lead down to the water's edge, and a platform big enough to get a running start on that sits about 10 feet above the water. The boards are still nailed to that very same cypress tree, and during my recent visit, a local teenage boy climbed to the top and did a few flips on his way down.

The park has nearly a dozen picnic tables with charcoal grills, spread out just enough to give you a bit of space from your neighbors. There are porta-potties on-site, and a public boat ramp next to the park gives you easy access to the Upper Suwannee River. I loved it then; I love it now! Royal is still one of my favorites.

This platform at Royal Springs sits about 10 feet above the water.

General description: Clear green water pours up from this perfectly circular spring, and you can see the river passing by as you sun on the grassy banks that surround it. The Suwannee River Rendezvous Resort, where Convict Spring is located, has a campground, lodging, swimming pool, canoe/kayak rentals. The best part is that this 40-acre parcel of land sits right beside the historic Suwannee River.

Location: 828 NE Primrose Rd., Mayo; about 5 miles east northeast of Mayo

Development: Developed

Best time to visit: Year-round

Restrictions: Side-mount SCUBA diving only; proof of certification required

Access: Drive to

Fees: $

Water temperature: 70.5°F

Nearby attractions: Mallory Swamp Wildlife Management Area

Services: Food, lodging, restrooms on-site; all services in Mayo

Camping: On-site

Management: Suwannee River Rendezvous Resort and Campground

Contact: (386) 294-2510; www.suwannee riverrendezvous.com

Map: *DeLorme: Florida Atlas & Gazetteer:* Page 53 D3

GPS coordinates: N30 05.280' / W83 05.777'

Finding the spring: From the junction of CR 354 and US 27 near Mayo, drive north on CR 354 for 1.6 miles to a right onto NE Primrose Road. Travel for 0.8 mile to the resort, at the end of the road.

From the junction of CR 354 and FL 51 near Mayo, drive east on CR 354 for approximately 5 miles to a left onto Primrose Road and follow directions above.

The Spring

As you head into the Suwannee River Rendezvous Resort and Campground, don't be discouraged by the RV campground, where although the sites are large, they seem to sit on top of one another, and there's seemingly little tree cover. Once you get past that portion of this 40-acre property, you'll find it's quite lovely and shaded by large oak trees. Tent campsites are dispersed among the trees and along the riverbanks; they also have a variety of other lodging opportunities, from A-frame cabins to hilltop motel rooms. Some of the rooms even overlook the spring, which got its name because in the early 1900s this location was used as a remote prison camp.

Today swinging benches and Adirondack chairs overlook the spring and Suwannee River as it swiftly passes by. Canoe and kayak rentals are available on-site, and the rates are extremely reasonable. They also have a narrow, steep private boat ramp on the property, if you want to bring your own. All visitors must check in at the office before heading off to swim in the spring or explore the property. Crystal-clear green water fills this natural pool, making it ideal for swimming and snorkeling. A shallow concrete ledge surrounds the circular spring, giving visitors a perfect place to sit in the cool springwater while soaking in the sun at the same time. Grassy banks slope down to the water's edge, providing additional space for lying out and warming up after taking a dip. An extremely advanced cave system lies below the surface and requires a side-mount entry. SCUBA divers must show proof of special certifications before being allowed to dive here.

The spring run makes a 90-degree turn and flows out to the Suwannee River. Fishing is a popular pastime here, and if you want something a bit more active, a paved path runs alongside CR 354. The path is suitable for bikes, inline skates, or runners and offers an enjoyable ride along a country road. A newly built swimming pool is also found on the property, giving visitors an additional option for swimming. The resort is very dog friendly; they even have a dog park on the premises. They also have their own resident pooch, a Yellow Lab named Charlie, so feel free to bring your pups along and enjoy the rendezvous.

Convict Spring was once the site of a remote prison camp.

General description: Due to its close proximity to the Suwannee River, the beauty of Telford Spring is highly dependent on river levels. At its best, the spring can be as bright blue as they come; at its worst, it's hard to believe that there's a spring below the brown river water. Sloping sandy banks surround the spring, and in summer it transforms into a popular local swim hole, despite the many signs that say "No Trespassing Allowed."

Location: Along the west bank of the Suwannee River, about 0.5 mile downstream from the FL 51 boat ramp; about 5 miles north of Mayo and 1 mile south of Luraville

Development: Primitive

Best time to visit: Year-round

Restrictions: Surrounded by private property

Access: Boat to; 0.75 mile upstream

Fees: No fee

Water temperature: 72°F

Nearby attractions: Peacock Springs State Park, Divers Outpost dive shop, Lafayette Blue Springs State Park

Services: All services in Mayo

Camping: Suwannee River State Park

Management: n/a

Contact: n/a

Map: *DeLorme: Florida Atlas & Gazetteer:* Page 53 D2

GPS coordinates: N30 06.430' / W83 09.945'

Finding the spring: From the junction of FL 51 and US 27 in Mayo, drive north on FL 51 for approximately 3 miles to the boat ramp, on your right before crossing the bridge.

From the junction of FL 51 and CR 252, drive south on FL 51 for approximately 5.5 miles to the boat ramp, on your left after crossing the bridge.

The Spring

Once a popular local swimming hole and easily reached by land, now Telford Spring is gated off, littered with "No Trespassing" signs, and only reachable by boat. Be sure to stay in your boat or in the water when you visit. If you step foot on dry land surrounding the spring, you will be trespassing.

From the boat launch on FL 51, follow the river upstream for about 0.75 mile. As you head north in between curves on the river, an obvious small cove will appear on the left (west) bank. The spring is strong, and unless the river is extremely high, clear blue water will form an obvious boil above it. If you plan on taking a dip, be sure to tie off or anchor your canoe or kayak or it will be swept away by the current.

The occasional SCUBA diver will access this spring from the southern end of 203rd Road and then wade with their gear less than 0.1 mile downstream to the spring. While you could do the same, or even put a canoe in at this locale, there is no parking. This is not a designated public boat launch, so you may get a ticket or be towed if you park here.

General description: Several springs and sinks connected by 33,000 feet of underwater passages are found within this peaceful state park, and they are very popular within the cave-diving community. People come from all over the world to dive in this elaborate cave system. Although this park gets very busy on the weekends, during the week you'll find it practically barren. Whether you drive right up or take a short hike to view the sinks and springs within this park, I recommend exploring them all. Each has its own unique beauty, both above and below the surface.

Location: 18081 185th Rd., Live Oak; about 2 miles east of Luraville

Development: Primitive

Best time to visit: Year-round

Restrictions: Open 8 a.m. to sunset; swimming and SCUBA diving allowed in Peacock and Orange Grove *only*; pets allowed in the park but not in the springs

Access: Drive to; hike to Olsen, Pothole, and Challenge Sinks

Fees: $

Water temperature: 72°F

Nearby attractions: Divers Outpost dive shop, Lafayette Blue Springs State Park, Convict Spring, Telford Spring, Royal Spring

Services: Gas, food available in Luraville; all services in Mayo

Camping: Full-service at Suwannee River Rendezvous Resort & Campground; primitive at Lafayette Blue Springs State Park

Management: Florida Park Service

Contact: (386) 776-2194; www.florida stateparks.org/peacocksprings/default.cfm

Map: *DeLorme: Florida Atlas & Gazetteer:* Page 53 D2

Finding the spring: From the junction of FL 51 and CR 354 near Mayo, drive north on FL 51 for 2 miles to a right onto 180th Street (at the caution light). Travel for 2.2 miles to the park, on your right.

From the junction of FL 51 and CR 252 near Luraville, drive south on FL 51 for 3.8 miles to a left onto 180th Street (at the caution light) and follow directions above.

ORANGE GROVE SINK

GPS coordinates: N30 07.638' / W83 07.848'

The Sink

As you travel along the dirt road through the park, the first parking area and sink you'll come to is Orange Grove. Depending on recent rainfall, this sink may be a rich navy blue one day and a month later be dark espresso brown water and covered with duckweed. You may want to call ahead for conditions before you waste a trip out there. Orange Grove is one of two places in the park where you're allowed to swim and snorkel, and it's the *only* place in the park where you can dive with an open-water SCUBA certification. You can also access the cave-diving system from here if you have the proper cave diving certification.

Tall limestone walls surround a good portion of the sink and a striking contrast is cast between the light-colored stone and the darker tones of the water. Several paths lead through a picnic area near the sink, and benches designed for divers line the parking lot as well as the picnic area. A steep set of steps leads into the water, but there's also a ramp that allows you to wheel your gear down if you'd rather. There is no lifeguard on duty anywhere within the park, so swim at your own risk.

PEACOCK SPRINGS I, II, III

GPS coordinates: Peacock I: N30 07.399' / W83 07.990'; Peacock II: N30 07.354' / W83 07.948'; Peacock III: N30 07.344' / W83-07.934'

The Springs

After stopping off at Orange Grove Sink, the dirt road leads through this wonder-fully wooded park to Peacock Springs. There are actually three distinct springs, but unless you're a cave diver, you wouldn't really be able to tell. Visitors are welcome to swim and snorkel in any of the three Peacock Springs, but these springs see more traffic from cave divers than any other group.

A sign at Peacock Springs reminds you to dive within your limits.

Peacock I is accessed from the northwest corner of the parking lot. Follow the boardwalk that leads due west and you'll quickly come to a small set of steps descending into the water. This is also the trailhead for the Interpretive Springs Trail, which leads you past Olsen and Pothole Sinks. You'll see a large free-standing information board at the trailhead (more on that below, where I describe the hike to those sinks). Peacock I's water is so calm and peaceful, it's almost unsettling. Large limestone rocks are visible through the transparent green water here and at the other Peacock Springs. An intricate cave system lies below this serene surface, forming a network of tunnels and rooms that connects several of the park's springs and sinks. You *must* show proof of your cave-diving certification to park staff, or by leaving a copy of your dive card on your dashboard while diving.

To reach Peacock II, walk a bit past the south end of the parking lot; you'll see a bench overlooking the dirt path that leads to the water's edge. Limestone rocks line the bank, and fish congregate near the stony edges of the underwater entrance to the spring. Use caution if you swim anywhere within Peacock Springs, but especially in this area, because large limestone boulders lie below the surface.

Peacock III is just a bit farther south from Peacock II; cypress knees line the banks near this one.

OLSEN AND POTHOLE SINKS

GPS coordinates: Olsen: N30 07.578' / W83 07.984'; Pothole: N30 07.467' / W83 07.986'

The Sink

At the trailhead near Peacock I Spring, you'll see a trail map on the kiosk for the Interpretive Springs Trail. The obvious path is very well marked, and along the way you'll see several informational signs. You'll enjoy the photos on the signs and reading about the extensive cave system beneath your feet. It's quite possible that SCUBA divers could literally be right under your feet at any given moment.

The pleasant stroll makes a loop leading back to the trailhead and takes about 20 minutes to complete. Along the way you'll see Pothole and Olsen Sinks. Both are unique, and clear blue water ties these sinks to the three Peacock Springs via the tunnels of this extensive cave system. Reading the signs and seeing these sinks gives you a bit of perspective as to exactly how far reaching this cave system really is.

CHALLENGE SINK

GPS coordinates: N30 07.765' / W83 07.991'

The Sink

Challenge Sink is very easy to get to, but it's often overlooked because people don't even know it's there. To access the sink, pull into the park, pay the fee, and park in the small parking area just past the pay station. Walk back out of the park to 180th Street. Carefully cross the street to the grass on the opposite side of the road from the park entrance, and walk left (west). About 250 feet from the park entrance, you'll see a small post in the middle of the grass and a cable box next to the post. Near this post, at the edge of the woods, you'll see another post, just a bit taller than the first, with a state park boundary sign on it. An obvious narrow trail leads northwest from this post for about 100 feet and takes you directly to the sink—a small pool of beautiful, amazingly clear water. Steep banks lead to the sink, but please view it from the path only. You get a better vantage point from here anyway, especially at high noon, when the rays of the sun hitting the spring from straight overhead really make the color pop.

General description: Lafayette Blue Springs State Park is a little different—it has two different locations to access different parts of the park. Make sure you use the southern entrance to access Lafayette Blue Spring. High limestone walls surround the spring, giving it a kind of primitive feel. A ramp on one side and a set of steep steps on the other lead down into the spring and to the edge of the river, and a string of buoys is all that separates the two.

Location: 799 NW Blue Springs Rd., Mayo; about 7 miles northwest of Mayo

Development: Primitive

Best time to visit: Year-round

Restrictions: Open 8 a.m. to sundown

Access: Drive to

Fees: $

Water temperature: 72°F

Nearby attractions: Allen Mill Pond Spring, Charles Springs, Telford Spring, Peacock Springs State Park, Divers Outpost dive shop

Services: Restrooms on-site; all services in Mayo

Camping: Full service tent-only camping and fully furnished cabins on-site; full-service at Suwannee River Rendezvous Resort & Campground, Suwannee River State Park

Management: Florida Park Service

Contact: (386) 294-3667; www.florida stateparks.org/lafayettebluesprings/default .cfm

Map: *DeLorme: Florida Atlas & Gazetteer:* Page 53 C2

GPS coordinates: N30 07.55' / W83 13.567'

Finding the spring: From the junction of CR 292 and US 27 near Mayo, drive north on CR 292 for 2.1 miles to a right onto NW Blue Springs Road. Travel for 0.6 mile to the park, at the end of the road.

From the junction of CR 292 and CR 251 near Dowling Park, drive west on CR 292 for 3.3 miles to a left onto NW Blue Springs Road and follow directions above. ***Note:*** When coming from CR 251, as you travel on CR 292 you'll pass the northern entrance to Lafayette Blue Springs State Park. Be sure to follow CR 292 all the way to a left onto NW Blue Springs Road to access the park's southern entrance.

The Spring

There are two distinct sections of this state park, and they both sit off CR 292 about 2 miles from each other. While you can hike to Allen Mill Pond Spring (#65) from the northern portion of the park, the main attraction by far is Lafayette Blue Spring, for which the park was named. This first-magnitude spring is accessed via the park's southern entrance. Along with the spring, there's a boat ramp, a lovely picnic area, rental cabins, and tent-only campsites. From the parking area, a sidewalk leads southeast, straight to the spring overlook and swimming area. The water has hints of blue, green, and brown, and the predominant color is heavily dependent on the river levels.

For easy access to the spring, a boardwalk ramp zigzags down to the mouth of the spring run, where it meets the river. Or you can take a set of steps that lead directly down near the spring head. The river is clearly visible from the spring, and this comparatively short run plays a role in why this spring is so dependent on the river levels. You can go online to www.mySuwanneeRiver.com to check river

An elegant palomino grazes on the grass.

levels daily, which are measured at over fifty monitoring stations along the river, including at Lafayette Blue Spring.

A large picnic area sits between the parking lot and the spring, or you can follow a little boardwalk out to a handful of picnic tables that sit right on the edge of the Suwannee River. Tall, steep banks surround this beautiful first-magnitude spring, and limestone walls encircle it underwater. This is great place to swim and snorkel, and when the river is low, a natural limestone land bridge divides the spring into two pools, adding to the picturesque landscape. An extensive cave system lies below, and SCUBA divers must show proof of their cave-diving certification before making their descent.

There are restrooms near the parking area, but you have to climb some stairs or take the elevator to reach them. Beautiful cabins that look like houses on stilts can sleep six, and each cabin has a fireplace for the cool nights and a screened-in porch for the warm ones. Although on a map they appear to be right on the river, there is too much brush between the river and the cabins to actually get a good view except in late fall and winter when the tree canopy thins a bit. The paved boat ramp is fairly steep, and there are canoe racks near the ramp, which is appropriate, considering that the park is found along the famous Suwannee River Wilderness Trail. This paddle trail spans 170 miles from the town of White Springs all the way out to the Gulf of Mexico. Lafayette Blue is one of nine state parks located along the route, and the full-service tent-only campground is often a pit stop for paddlers along the way. The camping is not only limited to paddlers though. Anyone can camp here, but this is a hike-in, tent-only campground, although each site does come equipped with water and electric.

General description: Within the northern portion of Lafayette Blue Springs State Park, Allen Mill Pond Springs is reached by hiking about 0.5 mile. The spring and area surrounding it are pristine and natural. Enjoy the pleasant hike, since you're likely to have this one to yourself.

Location: 4298 NW CR 292, Mayo; about 7 miles northwest of Mayo

Development: Primitive

Best time to visit: Year-round

Restrictions: Open 8 a.m. to sundown; no swimming (swimming allowed in Lafayette Blue Spring, at the southern entrance to the park)

Access: Hike to; 0.5 mile one way

Fees: $

Water temperature: 72°F

Nearby attractions: Lafayette Blue Spring, Charles Spring, Telford Spring, Peacock Springs State Park, Divers Outpost dive shop

Services: Restrooms on-site; all services in Mayo

Camping: Full service tent-only camping and fully furnished cabins on-site; full-service at Suwannee River Rendezvous Resort & Campground, Suwannee River State Park

Management: Florida Park Service

Contact: (386) 294-3667; www.florida stateparks.org/lafayettebluesprings/default .cfm

Map: *DeLorme: Florida Atlas & Gazetteer:* Page 53 C2

GPS coordinates: N30 09.765' / W83 14.581'

Finding the spring: From the junction of CR 292 and US 27 near Mayo, drive north on CR 292 for 4.1 miles to a right into the northern entrance to the park. ***Note:*** As you travel on CR 292, you'll pass the southern entrance to the park; continue driving until you reach the northern entrance to the park.

From the junction of CR 292 and CR 251 near Dowling Park, drive west on CR 292 for 1.3 miles to a left into the northern entrance to the park.

The Spring

When you visit the area, you'll see that there are two distinct sections of Lafayette Blue Springs State Park. The southern portion is home to Lafayette Blue Spring (#64), and along with the spring/swimming area, there's a boat ramp, canoe launch, cabin rentals, and tent camping. I highly recommend that you visit this first-magnitude spring while you're in the area. The portion of the park accessed by the northern entrance has an extensive trail system for hiking and horseback riding. You can also fish here, and wildlife viewing is optimal. This is also where you'll find the undeveloped Allen Mill Pond Spring.

After entering the park, the main park road becomes a dirt road. Follow this road back and at 0.2 mile you'll come to a fork, which the park rangers call "the triangle." Head left at this fork and you'll immediately see a gated forest road to your left. This gate is the trailhead, and reaching the spring requires an easy 0.5-mile hike. Parking is available by the ranger station near the entrance to the park, or in the parking area a short distance farther down the service road.

When you get out on the trails, this section of the park is surprisingly hilly, which is quite a refreshing change from the typical Florida flatlands. From the gate, follow the wide road-like trail north-northeast back into the forest. As you begin the hike, you can smell the pine trees and turpentine in the air. The trail bends a bit northwest along the way, but in general it follows a northerly direction. After 0.3 mile you'll see a narrow trail to the left (west) that leads to some houses that are visible through the trees. Ignore this side trail; continue hiking north and almost immediately come to a fork. Go right (north-northeast) at the fork as you hear the occasional car passing by on CR 292. The only other sounds you may hear on this peaceful hike are the leaves crunching beneath your feet, the tweeting of birds, or the screech of a hawk as it flies high overhead searching for prey.

After hiking less than 0.2 mile from the fork, you'll see the remnants of an old building on your left, just before reaching a T in the trail. After appreciating its rustic beauty, continue on to the T, where the left heads west and the right heads east and downhill. Go right (east) and in less than 0.1 mile you'll arrive at Allen Mill Pond Spring. A single picnic table sits beside the spring, and a staff gauge in the spring measures the water levels remotely. Other than that, this area is completely primitive and undeveloped, tucked away in the middle of the woods.

Water flows down the spring run, forming a small wooded creek, like one you would see up North. It even forms its own small rapid where the spring run bends to the right. This rapid generates the wonderful sound of moving water as you sit at the picnic table alongside the spring. It's an interesting dynamic, because you really don't see where the water is moving that fast out of the spring head; there's no obvious boil or other telltale sign of the magnitude of water pushing forth. But based on the sound of the rapid just 200 feet downstream, it's evident that this second-magnitude spring is clearly moving at a decent rate. If you decide to stay awhile, you may want to bring some bug spray along. This remote spring can be a bit buggy at times.

White-tailed deer find refuge within many of Florida's state parks.

General description: For some reason, I'm drawn to the springs in this small, remote park. Perhaps it's the land bridge made from limestone rock, or the fact that you can see every crevice within it. Maybe it's the crystal-clear water that looks bright green when the sun hits it just right, or the wooded spring run with high banks that serenades you as it flows out to the river. I'm not really sure what it is, but whatever the enchantment, to me this spring has both character and personality.

Location: 15465 237th Dr., Live Oak; about 5 miles south of Dowling Park and 9 miles north of Mayo

Development: Primitive

Best time to visit: Year-round

Restrictions: Open 7 a.m. to 7:30 p.m. Apr–Oct, 7 a.m. to 6 p.m. Nov–Mar; no alcohol or pets

Access: Drive to

Fees: No fee

Water temperature: 72°F

Nearby attractions: Allen Mill Pond Conservation Area, Lafayette Blue Springs

State Park, Peacock State Park, Twin Rivers State Forest

Services: Restrooms on-site; all services in Mayo

Camping: Full-service at Suwannee River State Park, Suwannee River Rendezvous Resort & Campground; primitive at Lafayette Blue Springs State Park

Management: Suwannee County Parks and Recreation

Contact: (386) 362-3004; http://suwannee parks.com/charles-springs

Map: DeLorme: Florida Atlas & Gazetteer: Page 53 C2

GPS coordinates: N30 9.983' / W83 13.7'

Finding the spring: From the junction of CR 252/152nd Street and FL 51 near Luraville, drive west on 152nd Street for 4 miles to where the paved road bends right and becomes 225th Road and 152nd Street continues straight ahead as a dirt road. Drive straight ahead on the dirt road, and continue to follow 152nd Street as it bends left. After 1.2 miles the road ends at 237th Drive. The park is directly in front of you.

The Spring

Cows feed on lush green grass alongside bales of hay as you drive down the seemingly endless 152nd Street to get to Charles Springs Park. This is the only paved road in the area, so don't wash your car before you head out to these springs. When you pull into the park, there's a small parking area on the right (north); the springs are just beyond it. The south side of the park has a single picnic table with a charcoal grill that sits up on a plateau overlooking the Suwannee River. There's a paved boat ramp on the premises, with ample parking for boat trailers. The boat ramp gives boaters easy access to the river, and the park is primarily used by local anglers and water enthusiasts. A tall set of steps leads down to the springs from a high bluff overlooking them. Character oozes from the springs, and walls of limestone form a natural bridge, separating the springs into perfect little pools. The clear green water lures you in; the slow-moving spring run then flows out and mingles with the Upper Suwannee River.

The land surrounding the springs is steeped in history, and the Charles family ran a trading post and ferry at this very location. Ruben Charles was killed by

Indians around 1840, despite his reputation as a "sympathizer." Twelve years later, his wife, Rebecca, was also killed, but it's said that she was shot by white settlers due to her close relationship with the Native Americans. The Charles family kept the ferry running for another two decades before abandoning it. Today this area is recognized as a historic landmark.

General description: White Springs is a stop along the way to other places. While it's rich in history, and it's neat to see the remains of what once was a happening health resort, unfortunately that's all the spring has to offer. The fact that it sits alongside the Suwannee River is nice, but you can't swim, snorkel, dive, or even fish within the spring.

Location: On the north bank of the Suwannee River; just before entering the Stephen Foster Folk Cultural Center State Park in White Springs

Development: Developed

Best time to visit: Year-round

Restrictions: Open sunrise to sunset; no swimming or fishing allowed in the spring

Access: Drive to

Fees: No fee

Water temperature: 72°F

Nearby attractions: Stephen Foster Folk Culture Center State Park, Blue Sink, Spirit of the Suwannee Music Park, Falmouth Springs, Suwannee River State Park, Osceola National Forest

Services: Restrooms on-site; all services in Live Oak

Camping: On-site

Management: Florida Park Service

Contact: (386) 397-2733; www.florida stateparks.org/stephenfoster

Map: *DeLorme: Florida Atlas & Gazetteer:* Page 54 B2

GPS coordinates: N30 19.800' / W82 45.656'

Finding the spring: From I-75 near White Springs, take exit 439 and drive east on FL 136 (Duval Street) for approximately 3.1 miles to a left onto US 41. Travel for less than 0.1 mile to the parking area on the left, just before entering Stephen Foster Folk Culture Center State Park.

From the junction of US 41 and CR 137 near White Springs, drive south on US 41 for approximately 3.3 miles to the parking area on the right, just outside the state park.

The Spring

Right outside the Stephen Foster Folk Culture Center State Park, the very popular White Sulphur Springs Health Resort once stood tall. Remnants of the four-story "fountain of health," built back in 1908 to completely surround White Springs, still stand. But today the spring and the building's remains act only as a window to the past. An information kiosk shows photos of when this was a popular swimming hole and tourist destination known for its healing properties. Now, however, it's more of a stop off on your way into the state park—and understandably so, since you can't swim, snorkel, dive, or fish in the spring. If you're in the area, it's worth stopping by for the historical aspect and the structure itself. But the fact that you can't actually access the spring is a bit of a disappointment.

The things you see along a country road.

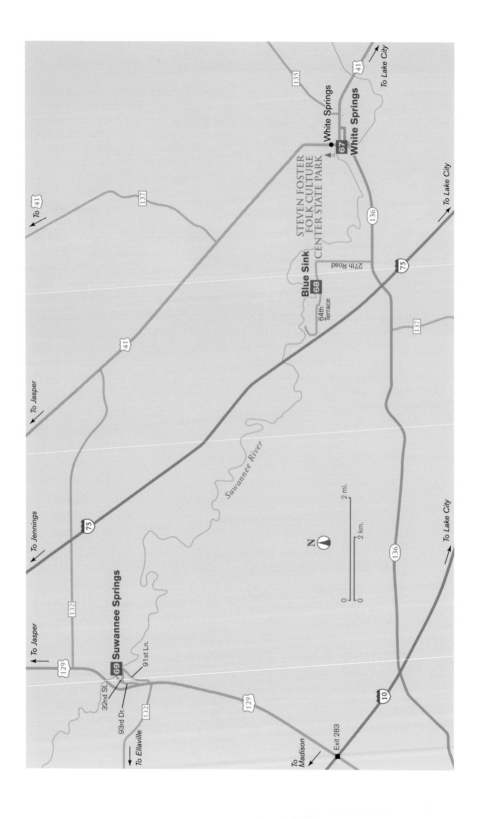

General description: Before you get your hopes up, you cannot swim in Blue Sink. The sink is, however, found within a conservation area that offers opportunities for hiking, biking, horseback riding, and fishing. I'm told that when water levels are right, the sink has a blue hue, although the few times I've been there, it's leaned more toward the tannic brown color of most of the rivers in Florida.

Location: Within a forested area of the Suwannee River Management District; about 3 miles west of White Springs and 13 miles northeast of Live Oak

Development: Primitive

Best time to visit: Year-round

Restrictions: Open sunrise to sunset; no alcohol

Access: Drive to

Water temperature: 72°F

Nearby attractions: Stephen Foster Folk Culture Center State Park, White Springs, Spirit of the Suwannee Music Park, Falmouth Springs, Suwannee River State Park, Osceola National Forest

Services: All services in Live Oak

Camping: Spirit of the Suwannee Campground

Management: Suwannee River Water Management District

Contact: (386) 362-1001; www.srwmd.state .fl.us/index.aspx?nid=274

Map: *DeLorme: Florida Atlas & Gazetteer:* Page 54 B2

GPS coordinates: N30 20.117' / W82 48.505'

Finding the sink: From the junction of FL 136 and I-75 near White Springs, drive east on FL 136 for 0.5 mile to a left onto 27th Road. Travel for 1.2 miles to a left onto 64th Terrace. Travel for 0.6 mile to the parking area, on the right.

From the junction of FL 136 and US 41 in White Springs, drive west on FL 136 for 2.6 miles to a right onto 27th Road and follow directions above.

The Sink

First and foremost, Blue Sink and the conservation area around it is not a designated swim site. If you're looking for a swimming hole, head over to Falmouth Spring (#70). However, if you're willing to stay on dry land, fishing is allowed in the sink.

The name Blue Sink may be deceiving, depending on how much rainfall the area has had. At the time of my last visit, the observation deck for the sink was underwater, and the sink was more brown than blue. I'm told that when the water level is lower, the water takes on a lighter hue, but I've been a few times and never seen it blue. I'm also told that this sink has a resident alligator, and on my last visit I did see a medium-size gator, about 5 to 6 feet, swimming across the far end of the sink. Several turtles also made an appearance, basking in the sun in the usual fashion—six or seven to a log, hanging on to whatever scrap of wood they can.

General description: Suwannee Springs is surrounded by public recreation land used for hiking and mountain biking. The main spring, one of a group of springs along the southern banks of the river, is isolated from the river by a tall stone wall. There are times when barely a trickle of water sits in the spring and other times when you can barely see the top of the wall. Either way, the river is beautiful, and when conditions are right, this is a popular local swim hole.

Location: On the south side of the Suwannee River; about 7.5 miles northeast of Live Oak

Development: Developed

Best time to visit: Year-round

Restrictions: Open summer hours 8 a.m. to 7 p.m., winter hours 8 a.m. to 6 p.m.; no alcohol, horses, or ATVs

Access: Drive to

Fees: No fee

Water temperature: 72°F

Nearby attractions: Spirit of the Suwannee Music Park, Stephen Foster Folk Culture Center State Park, Blue Sink, White Spring, Falmouth Springs, Anderson Spring, Suwannee River State Park

Services: Restrooms on-site; all services in Live Oak

Camping: Stephen Foster Folk Culture Center State Park, Spirit of the Suwannee Campground

Management: Suwannee River Water Management District

Contact: (386) 362-1001; www.srwmd.state .fl.us/index.aspx?nid=168

Map: *DeLorme: Florida Atlas & Gazetteer:* Page 54 A1

GPS coordinates: N30 23.656' / W82 56.037'

Finding the spring: From the junction of US 129 and CR 132 West near the town of Suwannee Springs, drive north on US 129 for 0.3 mile to a right onto 93rd Drive. Travel for 0.3 mile to a right onto 32nd Street. Travel for 0.3 mile to the parking area, at the end of the road.

From I-10 near Live Oak, take exit 283 and drive north on US 129 for approximately 4.3 miles to a right onto 93rd Drive and follow directions above.

From I-75 near Marion, take exit 451 and drive south on US 129 for 4.3 miles to a left onto 93rd Drive and follow directions above.

The Spring

Off the beaten path and surrounded by thick forest, you'll find the less-populated Suwannee Springs. Although it may seem desolate today, in the mid 1800s this spring was a popular health spa and tourist attraction. Now, however, a tall stone wall is all that separates the spring from the Suwannee River, and the wall acts not only as a barrier from the river but also as a reminder of days gone by. Since this spring seems to have many faces, it's hard to describe what to expect when you visit. At times of drought, there's barely a trickle of water behind the wall. Yet when the river is high, the spring may be filled to the brim and you're lucky to see just the top of the stone blockade. When Mother Nature does cooperate, it's a unique sight. There's a window-like opening in the wall, and when the water levels are just right, the spring overflows out into the river, making its own little spillway. While this spring is distinctive and rich in history, if you're looking for a swim hole and the conditions are poor, head over to Falmouth (#70) or up to Madison Blue Spring (#73).

This turtle seems almost aloof, perfectly perched in the sun.

General description: Although it's right off a main road, Falmouth Spring is primarily used by locals as a swimming hole. The spring is first magnitude but can still take on a brownish hue when the river levels rise. High banks surround the spring, and picnic tables near the parking area are the only amenity on-site.

Location: About 10 miles northwest of Live Oak

Development: Primitive

Best time to visit: Year-round

Restrictions: Open summer hours 8 a.m. to 7 p.m., winter hours 8 a.m. to 6 p.m.; no alcohol

Access: Drive to

Fees: No fee

Water temperature: 72°F

Nearby attractions: Suwannee River State Park, Madison Blue Spring, Lafayette Blue Spring State Park

Services: All services in Live Oak and Madison

Camping: Suwannee River State Park

Management: Suwannee River Water Management District

Contact: (386) 362-1001 or (800) 226-1066; www.srwmd.state.fl.us/index .aspx?nid=170

Map: *DeLorme: Florida Atlas & Gazetteer:* Page 53 B2

GPS coordinates: N30 21.721' / W83 08.072'

Finding the spring: From I-10 near Live Oak, take exit 275 and drive north on US 90 for 2.9 miles to the recreation area, on the left.

From the junction of US 90 and FL 132 in Ellaville, drive south on US 90 for 2.1 miles to the recreation area, on the right.

The Spring

Unlike most first-magnitude springs, Falmouth is usually not too crowded. Primarily used as a local swimming hole, the spring occupies a circular pool that reaches nearly 100 feet across. Typically the spring has clear greenish water in the basin, but on occasion, when the Suwannee River is at higher levels, the river backs up into the spring, causing the springwater to be on the browner side. Picnic areas are interspersed near the parking lot, and the recreation area has two boardwalks leading down to the spring. One is for swimmers, which becomes a series of steps that takes you directly down into the spring. The other skirts along the bank of the spring and has a small viewing platform that overlooks the spring.

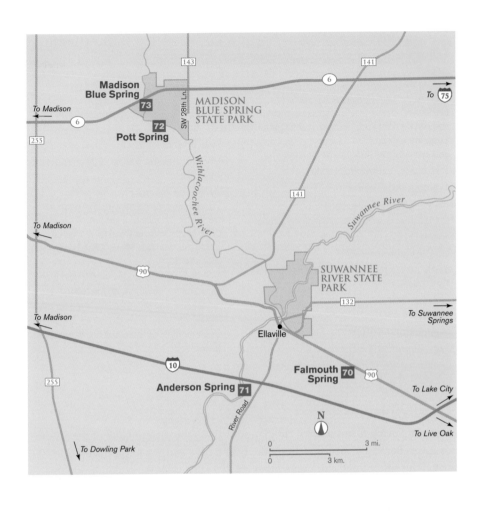

General description: Benches sit alongside the river on a small observation platform overlooking the spring. The spring is small and can be pretty, but because it sits right along the banks of the Suwannee River, its beauty fluctuates with the river levels.

Location: 5285 River Rd., Ellaville

Development: Primitive

Best time to visit: Year-round

Restrictions: Open 8 a.m. to 7 p.m.; no alcohol

Access: Drive to

Water temperature: 72°F

Nearby attractions: Suwannee River State Park, Falmouth Spring

Services: All services in Madison

Camping: Suwannee River State Park

Management: Florida Forest Service

Contact: (386) 208-1460; www.fresh fromflorida.com/Divisions-Offices/Florida -Forest-Service/Our-Forests/State -Forests/Twin-Rivers-State-Forest#rec and www.srwmd.state.fl.us/index.aspx?nid=172

Map: *DeLorme: Florida Atlas & Gazetteer:* Page 53 B2

GPS coordinates: N30 21.226' / W83 11.372'

Finding the spring: From the junction of US 90 and CR 132 in Ellaville, drive north on US 90 for 0.5 mile to a left onto River Road. Drive south on River Road for 2.1 miles to a right into the Twin Rivers State Forest (just after passing over I-10). Follow the dirt road back into the woods for 0.2 mile to the parking area, at the end of the road.

From the junction of US 90 and CR 141 near Ellaville, drive south on US 90 for 2.7 miles to a right onto River Road and follow directions above.

The Spring

Anderson Spring forms a small circular pool along the eastern bank of the Suwannee River. Because it sits right along the river's edge and is a lower magnitude spring, this one, along with many other smaller springs in the region, is highly dependent on the Suwannee River levels. If the river is up, you may not even be able to discern the spring from the river. But when the river is on the low side, a perfect little swim hole awaits within Twin Rivers State Forest, so named because the forest land surrounds the confluence of the Suwannee and Withlacoochee Rivers.

The Anderson Springs Tract sits on the southern portion of the forest. A peaceful picnic area along the river and a rope swing hanging near the wooden overlook are used regularly by locals, as are the two trails that begin at the southern end of the parking area. One trail is nearly 5 miles and dedicated to hikers; the other pushes over 6 miles and is designed for mountain biking. Both are loop trails, and both closely follow the river for half the loop. Bring your bike, boots, and a towel. Explore the forest, and then top it off with a quick dip in the spring as a wonderful way to cool down.

In the US, Florida is second only to Alaska in bald eagle population.

General description: Pott Spring is heavily used by locals as a swimming hole, and unfortunately the land near the spring often ends up littered. But the spring itself is one of the prettier ones. It occupies a small cove right along the eastern bank of the Withlacoochee River.

Location: Within the Withlacoochee Tract of Twin Rivers State Forest; about 10 miles east of Madison

Development: Primitive

Best time to visit: Year-round

Restrictions: Open sunrise to sunset

Access: Drive to

Fees: No fee

Water temperature: 72°F

Nearby attractions: Madison Blue Springs State Park, Suwannee River State Park

Services: All services in Madison

Camping: Primitive camping at Twin Rivers State Forest; full-service at Suwannee River State Forest

Management: Twin Rivers State Forest; Suwannee River Water Management District

Contact: (386) 208-1460; www. freshfromflorida.com/Divisions-Offices/ Florida-Forest-Service/Our-Forests/State-Forests/Twin-Rivers-State-Forest

Map: DeLorme: Florida Atlas & Gazetteer: Page 53 A2

GPS coordinates: N30 28.299' / W83 14.039'

Finding the spring: From the junction of FL 6 and CR 143 North in Blue Springs, drive south on SW 28th Lane (which is on the south side of FL 6, directly across from CR 143). Travel for 0.45 mile to a right turn into Twin Rivers State Forest. Once you enter the forest, you'll come to a fork at Loop Road. Go left and follow Loop Road to a second fork. Go left here as well, onto Spring Road, and follow it to the parking area, at the end of the road.

The Spring

As far as springs go, Pott Spring is more of a local swim hole than a popular tourist attraction. A few picnic tables mixed in between the pine trees is really all you'll see when you first park your car. As you start to approach the river, you'll see a small wooden overlook and a set of steps that lead down to the river. The spring sits in a tiny cove right along the eastern bank of the Withlacoochee River. As a result, the water clarity is dependent on river levels. When the river is up, it's hard to even imagine that a gorgeous spring lies below the brown tannic river water. But when the river is low, the area transforms into a beautiful, inviting clear-watered pool. Along with the spring, this tract of Twin Rivers State Forest is popular with equestrians but it's also open to hikers and mountain bikers. Wildlife is abundant, so bring your camera.

General description: Water pours out of this cone-shaped spring at a rate of about 75 million gallons a day, which is enough to keep this spring blue most of the year. However, the spring sits in a wide, deep cove off the Withlacoochee River, with a very short spring run. Occasionally the river gets so high that it tries to overtake the spring, infusing the blue water with darker hues. The large swimming area makes this spot ideal for swimming and snorkeling.

Location: 8300 NE SR 6, Lee; about 10 miles east of Madison on the west bank of the Withlacoochee River

Development: Developed

Best time to visit: Year-round

Restrictions: Open 8 a.m. to sundown; no alcohol; proof of certification is required for cave diving

Access: Drive to

Fees: $

Water temperature: 72°F

Nearby attractions: Suwannee River State Park, Pott Spring, Twin Rivers State Forest

Services: Restrooms on-site; all services in Madison

Camping: Suwannee River State Park

Management: Florida Park Service

Contact: (850) 971-5003; www.florida stateparks.org/madisonbluespring/default .cfm

Map: *DeLorme: Florida Atlas & Gazetteer:* Page 53 A2

GPS coordinates: N30 28.864' / W83 14.672'

Finding the spring: From the junction of FL 6 and CR 143 North in Blue Springs, drive west on FL 6 for 1.5 miles to the park, on the left immediately after crossing the bridge.

From the junction of FL 6 and CR 255 near Madison, drive east on FL 6 for 3.4 miles to the park, on the right just before crossing the bridge.

The Spring

Within clear view of the Withlacoochee River, Madison Blue Spring has presented many faces over the years. From brilliant blue to aquamarine to heavy greenish hues, this first-magnitude spring is always a pleasant surprise. Interestingly, even though the spring dispenses more than 65 million gallons of water a day, its color and clarity are still often dependent on the river levels due to their close proximity. Yet even at its worst, a hint of blue almost always overrides the brown tannic tints of the river. Unfortunately though, there are still times when the swimming area must be closed off due to high river levels and poor visibility, so you may want to call ahead to confirm, especially during the rainy summer months.

A cone-shaped depression dips down to about 25 feet deep and makes this an ideal swim and snorkel site. Beyond this initial depression, an extensive cave system has also been mapped out, making this a popular cave-diving destination as well. SCUBA divers must sign in prior to diving, must show proof of cave-diving certification, and must be out of the water within an hour of the park closing. No open-water diving is allowed.

The park has benches to accommodate divers and a shaded picnic area with charcoal grills scattered throughout. Pets are allowed in the picnic area but not in the spring. But don't despair. This is one of the few places that allow you to leave your *well-behaved* pet unattended for a maximum of 30 minutes—just enough time to take a quick dip and snorkel around the spring a bit. If you do leave your pet, please make sure you leave them in the shade with a full bowl of water. It *is* Florida after all. A volleyball net adds to the fun, and there's a canoe launch, but you must bring your own canoe/kayak, since there is no on-site rental concession.

Cormorants are a common sight in Florida's springs and rivers.

PANHANDLE
REGION

The spring-fed Wacissa River is peaceful any time of day.

Perhaps the panhandle is best known for its golden white sandy beaches, with dolphins swimming by as their fins glisten in the sun. Or for the parties in Pensacola and Panama City. Or for Florida State University, where they've won several national college football championships—go Noles! But beyond these typical toutings is a little-known secret: The Panhandle is also home to some of Florida's hidden gems. Find a perfect swimming hole at Pitt and Ponce de Leon Springs. Jump off a platform at Wakulla or Camp Indian Spring. Paddle to springs like Cypress and Gainer, where your jaw will drop at the depth, color, and clarity of the water. Take a tour of the caverns at Florida Caverns State Park, where you'll see stalactites and stalagmites that have been growing for thousands of years. Rent a pontoon boat and explore Merritt's Mill Pond, where spring after spring pops up out of nowhere and spectacular Jackson Blue Spring forms the headwaters. Swing from a rope swing at Big Blue, and revel in the abundance of birds and wildlife you'll see as you make your way there along the wild and scenic Wacissa River. SCUBA dive at Vortex, or cave dive at Gator Hole. Whatever your pleasure, you'll find it here in Florida's precious Panhandle.

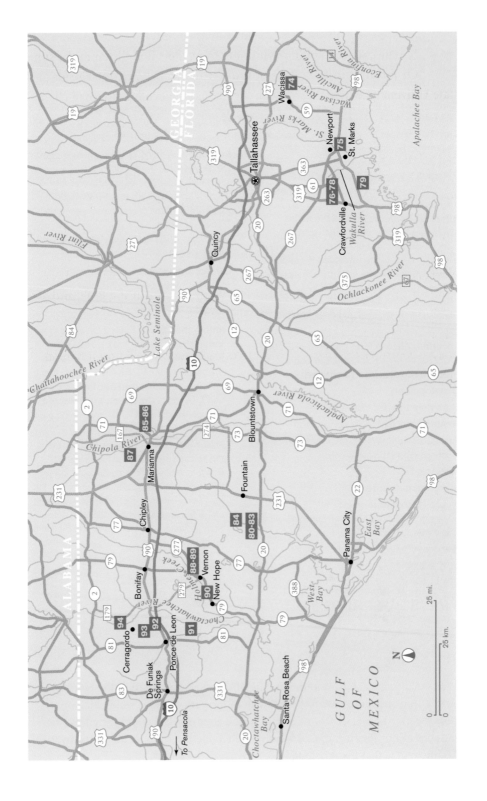

74

Wacissa Springs Group: Wacissa #1–#4, Horsehead, Log, Thomas, Maggie, Allen, Cassidy, Little Blue, Minnow, Buzzard Log, Garner, and Big Blue Springs

General description: A collection of twenty-two springs feed the 14-mile Wacissa River, and I've included fifteen of them here, all of which can be found within the first mile of the river. The only way to reach all but one of these springs is by boat, and you'll find specific details, directions, and descriptions for each individual spring below. If you visit every spring, you're likely to see turtles, alligators, snakes, and a large variety of birdlife on your adventure, so bring a camera along to capture the memories. If you only have time to visit one spring, make it Big Blue. Although it's the farthest away, it's worth the effort, especially if you remind yourself to make it about the journey and not the destination.

Location: Wacissa River Canoe Rental: 290 Wacissa Springs Rd., Monticello; about 19 miles southeast of Tallahassee

Development: Primitive

Best time to visit: Year-round

Restrictions: Open sunrise to sunset

Access: Drive to: Wacissa Spring #2; all other springs reached by boat only

Fees: No fee

Water temperature: 68°F

Nearby attractions: Aucilla Wildlife Management Area, Newport Spring, Edward Ball Wakulla Springs State Park

Services: Restrooms on-site; all services in Tallahassee

Camping: Tallahassee East Monticello KOA

Management: Jefferson County Recreation; Suwannee River Water Management District

Contact: Jefferson County Recreation: (850) 519-6640; www.jeffersoncountyfl.gov/p/recreation-tourism; Wacissa River Canoe & Kayak Rentals: (850) 997-5023 or (850) 545-2895; http://wacissarivercanoerentals.com/index.htm

Map: *DeLorme: Florida Atlas & Gazetteer:* Page 51 B2

GPS coordinates: Public boat ramp: N30 20.415' / W83 59.477'; Wacissa River Canoe & Kayak Rentals: N30 20.636' / W83 59.444'

Finding the spring: Public boat ramp: From the junction of FL 59 and FL 259 (Tram Road) in Wacissa, drive south on FL 59 for 0.7 mile to where FL 59 turns sharply to the right (west). Rather than take the bend west on FL 59, drive straight ahead on Wacissa Springs Road. Travel for 0.5 mile to the park, at the end of the road.

Wacissa River Canoe & Kayak Rentals: From the junction of FL 59 and FL 259 (Tram Road) in Wacissa, drive south on FL 59 for 0.7 mile to where FL 59 turns sharply to the right (west). Rather than take the bend west on FL 59, drive straight ahead on Wacissa Springs Road. Travel for 0.2 mile to the canoe rental, on your right.

WACISSA SPRING #1

GPS coordinates: N30 20.367' / W83 59.5'

The Spring

Wacissa Spring #1 sits out in the middle of the river, just south of the Horsehead Spring Run and about 300 feet southwest of the park. A large, solid patch of lily pads separate Spring #1 from the park, and a good-size alligator greeted us near the edge of this floating aquatic island. Quite honestly, I was so distracted by the healthy reptile that I barely took note of Wacissa Spring #1.

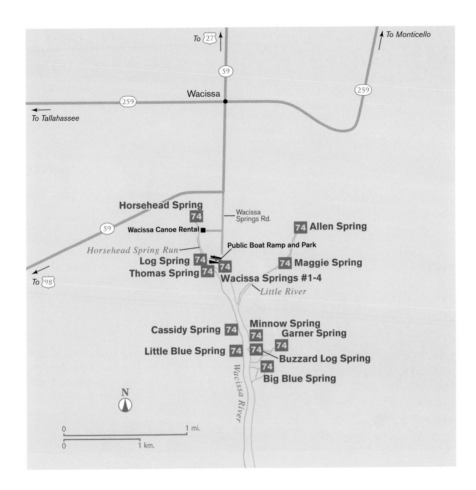

WACISSA SPRING #2

GPS coordinates: N30 20.4' / W83 59.483'

The Spring

The easiest spring to access on the Wacissa River is without a doubt Wacissa #2. Sadly, however, the spring is being choked out by hydrilla, an invasive plant—so much so that the spring was barely evident on my visit. Piles of hydrilla sat on the banks alongside the spring, where obvious efforts are being made to clear it out, because this spring truly is in dire straits. The spring can be found about 15 feet south of the cement diving platform. There is no boil, just an area of clear water that you can instinctively tell is the spring. A couple of rope swings hang over the spring, but they've been cut short. Apparently the county discourages rope swings here, but there's a fantastic one just a mile downstream at Big Blue Spring. You can, however, get a running start and leap into the spring from the platform.

A variety of canoes and kayaks are available at Wacissa Canoe Rental.

The county-run park has a couple of picnic tables, porta-potties, and a public boat ramp where you can launch a canoe or motorboat. Please use caution on the river. On my last visit there was an airboat whizzing around every corner. And as we finished our paddle, there were emergency vehicles meeting that same airboat at the boat launch, responding to an apparent accident on the river.

WACISSA SPRING #3

GPS coordinates: N30 20.433' / W83 59.45'

The Spring

Wacissa Spring #3 is right by the boat ramp on the northeast side of the park—not to be confused with the canoe launch, which is on the southeast end of the park. Several small sand boils form the spring, but the flow is minimal, and you may not even notice them.

WACISSA SPRING #4

GPS coordinates: N30 20.417' / W83 59.433'

The Spring

Wacissa Spring #4 lies just 90 feet downstream from spring #3. With the amount of hydrilla in this portion of the river, this spring too may not be noticeable. If the spring is visible, clear blue water creates a small boil that ruffles the surface of the water.

HORSEHEAD SPRING

GPS coordinates: N30 20.690' / W83 59.670'

The Spring

Upstream from both the park and the canoe rental, on the west side of the Wacissa River and at the head of the Horsehead Spring Run, is Horsehead Spring. This too is being invaded by hydrilla. There is a noticeable steady current as you paddle upstream, but the hydrilla has made it difficult to tell exactly where the spring is and where the water is coming from. There is certainly a clarity to it though, and the spring seems to be someone's secret fishing hole. A bench is propped perfectly on the water's edge, and you can easily picture someone sitting there with a cane pole cast in the water.

LOG SPRING

GPS coordinates: N30 20.433' / W83 59.583'

The Spring

Upstream from Wacissa Spring #1, and downstream from Horsehead Spring and the canoe rental, you'll notice an oddly clear patch of water on the eastern bank of the Horsehead Spring Run. This is Log Spring. The spring flows out near a private boat dock that belongs to a local fish camp. They seem to have all the toys you could wish for; boats, personal watercraft, canoes, and ATVs were all within view. There's a slight bend in the spring run near the spring, and the current really whips you by. Between the swift current and the distraction of the fish camp, you might not even notice that you passed right by Log Spring, except for the crystal-clear water that seems to occupy this small section of the spring run.

THOMAS SPRING

GPS coordinates: N30 20.383' / W83 59.533'

The Spring

As the narrow Horsehead Spring Run leads you out into the wide-open space of the Wacissa River, you'll again notice an oddly placed patch of clear water. This clear patch is Thomas Spring, and it sits just upstream from Wacissa Spring #1. It pours out from a large underwater crack in the ground. You might easily miss this one, because you're taken aback by nature's beauty as the scenery of the river unfolds before you.

MAGGIE SPRING

GPS coordinates: N30 20.400' / W83 58.967'

The Spring

About 0.4 mile south of the boat ramp, on the east side of the river, you'll see where the Little River flows out into the Wacissa. Follow the Little River upstream and about 0.5 mile from the confluence, on the west side of the Little River, you'll find Maggie Spring. Downed logs lying over the cracks in the limestone add to the character of this otherwise easily missed spring. The paddle up the Little River is quite pleasant, with the typical turtles and fish. On my last visit, my nephew and I were also fortunate enough to glimpse a red-shouldered hawk perched upon a cypress knee just 10 feet off the bow of our canoe. Keep a keen eye out. This was definitely a highlight!

ALLEN SPRING

GPS coordinates: N30 20.65' / W83 58.817'

The Spring

If you continue paddling upstream from Maggie Spring, after about 0.3 mile you'll come to Allen Spring, at the headwaters of the Little River. Look closely and you'll see a small boil with clear water welling up from below the surface. The spring is just before you run out of navigable waterway near the western bank of the river.

CASSIDY SPRING

GPS coordinates: N30 19.967' / W83 59.35'

The Spring

Just 0.1 mile downstream from the confluence of the Little and Wacissa Rivers, on the west bank of the Wacissa, Cassidy Spring sits in an obvious cove. There's a short spring run of about 100 feet, but it's hard to pinpoint exactly where the spring is, since the clear water is mixed with the tea-colored tannic water of the river. If you stop paddling for a minute, you can barely see a little boil where Cassidy Spring flows out from three different spring vents.

LITTLE BLUE SPRING

GPS coordinates: N30 19.811' / W83 59.304'

The Spring

Little Blue Spring sits directly across from Buzzard Log Spring, on the west side of the River and 0.7 mile downstream from the boat ramp. The very short spring run is wide and uneventful. Its mouth is covered in lily pads, so it's hard to even tell where the spring run begins. Once you realize that you have to paddle through the lily pads to reach Little Blue Spring, you also realize that, it's choked out with aquatic vegetation, and it's not that blue after all.

MINNOW SPRING

GPS coordinates: N30 19.867' / W83 59.183'

The Spring

Snake pit! As we neared Minnow Spring, we were not only greeted by a pair of water moccasins, obviously protecting their territory, but there was also a snake sunning itself on some cypress knees near the entrance to the spring run. Needless to say, I never did get a good look at the spring. While alligators may seem intimidating, they are likely to swim the other way as you approach. Water moccasins, on the other hand, are *not*! Known to be quite territorial, they can be aggressive, even toward a canoe. So please use caution!

BUZZARD LOG SPRING

GPS coordinates: N30 19.808' / W83 59.223'

The Spring

About 0.7 mile downstream from the public boat ramp, directly across from Little Blue Spring and resting at the mouth of the Garner Spring Run on the east side of the river, you'll notice a small patch of clear water and a heavier-than-normal current. Buzzard Log Spring is situated right here, pushing forth from the aquifer below. Take a quick peek before paddling up the spring run to see Garner Spring.

GARNER SPRING

GPS coordinates: N30 19.817' / W83 58.983'

The Spring

Massive downed cypress trees seem to form a triangle around Garner Spring as pretty blue water forces you to the outskirts of the cul-de-sac in which the spring sits, at the headwaters of the spring run. If you paddle to only one other spring besides Big Blue, make it Garner. It's one of the most distinct springs in the area and really has a lot of character.

BIG BLUE SPRING

GPS coordinates: N30 19.679' / W83 59.093'

The Spring

Big Blue Spring is the farthest downstream spring in this area, but it's by far the best. The spring runs (yes, there are two) enter the Wacissa River about a mile downstream from the public boat ramp. The spring itself is found less than

My nephew and I had fun on the rope swing at Big Blue Spring.

0.25 mile up the first spring run. Make sure you paddle up the first, wider spring run, which is the one that's upstream on the river. The downstream spring run is narrower and dead-ends at a difficult log-over. Save yourself the trouble, and paddle up the first.

Once you arrive at Big Blue, it's easy to see how the spring got its name. It's big—and it's blue. It's also pristine. A platform for divers, or anyone for that matter, is anchored out in the middle of the spring, and a rope swing sits off to the right (southern) bank. Although it's the hardest to reach, this spring is by far the climax of the day. As a result, it also sees more traffic than the others, relatively speaking, and you can clearly see why. It's a great place to take a dip. You can fly free from the rope swing or explore with a mask and snorkel. The spring is even open to SCUBA divers who have their open-water certification.

General description: In the oddest place, right off the side of a dirt road near the town of Newport, you'll find Newport Spring. A rope swing hangs from a large tree limb over the clear green water, and the spring is used almost daily as a swim hole and meeting place for local youth. The fairly long spring run flows east about 0.5 mile before merging into the St. Marks River.

Location: About 17 miles southeast of Tallahassee; near the community of Newport

Development: Primitive

Best time to visit: Year-round

Restrictions: None

Access: Drive to

Water temperature: 68°F

Nearby attractions: St. Marks National Wildlife Refuge, Aucilla Wildlife Management Area, Edward Ball Wakulla Springs State Park, Wacissa Springs Group

Services: All services in St. Marks

Camping: Newport Park Campground

Management: n/a

Contact: n/a

Map: *DeLorme: Florida Atlas & Gazetteer:* Page 50 C3

GPS coordinates: N30 12.518' / W84 10.49'

Finding the spring: From the junction of US 98 and FL 267 in Newport, drive east on US 98 for 0.2 mile to a left onto Old Plank Road. Travel for 0.9 mile to the parking area, on the left.

From the junction of US 98 and CR 59 in Newport, drive west on US 98 for approximately 0.3 mile to a right onto Old Plank Road and follow directions above.

The Spring

Reading about a spring that literally sits right beside the roadside doesn't really get your hopes up. The drive in on the barren, dusty dirt Old Plank Road might make you even more skeptical. But I have to say, Newport Spring was a pleasant surprise. A small sandy parking area sits on the west side of the road, and the spring sits on the east side. Lying in the shadow of a large oak tree with a rope swing hanging from one of its hefty limbs, an obvious boil wells up from the water below. A small flat area with a primitive fire ring also sits under the oak, and locals use the spring as a swimming hole and gathering place almost daily.

Clear green water flows from a crack in the earth and is visible from the small culvert-like bridge that was built right over the top of the spring. A slight sulfur smell rises from the water, but it's easily overlooked. You can see and hear a few rapids in the distance, adding to the spring's appeal. The land surrounding the spring run is private property, so other than taking a dip in the spring, don't venture too far from the road or you will be trespassing.

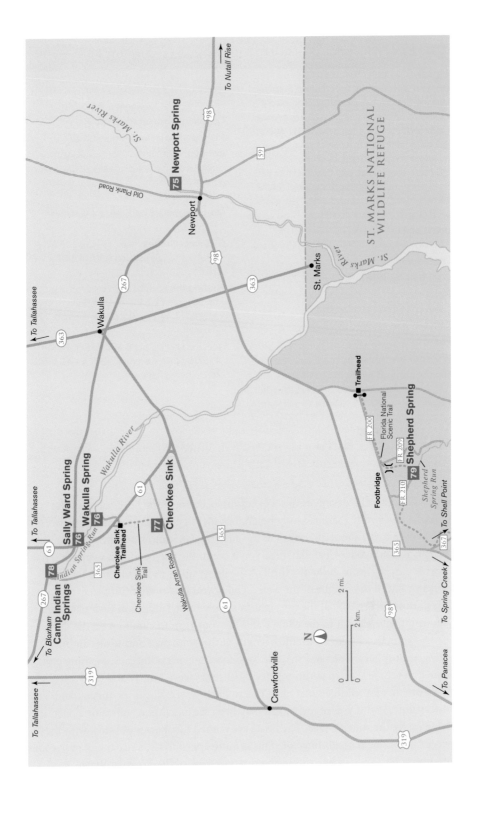

General description: To be honest, Sally Ward Spring wouldn't be included in this book if it stood on its own. But since you have to drive right past it as you enter Edward Ball Wakulla Springs State Park, I decided to include it. The real showcase here is Wakulla Spring. A massive swim area with floating docks and platforms you can jump off of is great for the kids, and the whole family usually gets a kick out of taking a tour on the glass-bottom boats.

Location: 465 Wakulla Park Dr., Wakulla Springs; about 20 miles south of Tallahassee

Development: Primitive

Best time to visit: Year-round

Restrictions: Open 8 a.m. to sunset; pets allowed in designated areas only

Access: Drive to

Fees: $

Water temperature: 68°F

Nearby attractions: Cherokee Sink, Newport Spring, Apalachicola National Forest, Wakulla State Forest, St. Marks National Wildlife Refuge

Services: Restrooms, food, lodging on-site; all services in Crawfordville

Camping: Newport Park Campground

Management: Florida Park Service

Contact: (850) 561-7276; www.florida stateparks.org/wakullasprings/default.cfm; lodge information and reservations: (850) 421-2000

Map: *DeLorme: Florida Atlas & Gazetteer:* Page 50 C2

GPS coordinates: Wakulla: N30 14.117' / W84 18.15'; Sally Ward: N30 14.483' / W84 18.65'

Finding the spring: From the junction of FL 267 and FL 61 in Wakulla Springs, drive east on FL 267 for 0.1 mile to the park, on the right.

From the junction of FL 267 and FL 363 in Wakulla, drive west on FL 267 for 4.9 miles to the park, on the left.

WAKULLA SPRING

The Spring

What a fun place! Not only is this a beautiful location, at the headwaters of the Wakulla River with a serene sandy beach, but there's also a large elevated platform that looks like it's about 20 feet up in the air. You can jump from the platform into the spring, and ladders just like those you'd see in the deep end of a swimming pool provide easy access to enjoy the thrill of the jump again and again. Two floating docks sit out in the middle of the water, giving you yet another fun place to play. The park service even had the foresight to supply three ladders on each platform, so you won't have to wait in the chilly water for your turn to climb up on the dock.

A sandy beach spans the entire length of the swim area and forms an interesting atmosphere. The sand sits side by side with cypress knees, something you almost never see. For an additional fee, boat tours leave hourly and take you downstream to a wildlife sanctuary. You're likely to see alligators, turtles, and birds galore, and if you're lucky, you may even see an elusive bobcat or a deer drinking by the water's edge. The boats are named for species of birds, with the exception of one named *Alligator*. This is quite appropriate, since many native and migratory bird species live within the riparian zone of the Wakulla River.

Wakulla Springs State Park is fun for the whole family.

The park office doubles as a mini museum, where they showcase mastodon bones and have other informative displays on the area and the springs. The Lodge is gorgeous and has benches overlooking the swim area. Built in the 1930s, it's listed on the National Register of Historic Places; reservations are recommended.

Clear water with a dark green hue gushes out, forming an obvious boil over the spring. Tannic tones add to the color, and eelgrass dances in the current, a great indication of a healthy spring. There are showers near the office, so you can rinse off before and after a quick dip. A large picnic area, with charcoal grills scattered throughout, makes this a perfect place to bring the whole family and spend the day. If that's not enough, the property also has hiking and mountain bike trails and a limited area where horses are allowed.

SALLY WARD SPRING

The Spring

While Wakulla Spring is the obvious highlight at Edward Ball Wakulla Springs State Park, Sally Ward Spring is worth a quick peek on your way to the main event. As you enter the park, less than 0.25 mile in on the main park road and before you reach the guard gate, you'll cross over a small culvert. Just after passing the culvert, on the east side of the road, you'll see an open grassy area where you can park to pop out and see the spring. The water you saw when you crossed over the culvert is where the spring is. A short, narrow path leads from the north end of the grassy parking area and gives you a good vantage point. The spring and spring run look inviting, but there is no swimming or fishing allowed in the shallow, crystal-clear water. Don't despair; you can swim all you want in Wakulla Spring.

General description: A fairly boring 1.1-mile hike leads to Cherokee Sink, where dark green water and limestone ledges make up most of the scenery above and below the water. It's surprisingly large for a sink and mostly used by, but not limited to, open-water SCUBA divers. The general public is welcome to take a dip in the spring as well, a refreshing treat after the humdrum hike.

Location: Within a remote section of Edward Ball Wakulla Springs State Park; about 20 miles south of Tallahassee

Development: Primitive

Best time to visit: Year-round

Restrictions: Open 8 a.m. to 5 p.m.; no pets, coolers, food, drink, or smoking in the spring area; no alcohol

Access: Hike to; 1.1 miles one way

Fees: $

Water temperature: 68°F

Nearby attractions: Wakulla Spring, Newport Spring, Apalachicola National Forest, Wakulla State Forest, St. Marks Wildlife Refuge

Services: Primitive restroom at trailhead; restrooms, food, lodging available at main body of the park; all services in Crawfordville

Camping: Newport Park Campground

Management: Florida Park Service

Contact: (850) 561-7276; www.floridastateparks.org/wakullasprings/default.cfm

Map: *DeLorme: Florida Atlas & Gazetteer:* Page 50 C2

GPS coordinates: N30 12.807' / W84 18.243'

Finding the sink: From the junction of FL 61 and FL 267 in Wakulla Springs, drive south on FL 61 for 1.2 miles to an unmarked road on your right at the sign for "Nature Trail." Travel for 0.1 mile to the parking area at the end of the road. ***Note:*** The unmarked road is directly across from the gated back entrance to the state park.

The Sink

Popular with SCUBA divers, Cherokee Sink is located within a remote section of Edward Ball Wakulla Springs State Park. A map of the trail can be found at the information kiosk near the trailhead, although you don't really need a map to find this one. From the kiosk, go around the gate and hike south on the wide dirt road. The 1.1-mile-long trail makes a perfectly straight line from the trailhead to the sink. In fact, you can practically see the sink from the trailhead. That's how straight the trail runs in a due south direction. After about a mile you'll come to a fork. Go right (west) at the fork to a wide open area. Hike through it; the trail leads southwest directly to the sink. Viewing platforms and a rocky ledge give you a few different vantage points to appreciate the beauty at this one. The sink is gorgeous, well worth the mundane hike.

The hike truly is uneventful, simply a walk in the woods on a road-like trail, with an occasional bumblebee buzzing by or a butterfly flitting about. Heat, mosquitoes, and ticks galore can put a damper on summertime hiking in Florida, and on this trail that seems to extend into spring and autumn as well. Bring lots of water and some bug spray to enjoy this hike. As long as you keep moving, the bugs don't seem that bad; but the second you stop, it's game on for those pesky predators. Also make sure you do a thorough tick check when you exit the forest.

All SCUBA divers must check in at the main park office and obtain a permit prior to diving. At the time of check-in, you can get the gate code or key so that you can drive on the trail to that large open area, which acts as a loading and unloading area for divers. I highly recommend that you visit Wakulla Spring while you're here. If you have extra time, take the boat tour as well.

A rocky ledge alongside Cherokee Sink makes a perfect place to perch yourself.

General description: The main focus of Camp Indian Springs is running children's summer camps, but when camp isn't in session, the property is open to the public. They offer a multitude of activities, both in and out of the water. The spring is filled with clear dark-green water, and you can snorkel, swim out to the float, jump off platforms, or simply slide down the slide. You certainly won't be at a loss for things to do, and whatever you choose, you're sure to have fun here.

Location: 2387 Bloxham Cutoff Rd., Crawfordville; about 20 miles south of Tallahassee

Development: Primitive

Best time to visit: Sept–May

Restrictions: All visitors must call ahead before visiting.

Access: Drive to

Fees: $$$

Water temperature: 68°F

Nearby attractions: Edward Ball Wakulla Springs State Park, Cherokee Sink, Newport Spring, Apalachicola National Forest, Wakulla State Forest

Services: Restrooms, lodging on-site; all services in Crawfordville

Camping: Newport Park Campground

Management: Privately owned

Contact: (850) 926-3361; www.indian springsretreatcenter.com

Map: *DeLorme: Florida Atlas & Gazetteer:* Page 50 C2

GPS coordinates: N30 15.05' / W84 19.317'

Finding the spring: From the junction of FL 267 (Camp Bloxham Cutoff Road) and FL 61 in Bethel, drive west on FL 267 for 0.7 mile to the camp, on the left.

From the junction of FL 267 (Camp Bloxham Cutoff Road) and US 319 near Hilliardville, drive east on FL 267 for 2.6 miles to the camp, on the right.

The Spring

Holy hotbed of activity! This 77-acre piece of property encompasses both sides of FL 267 and seems like 770 acres. You name it, they have it—from A to Z, literally! Archery, ATV rentals, basketball, canoe/kayak rentals, fishing, high ropes course, hiking trails, horseback riding, mountain bike trails, paintball fields, SCUBA diving, a swimming pool in the works, volleyball, and a zip line to boot. There's even a 1,500-square-foot indoor skate park with ramps and a half pipe; you can use traditional skates, inline skates, a bike, or a skateboard. And I haven't even gotten to the spring yet.

Indian Springs, is a large circular dark-green natural pool, with grassy banks on one side and forest surrounding the rest. Directly behind the camp's office, a tall stairway takes you down to a platform over the spring. You can see from the top of the steps that the spring is deep, and when you get a closer look, you can see where the limestone edges abruptly drop off. This particular platform sits a few feet above the surface, and there's enough room to get a running start and jump out into the clear green water. Several other smaller sets of steps lead down to the spring as well, so you can access it from a few different places.

On one edge there's an old-fashioned playground-type metal slide that you can slide down, landing in the chilly water. And in the center of the spring sits a

Activities galore at Camp Indian Springs.

floating dock that you can swim out to. If this isn't enough adventure for you, the camp has set up a high scaffolding-type platform that you can climb up and leap off. It looks to be about 20 feet high. Visitors also can rent out an inflatable prop the camp refers to as "The Blob"—a giant blow-up pillow that they secure at the base of the scaffolding platform. One person jumps down onto The Blob, and when the next person jumps down onto it, the first gets catapulted high into the air before landing out into the safety of the spring.

Bring a snorkel so that you can enjoy the many facets of the limestone walls. There is an extensive cave-diving system within Indian Springs, but due to the system's advanced nature, only very experienced divers, with a guide, are allowed. For more information on cave-diving this site, visit www.caveconnectionsflorida.com.

All the extra activities listed above require an additional fee, but if you simply want to visit the spring, you can do that too. Camp Indian Springs is primarily a summer camp for kids; they get lots of visitors via church and school groups as well. They are typically full June through August, but when camp is not in session, everyone is welcome. Whether you wanted to grab a group of friends and head out for the weekend or just go by yourself, they have a cabin rental to suit your needs. The only thing they require is that you call ahead before any visit. Even if you just want to pop in and take a quick dip, please call ahead, or you may not gain access. Visit their website for full details, call them if you have specific questions, and have fun!

General description: Shepherd Spring is found within a remote section of the St. Marks National Wildlife Refuge and is accessed by an easy hike on the Florida National Scenic Trail. Whether you're doing a through-hike on the trail or just popping in to see the spring, it's a refreshing sight. A boardwalk leads out to a platform with a bench near the virgin, blue-green spring, and this is all the development you'll see here.

Location: Within St. Marks National Wildlife Refuge; about 22 miles south of Tallahassee

Development: Primitive

Best time to visit: Year-round

Restrictions: Open sunrise to sunset; boat launch open 24 hours a day; no airboats, inboard motor thrust boats, or personal watercraft

Access: Hike to; 2.75 miles one way;

Fees: No fee

Water temperature: 68°F

Nearby attractions: St. Marks Historic Railroad Trail, St. Marks Lighthouse, Wakulla Springs State Park, Newport Springs, Apalachicola National Forest, Wacissa Springs Group

Services: All services in Crawfordville

Camping: Newport Park Campground

Management: St. Marks National Wildlife Refuge—Wakulla Unit

Contact: (850) 925-6121; www.fws.gov/ saintmarks/visit.html

Map: *DeLorme: Florida Atlas & Gazetteer:* Page 50 D2

GPS coordinates: N30 07.531' / W84 17.124'

Finding the spring: From the junction of US 98 and FL 363 (Woodville Highway) near St. Marks, drive west on US 98 for approximately 3.4 miles to a left onto Wakulla Beach Road. Travel for 0.9 mile to the entrance to St. Marks National Wildlife Refuge on the right.

From the junction of US 98 and CR 365 near Shadeville, drive east on US 98 for 3.8 miles to a right onto Wakulla Beach Road and follow directions above.

The Spring

While the gate at the entrance to the refuge may be open, unfortunately you are not allowed to drive in the refuge unless you are there for hunting purposes. So, park near the entrance, but do not block the road or gate if it is closed. The beginning of your hike is rather mundane as you hike southwest on FR 200, which is the main forest road that passes through this portion of the refuge. After 1.75 miles on the forest road, you finally reach FR 209, where you'll see the orange-blazed Florida National Scenic Trail cuts south southwest into the forest. Hop on the trail here and in less than 0.25 mile, you'll cross a footbridge, as you soon begin to enter what's known as the "Cathedral of Palms." Within this portion of the forest, you'll notice a stand of old-growth palm trees towering overhead. Much taller than any other trees in the area, this unique natural feature is a nice treat along the hike. As you continue through the forest, the trail follows a generally south direction for less than a mile until you reach a point where the trail crosses FR 210. From here, hike southwest back into the woods, and you'll almost immediately come to a fork with a bench in front of you. The bench is not only a resting place for weary travelers but also a signpost indicating that the spring is to the left and the Florida Trail continues to the right. At the fork, take the spur trail for a quick side trip and begin following the blue blazes and boardwalk back to the spring.

Mikey always knows which way to go.

A beautiful large pool rests at the end of the boardwalk. The spring is a welcome sight for hikers as they pass through this portion of the St. Marks National Wildlife Refuge. Clear, fresh water with a blue-green hue greets you. But remember that any water you drink from the forest, no matter how clear the source may be—even if it's a first-magnitude spring used by a bottled water company—should still be filtered prior to drinking it. Even the purest of springs contains bacteria and algae. You can even see some lyngbya along the shallow banks of Shepherd Spring.

Although most of this hike is along a forest road, the St. Marks National Wildlife Refuge is fairly swampy; you may want to apply bug spray before leaving the trailhead. Also, don't be surprised if you get your feet wet.

General description: At last this wonderful spring has been made available to the public via a day-use area. Visitors park near the entrance and walk 0.1 mile to the spring. A wide set of cement steps leads down to the water's edge, and you can clearly see Econfina Creek swiftly passing by.

Location: 5247-5273 Blue Springs Rd., Youngstown; about 7 miles northwest of Youngstown, 20 miles northeast of Panama City, and 30 miles west of Blountstown

Development: Primitive

Best time to visit: Year-round

Restrictions: No ATVs, alcohol, or SCUBA diving; no food, glass, or pets in the spring

Access: Hike to; 0.1 mile one way

Fees: No fee

Water temperature: 68°F

Nearby attractions: Pitt Springs, Sylvan Springs, Williford Spring, Econfina Creek Canoe Livery, Devil's Hole Spring, Econfina Creek Wildlife Management Area

Services: Restrooms on-site; all services in Youngstown and Fountain

Camping: Primitive camping on-site; full service at St. Andrews State Park, Falling Waters State Park

Management: Northwest Florida Water Management District

Contact: (850) 539-5999; www.nwfwater.com/lands/recreation/area/econfina/blue-spring/

Map: *DeLorme: Florida Atlas & Gazetteer:* Page 47 A1

GPS coordinates: N30 27.173' / W85 31.825'

Finding the spring: From the junction of FL 20 and US 231 near Fountain, drive west on FL 20 for 5.8 miles to a right onto Blue Springs Road. Travel for 1.3 miles to the parking area, on the left.

From the junction of FL 20 and FL 77 near Riverdale, drive east on US 20 for approximately 9.9 miles to a left onto Blue Springs Road and follow directions above.

The Spring

Good news! As of July 2014, a day-use area has been added to what was once strictly a group campsite. The campsite is still there and can be reserved seven days a week. Whether you're an individual, a family of four, or a Boy Scout troop, you can stay at this spring-side site. The campsite can accommodate up to twenty-five people, and online reservations are required. There is no fee to visit the springs, and there's a small parking area for day-use visitors, who then hike in about 0.1 mile to the spring.

A wide set of steps leads down to the creek, where you can swim in the clear running water or launch a canoe or kayak and explore even more of the swift-moving water. Several vents feed and form Blue Spring, although the water is more a clear green color than blue. The area is very peaceful and not too far off the beaten path. They have a portable toilet, picnic shelter, tables scattered about, and a few charcoal grills on-site. The typical alligator warning signs greet you as you near the spring, which is very pretty, in a more rustic and undeveloped way.

Washington Blue Spring sits right alongside Econfina Creek.

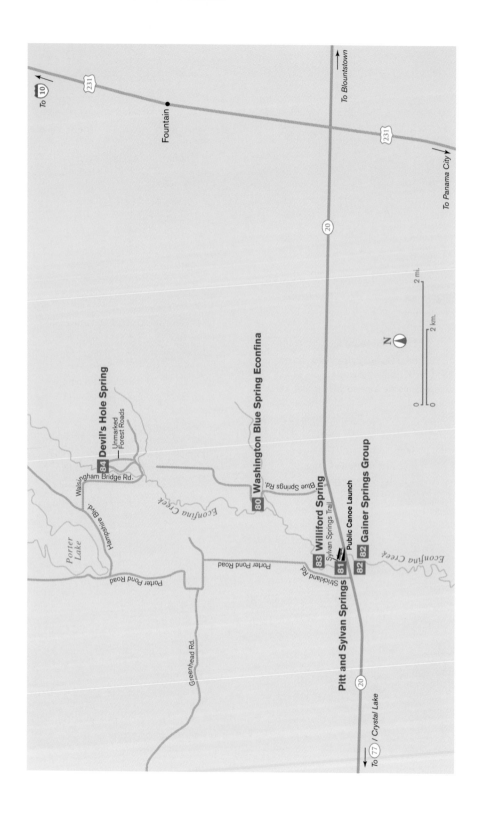

General description: Pitt is easily one of my favorite springs. The pale blue water is made even more beautiful by the sandy bottom surrounding the perfectly visible hole it pours out of. Cement steps lead down to the spring for ease of access. In contrast, a short hike is required to reach Sylvan Springs. And while it too is pristine, this group of small springs can only be viewed from the boardwalk. With the clarity and color of the water, it's hard to believe that Pitt Spring is only a third-magnitude spring, while Sylvan is a second.

Location: About 7 miles northwest of Youngstown, 20 miles northeast of Panama City, and 30 miles west of Blountstown

Development: Pitt: developed; Sylvan: primitive

Best time to visit: Year-round

Restrictions: Open sunrise to sunset; no food, drink, glass, or animals in the spring (these items are allowed in the picnic area); no alcohol

Access: Pitt: drive to; Sylvan: hike to; 0.2 mile one way

Fees: No fee

Water temperature: 68°F

Nearby attractions: Williford Spring, Econfina Creek Canoe Livery, Washington Blue Spring Econfina, Devil's Hole Spring, Econfina Creek Wildlife Management Area

Services: Restrooms on-site; all services available in Youngstown

Camping: Primitive camping at Econfina Creek WMA; full-service at St. Andrews State Park, Falling Waters State Park

Management: Northwest Florida Water Management District

Contact: (850) 539-5999; www.nwfwater .com/lands/recreation/area/econfina/pitt -sylvan/

Map: *DeLorme: Florida Atlas & Gazetteer:* Page 47 A1

GPS coordinates: Pitt Spring: N30 25.975' / W85 32.774'; Sylvan Springs: N30 25.907' / W85 32.896'

Finding the spring: From the junction of FL 20 and US 231 near Saunders, drive west on FL 20 for 6.9 miles to a right into the recreation area, just after crossing the bridge.

From the junction of FL 20 and FL 77 in Crystal Lake, drive east on FL 20 for approximately 8.8 miles to a left into the recreation area, just before crossing the bridge.

The Springs

Beautiful Pitt Spring is located on the northeast side of the parking lot. Pale aqua-colored water forms distinct rings in the sand around the spring, creating what looks like a perfect underwater Zen garden—that is, if you're lucky enough to have this popular local swimming hole to yourself. Not only is the spring gorgeous, but the Northwest Florida Water Management District has really done a fabulous job of redeveloping the entire recreation area. They've xeriscaped the landscape and sloped the land so that storm runoff ends up back in the spring run. There are composting toilets, and the boardwalk and benches are faux wood, a composite material made of recycled plastic. They really have made every effort to transform the area into a "green space" that's as earth-friendly as possible.

Schools of fish flock near the steps in hopes of getting a morsel of food from a friendly visitor. And the chilly 68°F water is just waiting for you to join them.

Pitt Springs is so clear it mimics a swimming pool in color.

On the exact opposite side of the parking lot from Pitt Spring, you'll see a boardwalk path. This boardwalk leads past the restrooms to a T. The right leg of the T leads to the inner tube launch, where visitors can enjoy a peaceful float down the spring run. The left heads toward Sylvan Springs. Sylvan is a group of spring vents that sit in the middle of the Pitt Spring Run, and they are as primitive as they come.

As you follow the boardwalk, it soon becomes a gravel path that heads downhill to another eco-friendly boardwalk. Follow the boardwalk and you'll see placards along the way, much like a self-guided interpretive trail, providing little tidbits of nature education as you hike. Once again the boardwalk quickly ends, and you're back on a gravel path heading west. Before you know it, there is yet another boardwalk. Follow this one for a short distance to a small area overlooking Sylvan Springs. This path continues past the spring and then uphill to the Strickland parking area off Strickland Road. You could park there and hike in if you just wanted to see Sylvan Springs, but it seems more logical to park at Pitt and visit both springs via the recreation area. Pitt Spring really is eye-catching. I highly recommend not skipping it.

Unlike Pitt, Sylvan Springs are primitive, untouched, and can only be viewed from the safe haven of the boardwalk. Although you can't swim here, the springs have a lot of character. As you look down from the boardwalk, you immediately can see where the water is pushing up. It almost looks like a pot of boiling water as it begins to bubble and bubble. The trail map at the trailhead, near the parking lot, shows that this trail goes all the way through to Williford Spring (#83). This is incorrect. A trail connecting the two recreation areas is under development, but it won't be completed until most likely 2016.

General description: It's a shame this group of springs can only be reached by boat, but perhaps that's why they remain unspoiled, unblemished, and unharmed by human influence. Aside from Gainer #2 being one of the clearest, prettiest springs I've ever seen, it's also fairly easy to reach. A long boardwalk leads from the unloading zone at the launch site, and from there it's a quick 0.4-mile downstream paddle to the mouth of the spring run.

Location: About 7 miles northwest of Youngstown, 20 miles northeast of Panama City, and 30 miles west of Blountstown

Development: Primitive

Best time to visit: Year-round

Restrictions: Surrounded by private property

Access: Boat to; 0.4 mile downstream

Fees: No fee

Water temperature: 68°F

Nearby attractions: Pitt, Sylvan, and Williford Springs, Econfina Creek Canoe Livery, Washington Blue Spring Econfina, Devil's Hole Spring, Econfina Creek Wildlife Management Area (WMA)

Services: Restrooms on-site; all services in Youngstown

Camping: Primitive camping at Econfina Creek WMA; full-service at St. Andrews State Park, Falling Waters State Park

Management: n/a

Contact: n/a

Map: *DeLorme: Florida Atlas & Gazetteer:* Page 47 A1

GPS coordinates: Canoe launch: N30 25.943' / W85 32.868'; Gainer #2: N30 25.65' / W85 32.9'; Gainer #1C: N30 25.667' / W85 32.767'

Finding the spring: From the junction of FL 20 and US 231 near Saunders, drive west on FL 20 for 6.8 miles to the canoe launch on the right, just before crossing the bridge.

From the junction of FL 20 and FL 77 in Crystal Lake, drive east on FL 20 for 8.9 miles to the canoe launch on the left, just after crossing the bridge.

The Spring

This spring group can only be reached by boat, and perhaps that lack of exposure is why they remain perfectly pristine to the nth degree. Collectively this group of springs is stunning, but two springs in particular really stand out from the crowd. Spring #2, which is also aptly named Emerald Spring, is the pinnacle of beauty. As you paddle downstream from the canoe launch, you'll go under the FL 20 bridge. At 0.4 mile from the launch site, on the west side of Econfina Creek, it's nearly impossible to miss the crystal-clear water of the spring run as it enters the creek. Paddle up the spring run to arrive at the bluest of blue-water springs you have ever seen. Without a doubt one is my favorites, and it's well worth the minimal paddle it takes to reach the spring. Unfortunately the spring is surrounded by private property, so make sure you stay in your canoe or kayak, or in the water if you opt to take a dip.

Directly across from the mouth of Gainer Spring #2, you'll see the mouth of Gainer #1C on the east side of Econfina Creek. A quick 0.1-mile paddle up the spring run leads you to Gainer Spring #1C. While the springs are immaculate and unspoiled, the canoe launch had trash all over the ground. I'd like to attribute it to raccoons getting into the trash bins, but I fear that it's more likely to be sheer negligence on the part of visitors. Please place your trash *in* the bins, and if you bring any food or drink along with you on the creek, I urge you to paddle-it-in, paddle-it-out so that these unspoiled splendors can remain pristine for years to come. If you're unable to paddle, don't despair. You can head up the road a short distance and visit Pitt Springs (#81); it too is among my favorites.

The presence of eelgrass is one of the signs of a healthy spring.

General description: Unfortunately this second-magnitude spring is closed for restoration until the summer of 2016. But when it reopens, it will be absolutely fabulous. A small recreation area is being developed around the spring, which will help protect it while, at the same time, giving the public easier access. I assure you, it'll be worth the wait. Williford Spring puts out an average of 18 million gallons of pale blue water a day, and it is simply stunning.

Location: About 7 miles northwest of Youngstown, 20 miles northeast of Panama City, and 30 miles west of Blountstown

Development: Primitive

Best time to visit: Year-round

Restrictions: Open sunrise to sunset; no food, drink, glass, or animals in the spring (these items are allowed in the picnic area); no alcohol

Access: Drive to

Fees: No fee

Water temperature: 68°F

Nearby attractions: Pitt Springs, Sylvan Springs, Econfina Creek Canoe Livery, Washington Blue Spring, Devil's Hole Spring, Econfina Creek Wildlife Management Area (WMA)

Services: Restrooms on-site; all services in Youngstown

Camping: Primitive camping at Econfina Creek WMA; full-service at St. Andrews State Park, Falling Waters State Park

Management: Northwest Florida Water Management District

Contact: (850) 539-5999; www.nwfwater .com/water-resources/springs/restoration -protection/williford

Map: *DeLorme: Florida Atlas & Gazetteer:* Page 47 A1

GPS coordinates: N30 26.267' / W85 32.783'

Finding the spring: From the junction of FL 20 and US 231 near Saunders, drive west on FL 20 for 7.4 miles to a right onto Strickland Road. Travel for 0.8 mile to the recreation area, on the right.

From the junction of FL 20 and FL 77 in Crystal Lake, drive east on FL 20 for approximately 8.3 miles to a left onto Strickland Road and follow directions above.

The Spring

Big plans are in store for this spring, as the area around it is being developed into a wonderful recreation area. The sad part is that we have to wait until summer 2016 for the redevelopment to be complete. In the meantime, enjoy Pitt Spring (#81), which is actually similar in appearance, almost like an older brother to Williford. Pale green water flows seamlessly from the spring as rings form on the sandy bottom from the force of the water. When the recreation area does reopen, it will have picnic pavilions, portable restrooms, and a boardwalk trail system, including one that will follow the spring run. There will be a canoe dock, so if you paddle in to see the spring, you can dock your canoe and hike a short distance to the swim area.

I urge you to stay on the designated paths when you're here, or at any spring for that matter. Straying from the path causes erosion and damages vital plant life that was purposely put there to help protect the spring. Unfortunately, some of our springs are literally being loved to death. Too many visitors cause silt to be kicked up, changing the spring opening and, over time, clogging the springs. People also inadvertently stand in vegetation that is vital to the health of the spring, damaging or killing it off. Please be conscious of where you step; better yet, *don't*. Instead grab a snorkel and a mask and float above the spring. I promise you'll get a much better view this way, making it a win-win situation. To get a sneak peek at the future site plan for the Williford Springs Recreation Area, visit the website listed above.

General description: Compared to its nearest neighbors, Williford (#83) and Pitt Springs (#81), Devil's Hole doesn't hold a candle. But if you've seen all the others and want to broaden your horizons, take a trip out to Devil's Hole. There is no swimming or fishing allowed in the spring, but the Florida National Scenic Trail passes right by. It's a great way to enjoy Econfina Creek and take a hike at the same time.

Location: Deep within the Econfina Creek Wildlife Management Area

Development: Primitive

Best time to visit: Year-round

Restrictions: Open sunrise to sunset; no swimming, fishing, or alcohol

Access: Drive to; high-clearance vehicles recommended

Fees: No fee

Water temperature: 68°F

Nearby attractions: Walsingham Park, Williford Spring, Econfina Creek Canoe Livery, Pitt Spring, Sylvan Springs, Washington Blue Spring

Services: Restrooms on-site; all services in Youngstown

Camping: Primitive camping on-site (reservations required); full-service at St. Andrews State Park, Falling Waters State Park

Management: Northwest Florida Water Management District

Contact: (850) 539-5999; www.nwfwater .com/lands/recreation/area/econfina/devils -hole

Map: DeLorme: Florida Atlas & Gazetteer: Page 47 A1

GPS coordinates: N30 29.433' / W85 31.317'

Finding the spring: From the junction of FL 20 and US 231 near Saunders, drive west on FL 20 for 7.4 miles to a right onto Strickland Road. Travel for 2.6 miles to a left onto Porter Pond Road. Follow Porter Pond Road for 2.3 miles as it bends right and then left and leads to a stop sign. Turn right here onto Hampshire Boulevard and follow it for 1.2 miles as it brings you around the south side of Porter Lake before bending left (north). Immediately after the bend, turn right onto Walsingham Bridge Road and travel 1.2 miles to a fork. Stay left at the fork and continue traveling under the power lines and over the bridge; the clay road becomes gravel. From the bridge over the creek, continue driving another 0.7 mile to a fork. Go left at the fork and travel for 0.6 mile to the parking area at the end of the road.

From the junction of FL 20 and FL 77 near Crystal Lake, drive east on FL 20 for approximately 8.3 miles to a left onto Strickland Road and follow directions above.

The Spring

At the northern end of the Econfina Creek Water Management Area (WMA), you'll find Devil's Hole Spring. The area surrounding the spring is currently under construction, but it should reopen by the summer of 2016. At that time they will have shored up the land around the spring and have developed a few primitive campsites that will be available by reservation only.

This second-magnitude spring ties into the Floridian aquifer, giving it a chilly 68°F temperature. Devil's Hole tends to hold a teal-like hue, although I've seen it dark green as well. The Florida National Scenic Trail passes right by the spring. If you enjoy hiking near the water, this is a great area to do it, since the Florida Trail closely follows Econfina Creek for several miles within the WMA.

I highly recommend paddling this creek, if you haven't before. It moves swiftly, and much like the Upper Suwannee River, it has high limestone walls, beautiful springs, and a lot of character. While you may find yourself having to portage here or there, it's well worth the effort to paddle on this pristine creek.

General description: The scenery at Jackson Blue Spring is just magnificent! A sloping grassy hill surrounds most of brilliant blue spring, and Merritt's Mill Pond forms the backdrop. I only wish this stunning spring was open to the public year-round.

Location: 5461 Blue Springs Rd., Marianna; about 5 miles east of Marianna

Development: Developed

Best time to visit: Open 7 days a week May 25—Aug 18 and on weekends through Labor Day; open to SCUBA divers year-round; diving permit required prior to arrival

Restrictions: Open 9:30 a.m. to 6 p.m.; no pets

Access: Drive to; also accessed by boat

Fees: $

Water temperature: 72°F

Nearby attractions: Florida Caverns State Park, the springs of Merritt's Mill Pond, Chipola River Greenway, Hinson Conservation Area, Bellamy Bridge Heritage Trail

Services: Restrooms, outdoor showers on-site; all services in Marianna

Camping: Florida Caverns State Park

Management: Jackson County Parks

Contact: (850) 482-2114 or (850) 718-0437; www.jacksoncountyfl.net/parks-and-recycling/blue-springs; Cave Adventures: (850) 482-6016; www.caveadventurers.com

Map: *DeLorme: Florida Atlas & Gazetteer:* Page 32 B1

GPS coordinates: N30 47.433' / W85 08.4'

Finding the spring: From the junction of CR 164 (Blue Springs Road) and CR 164A near Marianna, drive west on CR 164 for 0.2 mile to the park, on the left.

From the junction of CR 164 (Blue Springs Road) and FL 71 in Marianna, drive east on CR 164 for approximately 3.3 miles to the park, on the right.

The Spring

Forming the headwaters of one of the prettiest waterways in the state, Jackson Blue Spring doles out about 76 million gallons of water each day. The spring is found within a county-run recreation area that unfortunately is only open to the general public from late May through Labor Day. I say "general public," because cave divers can obtain a permit and gate code from a local dive shop and SCUBA dive in this bonny blue beauty year-round. Located on the northern bank of Merritt's Mill Pond, Cave Adventures is a full-service dive shop that also trains divers in cave, technical, and side-mount diving. If you're already certified, you can get a permit for Blue Springs or rent a boat from them and head out to one of the many other popular cave-diving sites on the millpond.

The spring-fed pond rivals the beauty of the Rainbow and Silver Rivers. During the off-season you can rent a boat or a glass-bottom kayak from Cave Adventures and explore the other amazing springs on the pond. (For more information on the springs of Merritt's Mill Pond, see entry #86).

The recreation area that houses Blue Spring is great fun for the entire family. A large grassy hillside surrounds most of the spring, and picnic tables are perfectly placed so that you can enjoy lunch while overlooking the spring and the millpond in the distance. There's a playground, a volleyball net, and hiking trails if

Jackson Blue Spring is simply stunning.

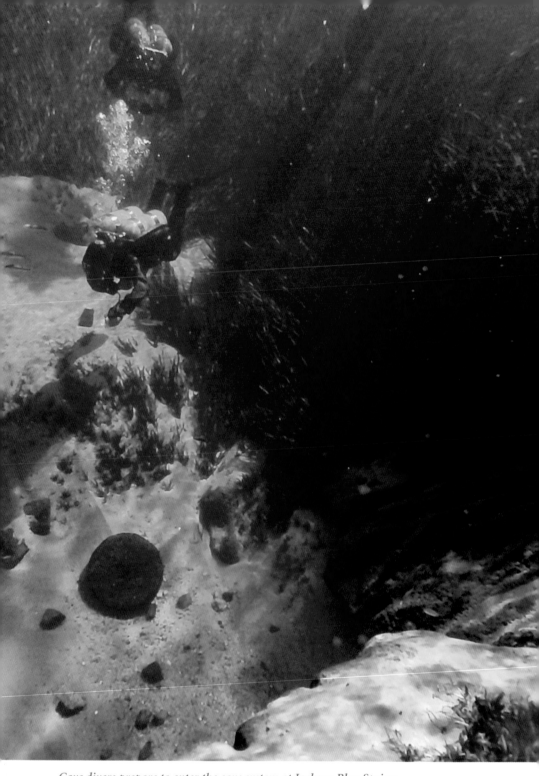
Cave divers prepare to enter the cave system at Jackson Blue Spring.

you choose to stay on dry land. But if you're a water baby like me, the spring has something for all ages. There's a sandy beach area near the shallows on one side of the head spring. An older looking metal slide sits on the other side of the spring, just waiting for you to take the plunge as it drops you out into the water amid the eelgrass. Make sure to get your swimsuit wet before heading down the slide, or you're sure to stick to it.

The park rents tubes, so you can float around in the swim area. Or you can rent a canoe, kayak, or pedal boat and head out to explore some of the other springs on the pond (see entry #86). And saving the best for last, there is a platform you can jump off and land right in the heart of the spring itself. A diving board used to sit on this platform, but on my last visit it was no longer there. This is not only a popular cave-diving site but also ideal for snorkeling. Fish and turtles swim on the outskirts, and rays of light can be seen streaming down into the large hole that forms the entrance to the spring. All in all, this is a fantastic park! Needless to say, Jackson Blue Spring and the entire Merritt's Mill Pond Springs group (#86) are among my favorites.

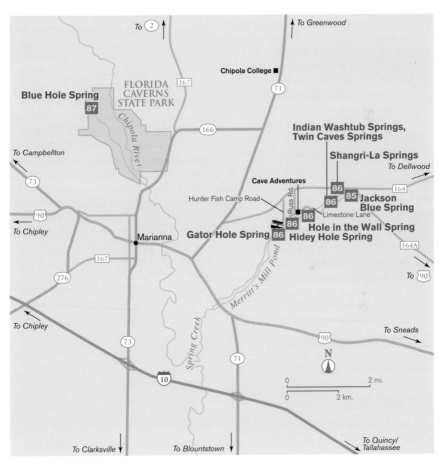

86

Merritt's Mill Pond Springs Group: Shangri-La, Twin Caves, Indian Washtub, Hole in the Wall, Hidey Hole, and Gator Hole Springs

General description: Indescribable! That's how astonishing Merritt's Mill Pond is. Much like the Rainbow and Silver Rivers, the millpond is spring fed. Numerous springs flow into the millpond, and I have included the top six, plus the head spring, Jackson Blue Spring, which is covered in its own individual write-up (#85). All these springs, with the exception of the head spring, are reached by boat only. The bluest of blue water flows from below to make up this 202-acre reservoir before merging into the Chipola River. The millpond is a popular cave-diving destination, but even if you're not a cave diver, I highly recommend taking a tour of this wonderful waterway! Paddling a canoe or kayak is ideal, or you can rent a pontoon boat from Cave Adventures at their waterfront location on the western bank of the pond. They not only rent kayaks and boats but are also a full-service dive shop. Owned and operated by one of the top technical cave divers in the country, Cave Adventures also trains divers on-site in cave, technical, and side-mount diving. They also have detailed maps of the area.

Location: 6 springs along the Merritt's Mill Pond southwest of the head spring (Jackson Blue Spring); 2 to 3 miles east of Marianna

Development: Primitive

Best time to visit: Year-round

Restrictions: SCUBA Cave-diving certification required for SCUBA diving

Access: Boat to; distances vary

Fees: No fee if you have your own watercraft and use the public boat ramp

Water temperature: 72°F

Nearby attractions: Jackson Blue Springs County Park, Florida Caverns State Park, Falling Waters State Park, Three Rivers State Park

Services: All services in Marianna

Camping: Florida Caverns State Park

Management: n/a

Contact: Cave Adventures: (850) 482-6016; www.caveadventurers.com

Map: *DeLorme: Florida Atlas & Gazetteer:* Page 32 B1

GPS coordinates: Public boat ramp: N30 46.767' / W85 10.1'; Cave Adventures access: N30 47.05' / W85 09.633'

Finding the spring: Public boat ramp: From the junction of CR 164 (Blue Springs Road) and FL 71 near Marianna, drive east on CR 164 for 1.7 miles to a right onto Hunter Fish Camp Road. Travel for 0.6 mile to the boat ramp, at the end of the road.

From the junction of CR 164 (Blue Springs Road) and CR 164A near Marianna, drive west on CR 164 for 2 miles to a left onto Hunter Fish Camp Road and follow directions above.

Cave Adventures access: From the junction of CR 164 (Blue Springs Road) and CR 164A near Marianna, drive west on CR 164 for 1.7 miles to a left onto Russ Road. Travel for 0.4 mile to a left onto Limestone Lane. Travel for less than 0.1 mile to 5211 Limestone Ln., on the right.

From the junction of CR 164 (Blue Springs Road) and FL 71 near Marianna, drive east on CR 164 for 2 miles to a right onto Russ Road and follow directions above.

SHANGRI-LA SPRINGS

GPS coordinates: N30 47.433' / W85 08.567'

The Spring

This is by far my favorite spring on the millpond, along with the head spring. If I were a cave diver, I might have a different opinion. But as a person simply observing from above, Shangri-La is astounding! A large limestone crack is made perfectly visible by the clear blue water that flows from it. On the northern bank, this is the farthest upstream spring on the pond aside from the head spring (Jackson Blue #85) and sits about 0.4 mile downstream from it. High cliff-like bluffs adjacent to the spring add to its appeal. If you skip every other spring on the pond, make sure you see Shangri-La! It's the most ideal spot for snorkeling in the region.

Shangri-La Springs is found within Merritt's Mill Pond.

TWIN CAVES SPRINGS

GPS coordinates: N30 47.217' / W85 08.7'

The Spring

About 0.1 mile downstream from Shangri-La, on the south side of the pond you'll see a small floating dock amid the cypress trees. The spring is about 50 feet north of the dock, and the dock is a perfect platform for boats to tie off to as SCUBA

A small platform gives cave divers easy access to Twin Caves Springs.

divers prepare for descent. A large log rests atop the entrance to one of the caves, and once again clear blue water pushes forth.

INDIAN WASHTUB SPRINGS

GPS coordinates: N30 47.267' / W85 08.733'

The Spring

Indian Washtub is directly across from Twin Caves Springs, on the north side of the pond. Located northeast of a private dock with a stainless-steel ladder, this spring is a bit smaller than the rest, so be sure to use the landmarks given.

HOLE IN THE WALL SPRING

GPS coordinates: N30 47.00' / W85 09.367'

The Spring

As the name implies, the entrance to this spring is literally a hole in the wall under the water at the base of a limestone bluff. Another of the more popular cave-diving sites, this one also has a small floating dock near the spring. If you have good eyesight, you can actually see it from the boat dock at Cave Adventures. It sits catty-corner to the boat dock, on the southern banks of the pond, and is approximately 0.7 mile downstream from the Blue Springs Recreation Area (#85).

HIDEY HOLE SPRING

GPS coordinates: N30 46.85' / W85 9.8'

The Spring

Hidey Hole is a perfectly circular hole in the middle of the pond, west of the obvious tree line that divides the pond in half. The only reason I even found this spring was because Edd Sorrenson gave me a personal tour of this portion of the pond. If you use the GPS coordinates, you may have some luck, but this spring is no more impressive than any of the others and is often impossible to see because it gets covered over with aquatic vegetation.

GATOR HOLE SPRING

GPS coordinates: N30 46.667' / W85 10.033'

The Spring

Directly across from the public boat ramp, you can find Gator Hole on the south side of the pond. From afar Gator Hole is very similar in appearance to Hole in the Wall, lying at the base of a high limestone bluff. As you ease your boat a bit closer, you notice a large crevice within the limestone wall. The spring lies below. Often covered with duckweed, it may not be that picturesque from above. But this too is a popular cave-diving site and said to be quite appealing below. It's also one that really begs the question: Who would even think to dive this? Pioneers like Edd Sorenson are opening up and exploring an entire new world that lies right below our feet. Keep up the good work!

General description: Blue Hole Spring is a popular swimming hole and a pretty little spring, but the dry cave tours are even more impressive. I say do both!

Location: 3345 Caverns Rd., Marianna; about 3 miles north of Marianna

Development: Primitive

Best time to visit: Year-round

Restrictions: Open 8 a.m. to sunset; cave tours not available on Tues, Wed, Thanksgiving, and Christmas; pets allowed in designated areas only

Access: Drive to

Fees: $

Water temperature: 68°F

Nearby attractions: Jackson Blue Springs, the springs of Merritt's Mill Pond, Chipola River Greenway, Hinson Conservation Area

Services: Restrooms, food on-site; all services in Marianna

Camping: On-site

Management: Florida Park Service

Contact: (850) 482-9598; www.florida stateparks.org/floridacaverns/default.cfm

Map: DeLorme: Florida Atlas & Gazetteer: Page 32 B1

GPS coordinates: N30 49.217' / W85 14.7'

Finding the spring: From the junction of FL 166 (Caverns Road) and US 90 in Marianna, drive north on FL 166 for 2.6 miles to the park, on the left.

From the junction of FL 166 (Caverns Road) and FL 167 in Marianna, drive south on FL 166 for 0.3 mile to the park, on the right.

The Spring

I almost feel sorry for Blue Hole Spring. Not because it's not pretty; it is. Not because it's not fun; it is. But because the cave tour at Florida Caverns State Park, where you'll find this spring, is so absolutely cool that it overshadows the spring by a mile. Make sure you take the cave tour when you visit this park. It's not only a rare adventure, where you can see amazing natural formations as you explore room after room of this underground world, but it's also educational. *Note:* The cave tours are closed on Tuesday, Wednesday, Thanksgiving, and Christmas, so plan accordingly.

The entire 1,300-acre park is a delight. The spring is made up of translucent milky blue water, and a string of buoys blocks off the swim area from the rest of the run. A footbridge crosses over the spring run and gives visitors a nice vantage point to view it in both directions. This huge park literally has something for everyone. The Chipola River runs right through the middle of the park, and I mean that literally. It even dips underground for about 0.5 mile. You may see people fishing from the road where it crosses right over the river. You can rent canoes every day of the week and enjoy an abundance of wildlife viewing while you're out on the river.

The park boasts a multiuse trail system that's about 6 miles long and is open to hikers, bikers, and those on horseback. In the center of the trail system is an equestrian center, with stables and a horse-washing station. The park's campground even has a few sites that have horse stalls near them, so you can camp with your equine friend. There are a few other trails just for hikers, and the terrain is surprisingly hilly for Florida's typical flatland. It's quite refreshing to enjoy a bit of topography as you hike on rocky bluffs and see unique open-air caves in the middle of the forest.

Florida Caverns State Park offers exceptional dry cave tours to the public.

General description: Easily the prettiest spring on Holmes Creek, Cypress Spring can only be reached by boat. There are several boat launch sites along the creek if you have your own canoe or kayak. If you don't, two nearby outfitters offer rentals and shuttles, so you can take your time and enjoy the creek.

Location: The spring run enters Holmes Creek from the northwest, about 0.35 mile downstream from Cotton Landing; about 12 miles south of Bonifay and southwest of Chipley

Development: Primitive

Best time to visit: Year-round

Restrictions: Open sunrise to sunset; no alcohol; road to canoe launch may be closed during times of high water

Access: Boat to; 0.35 mile downstream

Fees: No fee

Water temperature: 68°F

Nearby attractions: Beckton Spring, Hightower Spring, Morrison Springs, Ponce de Leon State Park, Vortex Spring, Falling Waters State Park

Services: All services in Bonifay

Camping: Primitive camping at Cotton Landing; full-service at Falling Waters State Park, Vortex Springs

Management: Northwest Florida Water Management District (NWFWMD)

Contact: (850) 539-5999; www.nwfwmd .state.fl.us/lands/recreation/area/ choctawhatchee-holmes/cotton-landing/

Map: *DeLorme: Florida Atlas & Gazetteer:* Page 30 C3

GPS coordinates: Cotton Landing Canoe Launch: N30 39.333' / W85 40.867'; Cypress Springs: N30 39.517' / W85 41.067'; Snaggy Bend Outfitters: N30 38.65' / W85 41.217'; Holmes Creek Canoe Livery: N30 37.819' / W85 42.585'

Finding the spring: From the junction of FL 277 and FL 79 in Vernon, drive northeast on FL 277 for 3.3 miles to a left into Cotton Landing. Follow the unmarked gravel road; after 0.1 mile the road makes a hard bend to the left. Continue to follow it for another 0.9 mile to where it ends at the canoe launch.

From the junction of FL 277 and CR 278A near Vernon, drive southwest on FL 277 for approximately 2.8 miles to a right into Cotton Landing and follow directions above.

The Spring

Without a doubt, Cypress Spring is the most beautiful spring on Holmes Creek. If you only have time to paddle to one spring on this creek, make it Cypress. Bright blue water flows constantly from this perfectly clear swimming hole. The spring is surrounded by private property and can only be accessed by boat, which contributes to its pristine nature. The easiest way to get to the spring is to put in at the Cotton Landing boat launch site. Paddle downstream from Cotton Landing, or simply let the current drift you down for about 0.35 mile to where you see the mouth of the spring run on your right (north bank). An additional 0.25-mile paddle up the spring run puts you right on top of Cypress Spring. The property owners surrounding the spring have been kind enough to keep this site open and allow people to tie off and snorkel about, so don't forget to bring your gear. Please be courteous and mindful of the property owner's rights, and as always pack it in, pack it out. We would like to keep this spring as pretty as it is now for years to come.

Cotton Landing is on NWFWMD land and offers more parking than most landings along the creek. But this is only a canoe launch; no motorized boats are allowed. Picnic tables and a set of steps leading down to the creek are all there is aside from the canoe launch. Cotton Landing has a bit of a nicer feel than Culpepper Landing, which is the next landing downstream. The NWFWMD people have been known to close and lock the gate if water levels rise too high, so it's a good idea to call ahead or monitor their website. If it is closed, you can still reach Cypress Spring if you want; you just have to put in at Culpepper Landing and paddle upstream about 0.5 mile to the mouth of the spring run, which will now be on the left. For directions to Culpepper Landing see Beckton Spring (#89).

If you don't have your own canoe or kayak, you're in luck. Snaggy Bend Outfitters (850-535-2004; www.snaggybendoutfitters.com) is right off FL 277. They not only offer rentals but also do shuttle services, so you can plan your paddle to be almost entirely downstream. Holmes Creek Canoe Livery (850-210-7001; www.holmescreekcanoelivery.com), located right on the creek near downtown Vernon, also offers rentals and shuttles and has a swim area, rope swing, and zip line on-site.

General description: Cypress and tupelo trees greet you as you paddle along Holmes Creek on your way to Beckton Spring. The spring is surrounded by private property but used as a local swimming hole. While this spring is not the most beautiful on the creek, it easily takes second place.

Location: The spring run enters Holmes Creek from the northwest, about 0.7 mile downstream from Culpepper Landing; about 12 miles south of Bonifay and southwest of Chipley.

Development: Primitive

Best time to visit: Year-round

Restrictions: Open sunrise to sunset; no alcohol

Access: Boat to; 0.7 mile downstream

Fees: $

Water temperature: 68°F

Nearby attractions: Cypress Spring, Hightower Spring, Morrison Springs, Ponce de Leon State Park, Vortex Spring, Falling Waters State Park

Services: All services available in Bonifay

Camping: Primitive camping at Cotton Landing; full-service at Falling Waters State Park, Vortex Springs

Management: Northwest Florida Water Management District

Contact: (850)539-5999; www.nwfwmd.state .fl.us/lands/recreation/area/choctawhatchee -holmes/

Map: *DeLorme: Florida Atlas & Gazetteer:* Page 30 C3

GPS coordinates: Snaggy Bend Outfitters: N30 38.65' / W85 41.217'; Holmes Creek Canoe Livery: N30 37.819' / W85 42.585'; Culpepper Landing Canoe Launch: N30 39.067' / W85 41.233'; Beckton Spring: N30 38.917' / W85 41.617'

Finding the spring: From the junction of FL 277 and FL 79 in Vernon, drive northeast on FL 277 for 2.1 miles to a left onto Culpepper Lane. Culpepper Lane bends right and left and is the only paved road in the neighborhood. Follow it for 0.4 mile to where it ends at the boat ramp.

From the junction of FL 277 and CR 278A near Vernon, drive southwest on FL 277 for approximately 4 miles to a right onto Culpepper Lane and follow directions above.

The Spring

The easiest, most direct route to see Beckton Spring is to use the boat launch at Culpepper Landing. Although there's not much parking, the ramp is smooth and gently slopes down to the creek. A self-pay station is on-site, so make sure you have singles on hand. The launch site has a few picnic tables and a charcoal grill, and a wall of beautiful bright pink bougainvillea bushes brightens up the area. To reach the spring, paddle downstream about 0.7 mile. Much like Cypress Spring, you'll see the mouth of the spring run on the right (northwest) bank of the creek. From the mouth, a quick and easy 0.15-mile upstream paddle leads you to the spring. While Beckton is pretty to see, I highly recommend taking the time to paddle up to Cypress Spring (#88) as well. Cypress is unmatched on Holmes Creek and is not to be missed.

If you don't have your own canoe or kayak, there's good news. There are two canoe rental places within easy reach, and they both rent canoes and offer shuttle services. Snaggy Bend Outfitters (850-535-2004; www.snaggybendoutfitters.com), located along FL 277 about 2 miles north of FL 79, is nearest to the launch sites.

They rent canoes and kayaks and offer hourly rentals as well as half-day or whole-day trips. The bonus if you do a shuttle is that you don't have to paddle upstream except for the spring runs. They have several different routes, so you can paddle upper Holmes Creek, lower Holmes Creek, or both. Holmes Creek Canoe Livery (850-210-7001; www.holmescreekcanoelivery.com) offers the same services and is located in Vernon off FL 79, right on the creek. They also have a swim area, rope swing, and even a zip line on-site.

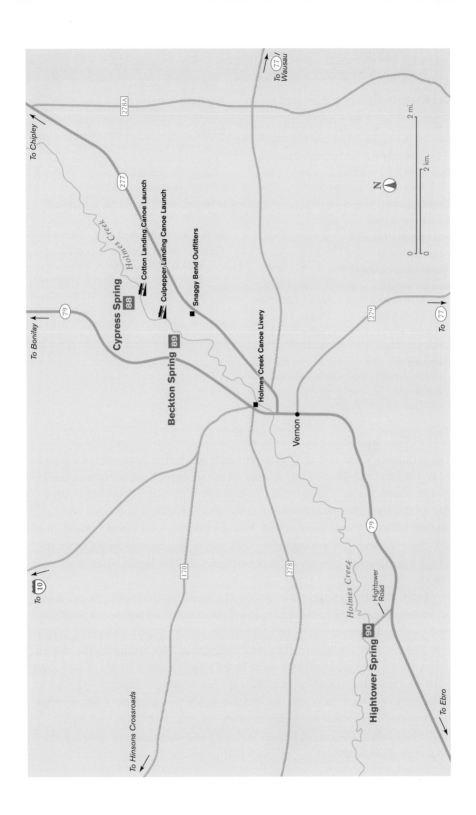

General description: Hightower once was a beautiful blue spring, but today there's no boil and the spring seems more like a murky bog. It's a perfect example of how a spring can change drastically if it's not treated properly.

Location: 3107 Hightower Rd., Vernon; about 3.5 miles south of Vernon

Development: Primitive

Best time to visit: Year-round

Restrictions: No ATVs

Access: Drive to

Water temperature: 68°F

Nearby attractions: Holmes Creek Canoe Livery, Morrison Spring, Ponce de Leon State Park, Vortex Spring

Services: Restroom on-site; all services in Ponce de Leon

Camping: Primitive camping on-site; full-service at Falling Waters State Park, Vortex Spring

Management: Northwest Florida Water Management District

Contact: (850) 539-5999; www.nwf water.com/lands/recreation/area/ choctawhatchee-holmes/hightower-landing/; Snaggy Bend Outfitters: (850) 535-2004; www.snaggybendoutfitters.com

Map: *DeLorme: Florida Atlas & Gazetteer:* Page 30 D2

GPS coordinates: N30 36.3' / W85 45.933'

Finding the spring: From the junction of FL 79 and CR 277 near Vernon, drive south on FL 79 for 4 miles to a right onto Hightower Road. Travel for 0.4 mile to the boat ramp, at the end of the road.

From the junction of FL 79 and CR 284 in New Hope, drive north on FL 79 for 3.4 miles to a left onto Hightower Road and follow directions above.

The Spring

The spring sits to the west of Hightower Landing, which is composed of a wide boat ramp and a single campsite located on the southern bank of Holmes Creek. Holmes Creek is one of many scenic state paddle trails and is definitely worth a day on the water. Several springs add to the allure, wildlife is abundant, and I'm told the fishing is pretty good as well. You can put your own canoe or kayak in at any one of several boat landings along the creek or visit Snaggy Bend Outfitters, where you can rent a canoe, paddle downstream, and be shuttled back to your vehicle.

Sadly, Hightower Spring is what I'd call a very unhealthy spring. Small boils are visible, but this is a perfect example of how drastically a spring can be affected by the environment around it. An older couple who were born and raised in this area told me there was a time when locals called this "Blue Springs"—the clearest, bluest, prettiest spring you'd ever seen. Today there's barely a trickle of dark green water due to sediment and invasive plant species clogging the spring—a simple reminder to not stand in vegetation, which may kill the native plant life. Another way you can help protect the springs is to try not to kick up silt as you explore the springs below. Over time, this silt builds up and contributes to clogging the smaller magnitude springs.

A local couple fish in Hightower Spring.

The saddest part of the demise of Hightower, and many other springs, is that within our own lifetime we have made such a negative impact. This dramatic demise has happened right before our very eyes in a matter of decades. Not centuries but decades. Keep this in mind on your next visit to any spring. Here's a great website with lots of information on how *you* can help restore our springs: www .watermatters.org/springs.

Important safety note: There is an apiary full of honeybee hives just off the side of the road, right before you reach Hightower Landing. If you've never seen one, it's pretty cool. However, the bees often wander from the apiary down to the boat landing. Benedryl is good to have just in case, but if you have a known bee-sting allergy, I *highly* recommend that you carry an EpiPen along with you.

General description: The spring and recreation area surrounding Morrison Spring are just beautiful. The people of Walton County are lucky to have not only a great swimming area but also a wonderful picnic shelter and boat ramp.

Location: 874 Morrison Springs Rd., Ponce de Leon; about 26 miles southwest of Bonifay and about 19 miles southeast of DeFuniak Springs

Development: Developed

Best time to visit: Year-round

Restrictions: Open sunrise to sunset; no alcohol or pets

Access: Drive to

Fees: No fee

Water temperature: 68°F

Nearby attractions: Ponce de Leon State Park, Vortex Spring

Services: Restrooms, outdoor showers on-site; all services in Ponce de Leon

Camping: Vortex Spring

Management: Walton County Parks

Contact: (850) 892-8108; http://www.waltonoutdoors.com/morrison-springs

Map: *DeLorme: Florida Atlas & Gazetteer:* Page 30 C1

GPS coordinates: N30 39.45' / W85 54.3'

Finding the spring: From the junction of CR 181 and FL 81 near Ponce de Leon, drive east on CR 181 for 1.6 miles to a right onto Morrison Springs Road. Travel for 0.4 mile and bear left at the fork. Continue for another 0.3 mile to the park, at the end of the road.

The Spring

The people of Walton County are lucky to have such a wonderful facility at their fingertips. A beautiful picnic shelter overlooks the spring, and it even has ceiling fans. I don't think I've ever seen that in an open-air pavilion. Unfortunately, at the time of my visit the river was so high that even this second-magnitude spring, that's usually as blue as they come, gushing out nearly 50 million gallons of water a day, was flooded out and not its usual beautiful blue self. Most of the boardwalk, many of the picnic tables, and the entire swim area were underwater. All that means is that I got some disappointing photos and was unable to take a dip. I'm sure the fish didn't know what to do with all this uncharted territory. Picnic tables, trash cans, and trees were all submerged.

But Morrison Springs still remains on the Author's Favorites list and is highly recommended. In its typical state, when it's not flooded over, the spring is beautiful and blue. There's a large swim area and a floating dock that sits out in the middle of the water and is always fun to swim out to and jump off. A well-built boardwalk leads out to the spring, and the picnic pavilion affords a perfect view from its elevated position. Along with restrooms, the park has outdoor showers and a SCUBA gear rinsing station.

The visibility for open-water SCUBA diving is hit or miss, but when you get to the caverns below, it usually clears up. With that in mind, if you're an open-water diver, you may want to head over to Vortex Spring (#93) to dive instead. A road leads from the day-use area about 0.5 mile back to a very nice boat ramp on the far side of the spring run. This launch site gives boaters a good access point to explore the Choctawhatchee River, which is where the 0.7-mile spring run leads.

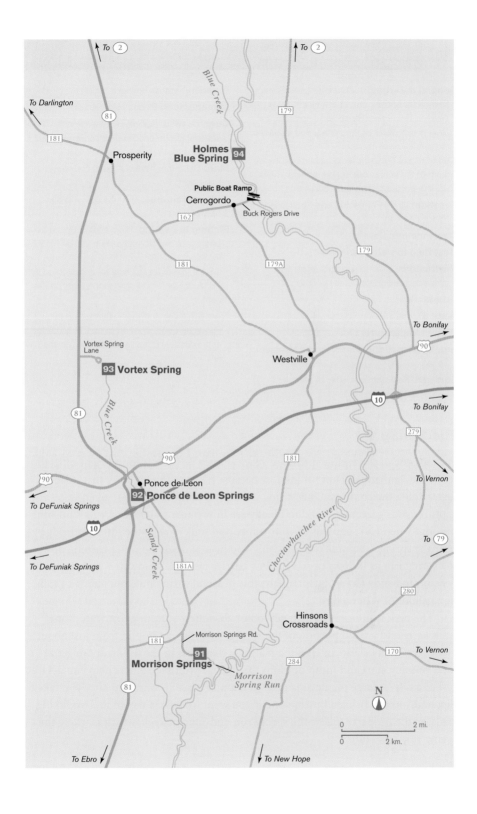

General description: Ponce de Leon Springs State Park houses one of the nicest swim areas in the region. Stone walls surround the clear green water of the spring, and a shaded picnic area gives the family a nice place to enjoy lunch. The park remains barren through most of the winter, but during summer it fills up with people by the hundreds.

Location: 2860 Ponce de Leon Springs Rd., Ponce de Leon

Development: Developed

Best time to visit: Year-round

Restrictions: Open 8 a.m. to sunset; pets allowed in designated areas only

Access: Drive to

Fees: $

Water temperature: 68°F

Nearby attractions: Vortex Spring, Morrison Spring

Services: Restrooms on-site; all services in Ponce de Leon

Camping: Vortex Spring

Management: Florida Park Service

Contact: (850) 836-4281; www.florida stateparks.org/poncedeleonsprings/default .cfm

Map: *DeLorme: Florida Atlas & Gazetteer:* Page 30 C1

GPS coordinates: N30 43.267' / W85 55.833'

Finding the spring: From I-10 in Ponce de Leon, take exit 96 and drive north on FL 81 for approximately 0.8 mile to a right onto US 90. Travel for 0.2 mile to a right onto CR 181A. Travel for 0.4 mile to the park, on the right.

From CR 181A and the I-10 overpass in Ponce de Leon, drive north on CR 181A for approximately 0.5 mile to the park, on the left.

The Spring

Perhaps one of the easiest springs to reach, Ponce de Leon is found right off I-10 up in the Panhandle. Don't think just because it's near the highway that it lacks luster; quite the contrary. This spring is simply beautiful. Its clear, green water just captures your gaze, and you don't really see how much water the spring's pushing out. But when you snap out of your trance and walk over to the little footbridge near the spring, holy smokes! Suddenly you hear and see the water rushing down the spring run as it flows over a shallow barrier near the headwaters and makes its way out to Sandy Creek. Surprisingly, this peaceful spring puts out about 14 million gallons of water a day.

The park is not only easy to get to but absolutely stunning. Intricate stone walls surround a good portion of the spring, and you can hop in from just about anywhere. There's also an elevated platform that adds to the fun; you can get a little running start and jump out into the spring. Multiple ladders help you get out just as easily. A large picnic area gives you a nice place to warm up after you take a dip, and you can bring a lunch along if you want to make a day of it. Two hiking trails on the property follow the spring run and Sandy Creek, which is where the spring run flows into.

Ponce de Leon Springs has a wonderful swim area.

The park hardly sees any traffic in the fall and winter months, and they often have the public use a self-pay station, so make sure you have singles if you visit during this time. However, in the spring and summer this small park fills up with people by the hundreds. During those months, I recommend arriving early if you want to guarantee access. Ponce de Leon Springs and state park are often confused with another spring and state park with a similar name, De Leon Springs. To add to the confusion, the town in which De Leon Springs is found is also named De Leon Springs. When you're planning your trip to this one, make sure you put the "Ponce" in the name so that you don't get misdirected.

General description: This is easily one of the most fun spring locations in the state. Not only is it a hot spot for the SCUBA community, but the whole family can enjoy jumping off platforms and slides and landing in the sparkling blue water of Vortex Spring. This gorgeous second-magnitude spring flows about 28 million gallons a day and has landed squarely on the Author's Favorites list.

Location: 1517 Vortex Spring Ln., Ponce De Leon; about 3.5 miles north of Ponce de Leon

Development: Developed

Best time to visit: Year-round

Restrictions: Open 8 a.m. to 5 p.m. Mon—Thurs, 7 a.m. to 7 p.m. Fri—Sun; closed on Christmas and Thanksgiving; no pets; no glass containers near the spring

Access: Drive to

Water temperature: 68°F

Nearby attractions: Ponce de Leon Springs State Park, Morrison Springs

Services: Restrooms, food, lodging on-site; all services in Ponce de Leon, DeFuniak Springs

Camping: On-site

Management: Vortex Spring Inc.

Contact: (850) 836-4979 or (800) 342-0640; www.vortexspring.com

Map: *DeLorme: Florida Atlas & Gazetteer:* Page 30 B1

GPS coordinates: N30 46.233' / W85 56.917'

Finding the spring: From the junction of FL 81 and US 90 in Ponce de Leon, drive north on FL 81 for 3.7 miles to a right onto Vortex Spring Lane. Travel for 0.6 mile to the entrance to the park, on your left.

From the junction of FL 81 and CR 181 in Prosperity, drive south on FL 81 for 5.5 miles to a left onto Vortex Spring Lane and follow directions above.

The Spring

Family owned and operated since the 1970s, Vortex Spring is just good clean fun! If it's been a while since your last visit, I have two words for you: Go again! The spring is as pretty as ever, and the props and activities just keep improving. There are slides and platforms to jump off. You can rent a canoe or pedal boat. Or just enjoy taking a dip and snorkeling about in the brilliant blue water of this dazzling spring.

Vortex Spring is also a SCUBA diving hot spot, and people come from all over the world to dive here. There are options available for every level. Whether your certification is for open water, cavern, or cave, they've got a dive for you. They even have night dives available. The office doubles as a mini store with food and general necessities, and is also a full dive shop where you can purchase or rent essential gear to enhance your diving experience. They offer almost any SCUBA class you could want. Simply call ahead, and they will make it happen. They'll not only find an instructor to suit your needs but even get one that speaks your language if it's not English. At the time of my last visit, they were clearing up the grotto to the left of the spring. When they're done, they will be developing that into a second swim area, adding to the fun.

Vortex Spring is both beautiful and fun.

If you also enjoy exploring by land, they have an extensive trail system on this 420-acre property. The trails, which once were open to ATVs, are now open only to hikers and mountain bikes. I recommend staying at the campground or in one of their several lodging options and spending at least a few days enjoying everything this fabulous park has to offer.

General description: Sapphire blue water flows from an almost perfectly circular hole in the center of the spring. An upstream paddle against a slow-moving current is the best way to reach the spring, since it's surrounded by private property.

Location: 1.5 miles upstream from the boat launch in Cerrogordo; about 16 miles northwest of Bonifay and 12 miles northeast of Ponce de Leon

Development: Primitive

Best time to visit: Year-round

Restrictions: None

Access: Boat to; 1.5 miles upstream

Fees: No fee

Water temperature: 68°F

Nearby attractions: Vortex Spring, Ponce de Leon State Park, Morrison Springs

Services: All services in Ponce de Leon

Camping: Vortex Spring

Management: n/a

Contact: n/a

Map: *DeLorme: Florida Atlas & Gazetteer:* Page 30 B1

GPS coordinates: Canoe launch: N30 50.117' / W85 52.717'; Holmes Blue Spring: N30 51.104' / W85 53.169'

Finding the spring: From the junction of CR 179A and US 90 in Westville, drive north on CR 179A for 5 miles to a right onto Buck Rogers Drive. Travel for 0.5 mile; the road bends left and continues for another 0.1 mile to the boat ramp, at the end of the road.

From the junction of CR 181 and FL 81 in Prosperity, drive southeast on CR 181 for 2.4 miles to the unmarked CR 162 (across from Hickory Hill Baptist Church). Travel for 2.3 miles to a stop sign at CR 179A. Drive straight across onto Buck Rogers Drive and follow directions above.

The Spring

Holmes Blue Spring is found on the western bank of the Choctawhatchee River, about 1.5 miles upstream from the boat ramp. Although the water from Vortex and Ponce de Leon Springs eventually ends up in the Choctawhatchee, Holmes Blue is the only spring of any significance that is practically right on this river. The spring can only be reached by boat, which in itself is not typically a problem. However, the nearest canoe/kayak rental is more than 20 miles away in the town of Vernon. Holmes Creek Canoe Livery is willing to take you up the river and provide a shuttle service, but it will cost a bit more than their typical canoe rental and shuttle, which runs along Holmes Creek (see map on page 235). The livery requires that you make reservations in advance of your trip. For specific details, visit www.holmescreekcanoelivery.com or call (850)210-7001.

Now, back to those of you who do have your own boat. The easiest way to reach Holmes Blue Spring is to use the boat ramp in the tiny town of Cerrogordo. On your way to the launch site, take note of the old blue Chevy truck in the yard at the corner of Buck Rogers Drive and CR 179A; it's quite a sight. You may also notice the historical marker about 0.5 mile down Buck Rogers Drive on your left. The marker commemorates the fact that Cerrogordo was home to the first-ever courthouse in Holmes County. The courthouse stood in town for nearly fifty years before being moved to Westville in 1895.

After enjoying the views, and getting a small history lesson, launch your craft and head upstream for about 1.5 miles to where you see a shallow, narrow spring run flow into the river on the left (west bank). The spring run is a mere 150 feet, so you can practically see it from the river. As you make your way upstream, don't be fooled by Blue Creek, which you will pass on your way to the Blue Spring run. Instead, when you see Blue Creek, (which is also on the western bank), keep paddling past it and around the bend to the left, and then halfway around the bend to the right you'll see the Blue Spring run on the left, about 0.5 mile past Blue Creek. This second-magnitude spring is highly dependent on river levels. If the river is less than 6 feet, you're in for a real treat. Almost dead center of the spring pool you'll see a distinct opening in the ground pouring out some of the bluest of blue water you've ever seen. This spring is pure, untouched, and definitely worth the trip, provided the river isn't too high. To check daily river levels for this and all the rivers in the area, visit www.water.weather.gov/ahps/riversummary.php?wfo=tae.

INDEX

ABOUT THE AUTHOR

Melissa Watson is a professional fire-fighter and paramedic who has been a Florida resident since 1978. Nearly a native child of the Sunshine State, naturally she was thrilled when the opportunity arose to share with you the amazing beauty found within her own back yard. From rivers running blue, to small local swim holes, Melissa has been spring hopping her way around the state for more than twenty-five years. She is always exploring, searching for new and unique swim holes, snorkel spots, and dive sites among the springs of Florida. Tireless research precedes each trip, as she delves into new territory with a map and a compass in hand, a pack on her back, a camera at the ready, and her trusty dog Mikey by her side.

This time around, she added a mask, snorkel, underwater camera, and towel to her repertoire of gear so she could literally submerge herself completely into her research. Melissa is dedicated to the journey, as you can clearly see in each Falcon-Guides book she has written: *Hiking Waterfalls in Georgia and South Carolina, Hiking Waterfalls in North Carolina, Camping North Carolina,* and *Camping South Carolina.* For more information, visit her website at www.trailtimenow.com or send her a friend request on facebook. You can also visit her author page on the FalconGuides website at falcon.com/search/node/watson.